FOUR
VIEWS
ON

DIVINE PROVIDENCE

Books in the Counterpoints Series

Church Life

Bible and Theology

FOUR VIEWS ON DIVINE PROVIDENCE

Paul Kjoss Helseth

William Lane Craig

Ron Highfield

Gregory A. Boyd

Stanley N. Gundry, series editor
Dennis W. Jowers, general editor

ZONDERVAN.com/
AUTHORTRACKER
follow your favorite authors

ZONDERVAN

Four Views on Divine Providence
Copyright © 2011 by Dennis Jowers, William Lane Craig, Ron Highfield, Gregory Boyd, and Paul K. Helseth

This title is also available as a Zondervan ebook. Visit www.zondervan.com/ebooks.

This title is also available in a Zondervan audio edition. Visit www.zondervan.fm.

Requests for information should be addressed to:

Zondervan, *Grand Rapids, Michigan 49530*

Library of Congress Cataloging-in-Publication Data

Four views on divine providence / [edited by] Dennis W. Jowers.
      p. cm. — (Counterpoints: Bible and theology)
   ISBN 978-0-310-32512-3
    1. Providence and government of God — Christianity — Comparative studies. I. Jowers,
Dennis W.
BT135.F68 2011
231'.5 — dc22   2010044403

Cover design: Tammy Johnson
Cover photography: Visuals Unlimited / Masterfile
Interior design: Matthew VanZomeren

Printed in the United States of America

HB 04.22.2024

CONTENTS

INTRODUCTION

DENNIS W. JOWERS

Faith in divine providence has waned considerably during the past century. The brutality of such events as two world wars, China's Cultural Revolution, and the 9/11 attacks, coupled with sharply declining belief in the authority and trustworthiness of the Bible, have led countless persons, even among those who profess to be Christians, to abandon entirely the doctrine of divine providence. Numerous clergy and theologians, in fact, have come to regard this doctrine, which teaches that God not only creates and sustains the world but also concerns himself with and intervenes in its daily affairs, as an anachronism and an embarrassment. To affirm divine providence in a contemporary context, such persons argue, would be either to sanction implicitly the cruelty of Auschwitz and the killing fields of Cambodia by attributing them to God's righteous will or to incriminate God for tolerating and even ordaining such manifest evils.

Persons who uphold the authority and inerrancy of Scripture, nevertheless, cannot consistently disavow the doctrine of providence, for Scripture unmistakably teaches it. Such persons, rather, must confess this doctrine and account for it as best they can. In the present volume, Paul Kjoss Helseth, William Lane Craig, Ron Highfield, and Gregory Boyd articulate four distinct conceptions of what the Bible teaches about divine providence.

In the following, by way of preface to these authors' discussions, we will briefly explore the scriptural foundations of the doctrine of divine providence, sketch the history of theological reflection on this topic, and introduce the perspectives advocated in this volume, which the principal authors will explain in detail.

Scriptural Foundations

That Scripture teaches the doctrine of divine providence seems undeniable. From God's creation of a helpmate for Adam, to the deluge, to the ten plagues, to the parting of the Red Sea, to the inspiration of the prophets, the Old Testament is replete with instances of God's care for his creation. The first testament, moreover, attributes the works of nature to God. One reads in Psalm 147, for instance,

> He covers the heavens with clouds;
> > he prepares rain for the earth;
> > he makes grass grow on the hills.
> He gives to the beasts their food,
> > and to the young ravens that cry....
> He gives snow like wool;
> > he scatters hoarfrost like ashes.
> He hurls down his crystals of ice like crumbs;
> > who can stand before his cold?
> He sends out his word, and melts them;
> > he makes his wind blow and the waters flow.
> > > *Psalm 147:8–9, 16–18 ESV[1]*

Human labor, declares the psalmist, cannot prosper without God's assistance.

> Unless the LORD builds the house,
> > those who build it labor in vain.
> Unless the LORD watches over the city,
> > the watchman stays awake in vain.
> > > *Psalm 127:1*

Hebrew Scripture portrays a God who shows special favor to the poor and oppressed ("who executes justice for the oppressed, who gives food to the hungry," Ps. 146:7) and cares for the temporal needs of the righteous ("I have not seen the righteous forsaken or his children begging for bread," Ps. 37:25). Likewise, Scripture emphasizes God's patience and mercy toward human beings. "His anger is but for a moment," declares David, "and his favor is for a lifetime. Weeping may tarry for the night, but joy comes with the morning" (Ps. 30:5). The Old Testament, in sum, depicts a God who is benevolent to the entirety of his creation. "The LORD is good to all, and his mercy is over all that he has made" (Ps. 145:9).

---

1. Unless otherwise noted, all further Scripture quotations in this introduction are from the ESV.

The God of the Old Testament, however, is no harmless or one-dimensional character. Though he is "of purer eyes than to see evil" (Hab. 1:13) and "hate[s] all evildoers" (Ps. 5:5), he hardens Pharaoh's heart (Ex. 4:21; 7:3, 13; 9:12; 10:1, 20, 27; 11:10; 14:4, 8) and moves David to number Israel (2 Sam. 24:1).[2] Though "lying lips are an abomination to the LORD" (Prov. 12:22), he sends a lying spirit into the mouths of Ahab's prophets (1 Kings 22:23; 2 Chron. 18:21–22) and declares, "If the prophet is deceived and speaks a word, I, the LORD, have deceived that prophet" (Ezek. 14:9).

Though God declares, "My counsel shall stand, and I will accomplish all my purpose" (Isa. 46:10), he expresses disappointment at his people's failure to hearken to his pleas.

> What more was there to do for my vineyard,
>> that I have not done in it?
> When I looked for it to yield grapes,
>> why did it yield wild grapes?
>
> *Isaiah 5:4*

Indeed, the God of the Old Testament expresses regret for creating the human race. According to Genesis 6:6–7, "The LORD was sorry that he had made man on the earth, and it grieved him to his heart. So the Lord said, 'I will blot out man whom I have created from the face of the land, man and animals and creeping things and birds of the heavens, for I am sorry that I have made them.'" The Old Testament, then, depicts God's providential control over creation in somewhat ambiguous terms.

Tensions similar to those that complicate the Old Testament account, moreover, resurface in the New Testament's teaching on divine providence. Once more, God expresses seeming disappointment at human beings' unwillingness to cooperate with his salvific initiative. "O Jerusalem, Jerusalem," Jesus cries out, "the city that kills the prophets and stones those who are sent to it! How often would I have gathered your children together as a hen gathers her brood under her wings, and you would not!" (Matt. 23:37). Yet the New Testament also contains some of Scripture's most emphatic affirmations of divine sovereignty

---

2. God punishes the latter act, incidentally, with a plague that slays 70,000 Israelites (see 2 Sam. 24:15; 1 Chron. 21:14).

over human beings' eternal destinies. After one of Paul's exhortations, Luke writes, "As many as were appointed to eternal life believed" (Acts 13:48). Romans 9, likewise, contains one of the most famous, or infamous, statements of God's foreordination of human beings to either salvation or eternal punishment. "When Rebekah had conceived children by one man, our forefather Isaac," Paul writes, "though they were not yet born and had done nothing either good or bad — in order that God's purpose of election might continue, not because of works but because of him who calls — she was told, 'The older will serve the younger.' As it is written, 'Jacob I loved, but Esau I hated.' What shall we say then? Is there injustice on God's part? By no means! For he says to Moses, 'I will have mercy on whom I have mercy, and I will have compassion on whom I have compassion.' So then it depends not on human will or exertion, but on God, who has mercy" (Rom. 9:10–16).

Jesus himself, moreover, says in Matthew 22:14 that "many are called, but few are chosen." In the New Testament, as in the Old, an apparent breach emerges between emphatic assertions of God's righteousness and suggestions that he influences human beings to perform wicked acts. James, for instance, commands his audience, "Let no one say when he is tempted, 'I am being tempted by God,' for God cannot be tempted with evil, and he himself tempts no one" (James 1:13). Yet Paul declares of the followers of the man of lawlessness, "God sends them a strong delusion, so that they may believe what is false, in order that all may be condemned who did not believe the truth but had pleasure in unrighteousness" (2 Thess. 2:11–12). Again, writes Paul, "He has mercy on whomever he wills, and he hardens whomever he wills" (Rom. 9:18).

Scripture, then, supplies grounds for a range of answers to significant questions about God's providence. Does God ever foreordain evil acts? Does God always get what he wants? How can one reconcile human beings' moral responsibility with God's sovereignty over their acts? More broadly, how does God influence the affairs of this world at all? To answer these and additional questions, each of the authors of this volume will set forth his own vision of what Scripture teaches on these subjects and how that teaching coheres with the rest of what Christians know about God from Scripture and general revelation. The following review of the history of the doctrine of providence in postbiblical Christian theology will help the reader to place each of the theologies of providence advocated in this volume in its approximate historical context.

The History of the Doctrine of Providence

For convenience' sake, one may divide the history of Christian reflection on providence into six periods. These include (1) the ante-Nicene era, roughly AD 70 until the Council of Nicaea in 325; (2) the post-Nicene, 325 until the death of John Damascene in 787; (3) the medieval, 787 until the dawn of the Reformation in the sixteenth century; (4) the early modern, from the outset of the Reformation until the close of the seventeenth century; (5) the Enlightenment, which began in the seventeenth century and reached its zenith in the eighteenth; and (6) the post-Enlightenment, from the outset of the nineteenth century until the present.

In the first of these periods, the *ante-Nicene*, Christian writers broached the topic of divine providence most frequently when arguing for the existence of a loving God who cares for his world. Minucius Felix, for example, appealed to God's orderly arrangement of nature as evidence of God's fatherly concern for humankind. "If, on entering any house," he asserted, "you should behold everything refined, well arranged, and adorned, assuredly you would believe that a master presided over it, and that he himself was much better than all those excellent things. So in this house of the world, when you look upon the heaven and the earth, its providence, its ordering, its law, believe that there is a Lord and Parent of the universe far more glorious than the stars themselves, and the parts of the whole world."[3]

Lactantius, similarly, excoriated the Epicureans for their failure to acknowledge that a wise and benevolent God designed, created, and now governs the universe. "Since the world and all its parts are governed by a wonderful plan," he wrote, "since the framing of the heaven, and the course of the stars and of the heavenly bodies, which is harmonious even in variety itself, the constant and wonderful arrangement of the seasons ... the verdure and productiveness of the woods, the most salubrious bursting forth of fountains, the seasonable overflowings of

---

3. Minucius Felix *Octavius* 18 (ANF 4:182). ANF refers to *The Ante-Nicene Fathers: Translations of the Writings of the Fathers Down to AD 325*, ed. Alexander Roberts and James Donaldson, 9 vols. (New York: Scribner, 1896–1926).

rivers, the rich and abundant flowing in of the sea ... and all things, are fixed with the greatest regularity: who is so blind as to think that they were made without a cause, in which a wonderful disposition of most provident arrangement shines forth? If, therefore, nothing at all exists nor is done without a cause; if the providence of the supreme God is manifest from the disposition of things, his excellency from their greatness, and his power from their government: therefore they are dull and mad who have said that there is no providence."[4]

In this era, the subject of providence also commonly arose in discussions of the problem of evil. That evil exists in God's world constitutes no evidence against God's existence or his providence, ante-Nicene Christians typically argued, because all evil results from sin, and God could have prevented sin only at the cost of nullifying human freedom. God, wrote Tertullian, "did not intervene to prevent the occurrence of what he wished not to happen [viz., sin] in order that he might keep from harm what he wished [viz., human freedom]."[5]

Christian writers of this age also regularly invoked the doctrine of providence when disputing with Marcion and others who distinguished between the just, punishing God of the Old Testament and the good, merciful God of the New. Irenaeus, for instance, argued contra Marcion that justice and benevolence alike are indispensable to genuine deity. "Marcion," he wrote, "does in fact, on both sides, put an end to deity. For he that is the judicial one, if he be not good, is not God, because he from whom goodness is absent is no God at all; and again, he who is good, if he has no judicial power, suffers the same [loss] as the former, by being deprived of his character of deity."[6]

In the ante-Nicene period, then, Christian authors referred to the doctrine of providence mainly in the context of apologetic arguments against paganism and heresy. This apologetic emphasis continued in the *post-Nicene* period, but the Christianization of the Roman Empire and the palpable decline of Roman civilization that quickly followed lent a radically different character to Christian discussions of providence in the later patristic period. Whereas Christian apologists of the ante-Nicene period invoked providence to establish the unity, beneficence,

---

4. Lactantius *Institutes* 7.3 (ANF 7:198).
5. Tertullian *Against Marcion* 2.7 (ANF 3:303).
6. Irenaeus *Against All Heresies* 3.25.3 (ANF 1:259).

and justice of God, post-Nicene thinkers sought also to defend God's providence against pagans who blamed Christianity for the Roman Empire's demise. The theology of providence in the post-Nicene period, moreover, increasingly began to intersect with soteriology as the Pelagian and Semipelagian controversies focused attention on the dilemma of how to reconcile human freedom with divine sovereignty.

The influence of political events on this era's theology of providence appears especially clearly in the work of Eusebius of Caesarea, who extolled Constantine as God's chosen instrument for the conversion of humanity. In works such as his *Life of Constantine* and his *Oration in Praise of Constantine*, Eusebius articulated a triumphalist ideology, which identified Constantine's ascent as a manifestation of divine providence and equated, in all essential respects, the interests of the church with those of the empire. This ideology's popularity declined precipitously after Alaric's sack of Rome in 410, and a more jaded view of all earthly regimes, promoted by works such as Augustine's *City of God* and Salvian's *On the Government of God*, gradually supplanted Eusebianism in the fifth century.

When the Pelagian controversy broke out in the early fifth century, moreover, Augustine of Hippo began to address a number of issues relevant to the subject of providence in a manner that was, to a certain extent, unprecedented. Specifically, Augustine seems to have been the first to articulate a conception of freedom that allows one consistently to claim both (1) that human beings sin freely and thus deserve punishment for their sins and (2) that human beings, without the assistance of grace, cannot refrain from sinning.[7]

Augustine's opponents, followers of the British monk Pelagius, maintained that human beings cannot be morally accountable for their wrongdoing if they are not capable of behaving righteously. Hence, the Pelagians argued, all human beings naturally possess the ability to behave righteously. Augustine, by contrast, held that human beings, before God has regenerated them, can do nothing but sin.

Freedom, as Augustine understood it, consists not in the ability to do otherwise than one actually does but in the ability to do that which

---

7. See, e.g., Augustine *Man's Perfection in Righteousness* 2.3 (NPNF 1.5:160). NPNF refers to *A Select Library of Nicene and Post-Nicene Fathers of the Christian Church*, ed. Philip Schaff and Henry Wace, 28 vols. (New York: Christian Literature Co., 1890–1900).

one wishes.[8] In his view, accordingly, an act can be voluntary and thus liable to praise or blame, reward or punishment, even if one cannot refrain from performing it. For, Augustine argued, it would be the height of absurdity to claim that because human beings cannot fail to desire their own happiness, they do not desire to be happy voluntarily. Likewise, he asserted, it would be foolish to say that God is not righteous voluntarily, because he cannot be unrighteous.[9]

In Augustine's view, consequently, God can justly punish unregenerate human beings for their sins even though they are incapable of abstaining from sin. Inasmuch as human beings can do nothing but sin before God regenerates them, Augustine argued furthermore, they can believe in Christ unto salvation only after, logically speaking, God regenerates them and endows them with the will to believe. According to Augustine, therefore, it is God, not human beings, who ultimately determines which human beings receive salvation.

Although Augustine's view, in the main at least, came to dominate the Latin West by the end of the post-Nicene, or patristic, period, it received scant support in the Greek East. Over against Augustine, the Eastern Fathers held with virtual unanimity that voluntary acts are solely those that one may choose either to perform or not to perform. John of Damascus, for instance, equated voluntary acts with those "which we are free to do or not to do at our will."[10] Such acts, he continued, concern "equal possibilities: e.g.... to tell lies or not to tell lies, to give or not to give ... and all such actions as imply virtue or vice in their performance, for we are free to do or not to do these at our pleasure."[11]

The Eastern Fathers, moreover, considered human beings, not God, the primary determinants of who receives salvation. "Whence," asks John Chrysostom, "are some vessels of wrath, and some of mercy? Of their own free choice. God, however, being very good, shows the same kindness to both. For it was not those in a state of salvation only to whom he showed mercy, but also Pharaoh, as far as his part went. For of the same long-suffering, both they and he had the advantage. And if

---

8. See Augustine *The City of God* 5.9–10 (NPNF 1.2:90–93) and *On the Spirit and the Letter* 53 (NPNF 1.5:106).
9. Augustine *On Nature and Grace* 54, 57 (NPNF 1.5:139–40).
10. John of Damascus *On the Orthodox Faith* 2.26 (NPNF 2.9:40b).
11. Ibid.

he was not saved, it was quite owing to his own will: since, as for what concerns God, he had as much done for him as they who were saved."[12]

At the close of the patristic period, then, two radically opposed conceptions of divine providence dominated in the East and the West, respectively. The perspective of the East on the relation of God's providence to human freedom remained largely unchanged in the succeeding centuries. Views on divine providence vis-à-vis human freedom in the West, by contrast, fluctuated radically. It is on the West, therefore, that we shall focus in our treatment of the doctrine of providence in the medieval, early modern, Enlightenment, and post-Enlightenment eras.

Throughout the *medieval* period, moderately Augustinian and moderately anti-Augustinian theologies of providence and grace coexisted in the Western church. Whereas the Synod of Quiersy in 853 condemned Augustinian predestinarianism in the person of Gottschalk of Orbais, for example, the Synod of Valence in 855 countered Quiersy by endorsing Augustine's views on predestination emphatically. Again, whereas thinkers such as John Duns Scotus[13] and William of Ockham[14] held that human beings are always free to sin or not to sin, theologians like Thomas Bradwardine[15] and Gregory of Rimini[16] reaffirmed Augustine's contention that the unregenerate are incapable of refraining from sin. This ongoing diversity notwithstanding, theologies of providence and grace that emphasize the freedom of the human will over against divine sovereignty came overwhelmingly to predominate in Western Christendom immediately before the Reformation.

Augustinianism enjoyed a great resurgence, however, in the *early modern* period, the Reformation of the sixteenth century. The magisterial Reformers, the later Melanchthon alone excepted, uniformly endorsed the view that God primarily determines who is or is not

---

12. John Chrysostom *Homily 16 on Romans 9:22–24* (NPNF 1.11:469).

13. John Duns Scotus, *Ordinatio* II, dist. 28, q. 1, in *Opera Omnia*, ed. Luke Wadding et al., 26 vols. (Paris: Vivès, 1891–95), 13:255–56.

14. William of Ockham, *Reportatio in II Sententiarum*, q. 15, in *Guillelmi de Ockham: Opera theologica 5*, ed. Gedeon Gál and Rega Wood (St. Bonaventure, N.Y.: Franciscan Institute of St. Bonaventure University, 1981), 356, lines 6–11.

15. Thomas Bradwardine, *De Causa Dei contra Pelagianos*, ed. Henry Saville (London: Ex officina Nortiana, 1618), §2.7, pp. 490–91.

16. Gregory of Rimini, *In II Sententiarum*, dist. 26–28, q. 2, art. 1, in *Gregorii Ariminensis OESA lectura super primum et secundum sententiarum*, ed. Damasus Trapp et al., 7 vols. (Berlin: De Gruyter, 1979–87), 6:96–101.

saved: not putatively autonomous human beings. The Jesuits, perhaps the most formidable enemies of the Reformation, by contrast, insisted that human beings always possess the freedom to do otherwise than they actually do. On the basis of this robust conception of human freedom, then, the Jesuits maintained that human beings, rather than God, are the primary determinants of who does or does not attain salvation.

The most distinguished champion of the Jesuits' libertarian conception of providence in this period is unquestionably Luis de Molina (1535–1600). Like the Thomists, disciples of Thomas Aquinas, and the stalwart defender of their moderately Augustinian theology of grace, Domingo Bañez, Molina denied that God derives his knowledge of what will occur in the world from the world itself.[17] To assert that he who gives all others whatever they have receives something from these others, Molina and the Thomists agreed, would be patent nonsense.

The Thomists inferred from the truth that God does not derive his knowledge of human decisions from observing the decisions themselves that he must derive it from his knowledge of his own will. God knows what human beings will do, the Thomists held, because he has foreordained that they will do it. Molina, however, maintained that God's "middle knowledge," his knowledge of what free human beings would do in any set of circumstances, enables him to know in advance and even to control human decisions without predetermining them. If, Molina reasoned, God knows what free agents will do in any set of circumstances and can determine by his acts what circumstances they will face, he can foreknow and even control what those agents do without compromising their liberty in the slightest.[18]

The conflict between Thomists and Molinists grew so severe that in 1598 Clement VIII appointed a special commission, titled *Congregatio de Auxiliis*, to consider the points in dispute. *Congregatio de Auxiliis* literally means "congregation on helps," an appropriate name for the commission, given its assignment to investigate a controversy about what kind of help God gives human beings to perform salutary

---

17. Luis de Molina, *Liberi arbitrii cum gratiae donis, divina praescientia, providentia, praedestinatione et reprobatione concordia*, 2nd ed. (Antwerp: Officina typ. Joachimi Tragnæsii, 1595), disp. 49, in q. 14, art. 13, p. 208b. Hereafter cited as *Concordia*.

18. Ibid., disp. 53, memb. 3, in q. 14, art. 13, p. 263a.

acts, that is, acts that lead to salvation. The Thomist position was that God's saving grace is intrinsically efficacious: his grace is such that whoever receives it will certainly perform a salutary act.[19] The Molinist position, by contrast, was that the human will is always able either to cooperate with or to resist God's grace.[20] Although the commission voted several times to condemn the Molinist position, Clement VIII's successor, Paul V, ultimately disbanded it in 1607 and left the controversy unresolved.

These disputes exerted great influence on the course of Protestant and Catholic theology alike in the seventeenth century. Jacobus Arminius (1560–1609), the eponymous founder of the Arminian movement in Reformed Protestantism, for example, incorporated the notion of middle knowledge into his critique of Calvinistic belief in absolute predestination.[21] The notion of middle knowledge, moreover, became a key element of the Arminian theology constructed by Arminius's disciples Simon Episcopius[22] and Hugo Grotius,[23] which would guide Dutch Remonstrants and their sympathizers abroad for the next century. In response, Calvinist theologians of the seventeenth century frequently argued against Molinism.[24] As a general rule, moreover, they adopted the Thomistic doctrine of physical premotion, according to which nothing in creation can act in any way without being predetermined so to act by the operation of God. Not only the theological but also the philosophical arguments of the Thomists found their way into mainstream Reformed dogmatics, and the debate between Arminians and Calvinists raged throughout the seventeenth century on parallel lines to that between Molinists and Thomists.

---

19. See Thomas Aquinas, *Summa Theologiae* I, q. 23, arts. 4–5, 7.

20. See Molina, *Concordia*, disp. 29, in q. 14, art. 13, p. 125a.

21. See Jacobus Arminius, "Twenty-five Public Disputations," 4.43, 45, in *The Works of James Arminius*, trans. James Nichols and William Nichols (London: Longman, 1825–28 and Thomas Baker, 1875), 2:123–24; and the discussion of Arminius's views in Eef Dekker, "Was Arminius a Molinist?" *Sixteenth Century Journal* 27 (1996): 337–52.

22. Simon Episcopius, *Institutiones theologicarum* 4.2.19, in *Opera theologica* (Amsterdam: John Blaeu, 1650), 303–4.

23. Hugo Grotius, *Conciliatio dissidentium*, in *Opera omnia theologica* (Basel: Thurnissios, 1732), 4:352–54.

24. For bibliographical details and an account of the arguments generally employed, see Richard A. Muller, *Post-Reformation Reformed Dogmatics: The Rise and Development of Reformed Orthodoxy, ca. 1520 to ca. 1725*, 4 vols. (Grand Rapids: Baker Academic, 2003), 3:419–25.

During the *Enlightenment*, which began in the seventeenth century and flowered in the eighteenth, belief in providence declined precipitously as intellectuals gravitated to deism and atheism. Some deists of the time, admittedly, granted that God governs the world's affairs in some sense and that he metes out postmortem rewards and punishments to the righteous and the wicked, respectively. Nevertheless, all deists denied that God intervenes in nature by working miracles and that he reveals himself to human beings in a supernatural manner. Deists usually acknowledged only what came to be known as "general providence," that is, a loose superintendence over the world by God, who allows everything to proceed in accordance with physical laws.[25] Orthodox Christians of this period, naturally, objected vociferously to the notion that God exercises a merely general providence. John Wesley wrote:

> You say, "You allow a *general* providence, but deny a *particular* one." And what is a general, of whatever kind it be, that includes no particulars! Is not every general necessarily made up of its several particulars? Can you instance ... any general that is not? Tell me any genus, if you can, that contains no species? What is it that constitutes a genus, but so many species? What, I pray, is a whole that contains no parts? Mere nonsense and contradiction![26]

In the view of the orthodox theologians of this period, a denial of God's providential guidance of everything leads logically to a denial of his providential guidance of anything. Again, Wesley asked the proponent of a merely general providence: "Do you mean ... that the providence of God does, indeed, extend to all parts of the earth, with regard to great and singular events; such as the rise and fall of empires; but that the little concerns of this or that man are beneath the notice of the Almighty? Then you do not consider, that great and little are merely relative terms.... With regard to the Most High, man, and all the concerns of men, are nothing, less than nothing, before him."[27]

---

25. See the fourfold classification of deists in Samuel Clarke, *A Discourse Concerning the Being and Attributes of God, the Obligations of Natural Religion, and the Truth and Certainty of the Christian Revelation* (Glasgow: Richard Griffin, 1823), 2:140–55.

26. John Wesley, "On Divine Providence," sermon 67, in *The Works of John Wesley*, 3rd ed., 14 vols. (London: Wesleyan Methodist Book Room, 1872), 67.23, p. 322.

27. Ibid., 67.26, p. 323.

Such considerations notwithstanding, many professedly orthodox apologists for Christianity in the eighteenth century advocated relatively deistic accounts of divine providence. Whereas earlier theologians characterized God's preservation of the world as a continuous creation and underscored the impotence of creatures to act without God's *concursus*, that is to say, the anti-deist apologists of this era tended to depict the world as a machine that requires a God to operate it but does not continually receive from him its inmost being.[28]

These apologists, moreover, ultimately proved much less influential than the glib rationalists who abounded in German theological faculties during the last decades of the eighteenth century. These thinkers banished divine causality entirely from the world. Miracles they either denied or attempted to explain away in a naturalistic fashion.[29] Indeed, they frequently claimed that one can know, at least in the strictest sense of this term, nothing about God whatsoever.[30]

Matters improved somewhat, then, in the nineteenth century, the *post-Enlightenment* era. "After the shameful defeat of theology in the period of the 'Illumination' (*Aufklärung*)," wrote Abraham Kuyper, "we may affirm an undeniable *resurrection* of theology in the nineteenth century."[31] Rationalism, admittedly, continued to exert influence in the first half of the century.[32] In the Hegelian school, which largely supplanted that of the older rationalists, the tendency of the older rationalism to isolate God from his creation gave way to the even more destructive tendency to confuse God's being with that of the world.[33]

---

28. 28. See, e.g., William Derham, *Physico-Theology: Or, a Demonstration of the Being and Attributes of God from His Works of Creation* (London: Robinson & Roberts, 1768).

29. See, e.g., Karl Friedrich Bahrdt, *Würdigung der natürlichen Religion und des Naturalismus in Beziehung auf Staat und Menschenrechte* (Halle: Francke & Bispinf, 1791), 61–69; Johann Eberhard, *Neue Apologie des Sokrates, oder Untersuchung der Lehre von der Seligkeit der Heiden*, 2 vols. (Berlin: Nikolai, 1772–78), 1:125–32.

30. See, e.g., Karl Friedrich Bahrdt, *Katechismus der natürlichen Religion* (Halle: Francke & Bispinf, 1790), 3–11.

31. Abraham Kuyper, *Encyclopedia of Sacred Theology: Its Principles*, trans. J. Hendrik de Vries (New York: Scribner, 1898), §3.5.106, p. 672.

32. In this period, indeed, appears the rationalist dogmatician par excellence, Julius Wegscheider, whose masterwork, *Institutiones theologiae christianae dogmaticae*, 7th ed. (Halle: Libraria Gebaueria, 1833), is arguably the greatest work of systematic theology produced by the rationalist school.

33. See, e.g., Georg Wilhelm Friedrich Hegel, *Hegel's Science of Logic*, trans. A. V. Miller (London: Allen & Unwin, 1969), 1.1.2, pp. 137–49, where he identifies the truly infinite as the all-inclusive.

Elsewhere, even within Germany to an extent, more orthodox modes of depicting the relation between God and the world manifested themselves. Abraham Kuyper[34] and Herman Bavinck[35] of the Netherlands, for instance, at least arguably embraced the old Reformed and Thomistic doctrine of physical premotion, and leading Reformed theologians in the United States and Scotland, although they renounced the doctrine of physical premotion,[36] granted that God foreordains everything that occurs.[37] The revival of scholastic philosophy that swept through the Catholic Church in the nineteenth century, furthermore, led to renewed advocacy of physical premotion by Dominicans and of middle knowledge by Jesuits. Among the nineteenth-century Jesuits who disputed Aquinas's doctrine of physical premotion, ironically, were some of the architects of that century's revival of Thomistic philosophy.[38]

In the twentieth century, this dispute among Catholics continued until the Second Vatican Council of 1962–65, which unleashed a wave of theological liberalism in the Catholic Church and marked the end, for all practical purposes, of neoscholastic theology. Among Protestants, the central conflict of the century concerned whether it makes sense to say that God acts in history at all. From the emergence of neoorthodoxy as a major alternative in Protestant theology until its demise in the 1960s and 1970s, scholars who sympathized with the so-called biblical theology movement tended to emphasize God's "mighty acts" in history as the locus of his self-revelation. This school disintegrated, however, in the face of criticism by James Barr,[39] Langdon Gilkey,[40] and others that its proponents could not justify exempting the salvation history in

---

34. See Abraham Kuyper, *Dictaten Dogmatiek*, 2nd ed., 5 vols. (Kampen: Kok, 1910), 3:66–69.

35. See Herman Bavinck, *Reformed Dogmatics*, ed. John Bolt, trans. John Vriend, 4 vols. (Grand Rapids: Baker Academic, 2003–8), 2:614.

36. For America, see Charles Hodge, *Systematic Theology*, 3 vols. (New York: Scribner, 1872; repr., Grand Rapids: Eerdmans, 1989), 1:604–5; for Scotland, see John Dick, *Lectures on Theology*, 2 vols. (New York: Robert Carter & Brothers, 1878), 1:433–35.

37. See Hodge, *Systematic Theology*, 1:542; and Dick, *Lectures*, 1:353.

38. See, e.g., Matteo Liberatore, *Institutiones philosophicae*, 8th ed., 2 vols. (Rome: Propaganda Fide, 1855), 2:348–49; Giovanni Cornoldi, *La filosofia scolastica di San Tommaso e di Dante*, 7th ed. (Rome: Tipografia A. Befani, 1889), 472–74, 479–83.

39. See, e.g., James Barr, *The Bible in the Modern World* (London: SCM, 1973), 75–88.

40. See esp. Langdon Gilkey, "Cosmology, Ontology, and the Travail of Biblical Language," *Journal of Religion* 41 (1961): 194–205.

which they located God's revelatory acts from the naturalistic assumptions they applied to all other spheres of human life.

Unlike neoorthodox followers of the biblical theology movement, other Protestant theologians attempted throughout the twentieth century to speak meaningfully of divine influence on the world without invoking the concepts of intervention or miracle. One can divide these thinkers into two categories: process theologians and more conventional panentheists. The second group identify God with the act of being in which the being of every individual being consists. These thinkers regard all talk of divine action as incoherent, because, in their view, only beings act, and God, who is the act of being that all beings share, cannot himself be one of these beings. The most eminent twentieth-century representative of this viewpoint is Paul Tillich.[41]

Process theologians, although panentheists, typically admit the possibility of meaningful language about divine action on particular entities in the world. Nevertheless, they exclude the kind of divine action requisite to generate miracles. Since every entity, in their view, possesses a measure of freedom, God cannot unilaterally cause anything to occur. He can only contribute his influence, which he does by endowing each particular entity with an aim, which consists in the greatest self-realization achievable by that entity in its present situation. To ensure that this aim rather than any other comes to realization in a given instance is not possible for God, process theists hold, for two reasons: (1) each entity possesses a freedom and causality of its own, which can resist the divine purpose, and (2) God's loving character precludes his violating the freedom of particular things by determining what they will or will not do. God, in the view of process theists, acts only by persuasion.[42]

Both process theists and panentheists, moreover, reject the notion of particular divine interventions as inconsistent with their experience of the world as a closed nexus of natural causes and seek, by denying that

41. See Paul Tillich, *Systematic Theology*, 3 vols. (Chicago: University of Chicago Press, 1951–63), 1:115–17, 239–45. For a sketch of the trend toward panentheism in twentieth-century theology, see Michael Brierley, "Naming a Quiet Revolution: The Panentheistic Turn in Modern Theology," in *In Whom We Live and Move and Have Our Being: Panentheistic Reflections on God's Presence in a Scientific World*, ed. Philip Clayton and Arthur Peacocke (Grand Rapids: Eerdmans, 2004), 1–15.

42. For a brief discussion of divine action in process thought, see John B. Cobb Jr. and David Ray Griffin, *Process Theology: An Introductory Exposition* (Louisville, Ky.: Westminster John Knox, 1976), 41–62.

God can intervene in nature, to exempt him from responsibility for evil in the world.[43] The humanitarian bent of these theologies is much too strong to allow that God might refrain from righting grave injustices or alleviating extreme suffering if, in fact, he were capable of so doing.

Evangelical theologians of the twentieth and twenty-first centuries, admittedly, articulate a variety of orthodox views on divine action, and evangelical philosophers such as Alvin Plantinga and Nicholas Wolterstorff exert considerable influence in the academic philosophy of religion. Nevertheless, the sounder views advocated by these thinkers did not enter the mainstream of academic theology in the twentieth century and have yet to enter it in the twenty-first.

Views Advocated in This Volume

Ambiguities within Scripture's testimony to providence as well as massive conflicts of worldviews, then, have led theologians of all ages to advocate diametrically opposed conceptions of providence. In the present volume, Paul Kjoss Helseth, representing the Reformed tradition, argues that all events owe both their occurrence and the precise mode of that occurrence to God, who causes every creaturely act in such a way as to determine completely its nature and outcome. William Lane Craig, who argues on behalf of contemporary Molinists, maintains that God knows what creatures will do by virtue of his middle knowledge and that he controls the course of worldly affairs by means of this awareness without predetermining any of his creatures' free decisions.

Ronald Highfield, writing out of the Restorationist tradition, calls both traditional and recent conceptions of providence before the bar of Scripture and finds them wanting. He articulates, instead, what he considers a biblical perspective on the subject, which differs in content and emphases from the others in this volume. Gregory Boyd, finally, advocates open theism, according to which human decisions, in most circumstances, can be free only if God neither determines nor even knows what they will be.

---

43. See esp. Maurice Wiles, "Divine Action: Some Moral Considerations," in *The God Who Acts: Philosophical and Theological Explorations*, ed. Thomas F. Tracy (University Park: Pennsylvania State University Press, 1994), 13–30.

Conclusion

As we established at the outset of this introduction, none of these views possesses indisputable scriptural warrant. To arrive at a responsible position on the questions of what God controls and how he controls it, one must weigh a great deal of evidence, carefully work out the implications of alternative answers, and scrutinize the frequently intricate arguments employed for and against different models of divine providence. This is unquestionably an arduous task.

Contemporary Christians, nonetheless, must expend the labor necessary to attain a scripturally and rationally adequate account of providence. For in an increasingly chaotic and frequently tragic world, persons within and without the church demand answers as to how a good God can allow one billion people to languish on an income of a dollar or less a day; why God sends natural disasters, prolonged wars, and debilitating illnesses; and what relevance God has for their personal agony. One cannot credibly present the gospel in today's culture, it seems, without supplying defensible answers to such questions.

GOD CAUSES ALL THINGS

PAUL KJOSS HELSETH

True Courage

Shortly after the Battle of Manassas in Ronald Maxwell's film adaptation of Jeffrey Shaara's historical novel *Gods and Generals*, a shell-shocked captain in the Confederate army asks Lieutenant General Thomas "Stonewall" Jackson how he could remain so tranquil in battle when the fight was raging all around him. "General," the young captain asks in an almost reverential tone, "how is it that you can keep so serene and stay so utterly insensible, with a storm of shells and bullets raining about your head?" Jackson's response reveals his unshakable confidence in the absolute sovereignty of God over all things, including the seemingly random events that take place on the battlefield. "Captain Smith," Jackson thoughtfully responds, "my religious belief teaches me to feel as safe in battle as in bed. God has fixed the time for my death; I do not concern myself with that, but to be always ready, whenever it may overtake me. That is the way all men should live; then all men would be equally brave."

While Maxwell's portrayal of this exchange takes certain liberties with the historical record, it accurately depicts both the tone and the theological substance of the actual exchange.[1] Apparently, Jackson really was a profoundly courageous man, and his courage really was grounded in his belief in the all-encompassing sovereignty of God. At a

---

1. For examples of minor historical discrepancies, see John Selby, *Stonewall Jackson as Military Commander* (New York: Barnes & Noble, 1999), 25–26.

memorial service shortly after Jackson's death from pneumonia on May 10, 1863, the erstwhile adjutant general of the "Stonewall" Brigade, Southern Presbyterian theologian Robert Lewis Dabney, confirmed that the source of Jackson's courage was not found in one form of pagan fatalism or another, as some who "knew not whereof they affirmed" were apparently insisting.[2] It was found, rather, in his "strong" belief in the providence of God, a belief that viewed all events not as "fixed by an immanent, physical necessity in the series of causes and effects themselves," but as "directed by his most wise and holy will, according to his plan, and the laws of nature which he has ordained."[3] In short, Jackson's fearlessness, Dabney explained in a memorial address titled "True Courage," was grounded in his conviction that the providence of God "is over all his creatures, and all their actions."[4] As such, he was confident that

> there is no creature so great as to resist its power, none so min-
> ute as to evade its wisdom. Each particular act among the most
> multitudinous which confound our attention by their number, or
> the most fortuitous, which entirely baffle our inquiry into their
> causes, is regulated by this intelligent purpose of God. Even when
> the thousand missiles of death, invisible to mortal sight, and sent
> forth aimless by those who launched them, shoot in inexplicable
> confusion over the battle-field, his eye gives each one an aim and
> a purpose, according to the plan of his wisdom. Thus teacheth our
> Saviour.[5]

The Irresistible Ruler: No Mere "Godling"

That Jackson thought about the providence of God in such a fashion is not surprising given his confessional commitments. As a deacon in the Presbyterian Church, he subscribed to the Westminster Confession of Faith and also embraced the Westminster Larger and Shorter Catechisms. He stood, therefore, in the doctrinal mainstream of the

---

2. Robert Lewis Dabney, "True Courage," in *Discussions of Robert Lewis Dabney*, vol. 3 (Edinburgh: Banner of Truth Trust, 1982), 459.

3. Ibid.

4. Ibid., 457.

5. Ibid.

Reformed wing of the Augustinian tradition.[6] According to those in this wing of the tradition, "There is nothing that is, and nothing that comes to pass, that [God] has not first decreed and then brought to pass by His creation or providence."[7] As B. B. Warfield makes clear in his essays on the doctrines of providence and predestination, the God of Reformed believers is no mere "godling"[8] that is subject to forces acting "independently ... and outside of his teleological control."[9] Rather, "over against all dualistic [or deistic] conceptions" of God on the one hand and "all cosmotheistic [or pantheistic] conceptions" of God on the other, he is "the irresistible Ruler" who is the Creator of "all that is and, as well, the upholder and powerful governor of all that he has made, [and] according to whose will, therefore, all that comes to pass must be ordered."[10] In short, the God of Reformed believers is "an infinite Person" whose "cosmical purpose" is "eternal and independent, all-

---

6. According to the Westminster standards: "God, the great Creator of all things, doth uphold, direct, dispose, and govern all creatures, actions, and things, from the greatest even to the least, by his most wise and holy providence, according to his infallible foreknowledge, and the free and immutable counsel of his own will, to the praise of the glory of his wisdom, power, justice, goodness, and mercy" ("Of Providence," 5.1, in *The Westminster Confession of Faith* [Glasgow: Free Presbyterian Publications, 1994], 33–34).

"God's works of providence are his most holy, wise, and powerful preserving and governing all his creatures; ordering them, and all their actions, to his own glory" ("The Larger Catechism," q. 18, in *The Westminster Confession of Faith*, 137).

"God's works of providence are, his most holy, wise, and powerful preserving and governing all his creatures, and all their actions" ("The Shorter Catechism," q. 11, in *The Westminster Confession of Faith*, 289).

7. B. B. Warfield, "Predestination," in *Biblical Doctrines*, vol. 2 of *The Works of Benjamin B. Warfield* (1929; repr., Grand Rapids: Baker, 1991), 21.

8. B. B. Warfield, "Some Thoughts on Predestination," in *Selected Shorter Writings*, ed. John E. Meeter, 2 vols. (1970–73; repr., Phillipsburg, N.J.: P&R, 2001), 1:105.

9. Warfield, "The Significance of the Confessional Doctrine of the Decree," in *Shorter Writings*, 1:94. According to Warfield, those who insist that God rules the universe while simultaneously granting the existence of causes that can act independently and outside of his control in fact are "deny[ing] in detail what they [are] affirm[ing] in the mass" (ibid.). Among those who do this are not only those who insist that the eternal destinies of particular individuals are ultimately determined not by God but by the individuals themselves (cf. ibid., 100), but also those who "asseverate that though ... God had foreordained all that would come to pass, this was only because in his infinite wisdom he was able to forecast the future perfectly; because he thoroughly knew all the causes in operation, and could calculate their issues; and on this ground could foretell what would come to pass, and so ordain it" (ibid., 99). Conceiving of providence in this second sense betrays a deistic tendency that mars "the purity of our theism" just as surely as the first sense does, Warfield argues, for it "dethrone[s] God as the governor of the universe" (ibid.). Indeed, it makes him "rather govern himself by the course of events; and so under color of affirming the primal theistic implicate of purposive action, actually overthrow[s] the whole theistic conception, and enthrone[s] the 'course of events' as the real ruler of the world" (ibid.).

10. Warfield, "Predestination," 45, 9, 45.

inclusive and effective."[11] He is "the free determiner of all that comes to pass in the world which is the product of His creative act," yet he determines all things in such a way that "the real activity of second causes" is both affirmed and maintained,[12] and for this reason he is neither the "sole cause" of everything that transpires in the universe that he has made,[13] nor is he the author of evil.[14] Since God's "providential

---

11. Ibid., 62, 56, 62.

12. Ibid., 8, 9. Please note that although not all Reformed believers endorse the primary/secondary distinction, nevertheless it is, as far as I can tell, the majority position in the Reformed camp.

13. Warfield, "Confessional Doctrine," 98. Note that for philosophers like Keith Yandell, it is "dubious" for monotheists who are determinists to maintain that there really is more than "one agent" or cause in the universe (Keith E. Yandell, *Philosophy of Religion: A Contemporary Introduction* [New York: Routledge, 1999], 339; for Yandell's extended argument, see 303–40). Despite what philosophers like Yandell would have us believe, Reformed believers are not persuaded that "omnicausality" necessarily entails "monocausality." According to Warfield, "When the [Westminster] Confession was written as well as now, there were men who were accustomed to asseverate that to affirm that God had freely and unchangeably ordained whatsoever comes to pass were to declare God the sole cause operative in the universe, to destroy the freedom of the human will, and indeed the reality of all second causes, and to reduce all things to the control of a blind necessity or fate. Accordingly the Confession adds the caveat, that God's foreordination does not make him the author of sin, nor offer violence to the will of the creature, nor take away (but rather establish) the liberty or contingency of second causes. In other words, the Confession guards its readers against being misled into supposing that the divine government of the universe according to an eternal plan excludes the administration of that government through instruments; and protects the reality and real efficiency of all second causes, free and necessary alike, as the proximate producers of the effects that take place in the world, while affirming the reality and real efficiency of the first cause as the determiner of the course of events in accordance with the primal plan" (Warfield, "Confessional Doctrine," 98–99).

14. According to John Frame, there are two senses in which the phrase "author of evil" can be understood. In the first sense, the phrase "connotes not only causality of evil, but also blame for it. To author evil is to do it" (John M. Frame, *The Doctrine of God: A Theology of Lordship* [Phillipsburg, N.J.: P&R, 2002], 181). The second sense suggests that God's relationship to the world is like that of an author to his story. Conceiving of God's relationship to evil in this sense, Frame suggests, provides "a way of seeing that God is *not* to be blamed for the sin of his creatures," for not only does he transcend and rule over the created order much like an author transcends and rules over the world of his story, but more important, he is "the covenant Lord" who, as the author of his story, has prerogatives that, while always consistent with his character, nevertheless "are far greater than ours," and for this reason he is "not required to defend himself against charges of injustice" (ibid., 181, 180, 181). This analogy and the sense of authorship that it commends will perhaps make more sense when coupled with the typical Reformed distinction "between God as the 'remote cause' and human agency as the 'proximate cause'" of sin (ibid., 176). While Reformed believers typically insist that only the "proximate" cause is culpable for sin because only the proximate cause is "a doer of sin" (ibid., 288), they nevertheless acknowledge that the mechanics of how God can be the efficient cause of sin without actually doing, and thus being culpable for, sin is inscrutable. Calvin, Frame argues, "uses the proximate-remote distinction," not to demonstrate "*why* God is guiltless," but merely "to distinguish between the causality of God and that of creatures, and therefore to *state* that the former is always righteous" (ibid., 177). Thus, while the proximate-remote distinction is useful because it "stat[es] who is to blame for evil" and helps us to conceptualize divine authorship, it does not in itself provide a comprehensive solution to the problem of evil

control" extends to all his "works" and "all his creatures and all their actions of every kind,"[15] Reformed believers conclude that "all things without exception ... are disposed by Him, and His will is the ultimate account of all that occurs. Heaven and earth and all that is in them are the instruments through which He works His ends. Nature, nations, and the fortunes of the individual alike present in all their changes the transcript of His purpose."[16]

Preservation and Government

Among the most thoughtful and compelling articulations of the classical Reformed understanding of providence is that which is found in the second volume of Herman Bavinck's *Reformed Dogmatics*. According to Bavinck, "The providence of God ... is—in the beautiful words of the Heidelberg Catechism—'the almighty and ever present power of God by which he upholds, as with his hand, heaven and earth and all creatures and so rules them that ... all things, in fact, come to us, not by chance but from his fatherly hand' (Lord's Day 10, Q. & A. 27)."[17] When the doctrine of providence is understood in this fashion, it has, as Bavinck insists, "enormous scope," for it encompasses not just some of God's works but "the entire implementation of all the decrees that have bearing on the world after it has been called into being by creation."[18] Indeed,

> if the act of creation is excepted from providence, it is as full as the free knowledge of God (*scientia libera*) and the decrees of God, as is everything that exists and occurs in time. It extends to everything that is treated in dogmatics after the doctrine of creation and includes both the works of nature and of grace. All the works of God *ad extra*, which are subsequent to creation, are works of his providence.[19]

(ibid., 179). As such, it too calls us to trust the promises of God, all of which "find their Yes in him" (2 Cor. 1:20).

15. Archibald Alexander Hodge, *The Confession of Faith* (1869; repr., Edinburgh: Banner of Truth Trust, 1992), 91.

16. Warfield, "Predestination," 9.

17. Herman Bavinck, *Reformed Dogmatics*, 2:604.

18. Ibid.

19. Ibid.

For Bavinck and Reformed believers generally, then, the providence of God has to do with everything that God does to ensure that his purposes are accomplished in time. It does not have to do with the "works of God" per se but "limits itself to a description" of the relationship in which God always and everywhere stands "toward his creatures."[20] In short, God actively "works all things according to the counsel of his will" (Eph. 1:11 ESV)[21] not simply by preserving "all creatures in their own state (which is done by a conservation of essence in the species, of existence in individuals and of virtues to their operations)."[22] His providential activity has to do, in other words, with more than simply "giv[ing] and conserv[ing] to second causes the power of acting and permit[ting] them to act," as "the Jesuits followed by the Socinians and Remonstrants" were eager to maintain.[23] Rather, as Turretin puts it, God's providence "consists not only in the conservation of things, but also in the concourse of God; not indifferent and general [in the sense that it passively allows second causes to determine themselves], but particular and specific (by which it flows immediately into both cause and effect)."[24]

As such, Reformed believers are persuaded that God actively accomplishes all his good purposes not just by preserving and passively

---

20. Ibid. For Bavinck, God is related to his creatures as the primary cause that works through secondary causes. As such, secondary causes are the "formal" causes of everything that transpires. See note 25 on the next page.

21. Note that the active nature of God's providential control extends even to the manner in which he permits sin. According to Frame, God permits nothing passively, but his permission is "an *efficacious* permission" (Frame, *Doctrine of God*, 178). But what does this mean? Francis Turretin suggests that "this permission must not be conceived negatively, as if it was a mere keeping back *(anergia)* or cessation of his will and providence in evil works.... But it must be conceived positively and affirmatively; not simply that God does not will to hinder sin (which is an otiose negation), but that he wills not to hinder (which is an efficacious affirmation). Thus the permission involves a positive act of the secret will by which God designedly and willingly determined not to hinder sin, although he may be said to nill it as to the revealed will of approbation. In this sense, our divines do not refuse to employ the word 'permission' with the Scriptures. And if at any time they reject it ... they understand it in the Pelagian sense of otiose 'permission' which takes away from God his own right and sets up the idol of free will in its place" (Francis Turretin, *Institutes of Elenctic Theology*, ed. James T. Dennison Jr., trans. George Musgrave Giger, 3 vols. [Phillipsburg, N.J.: P&R, 1992–97], 1:516–17).

22. Turretin, *Institutes of Elenctic Theology*, 1:501.

23. Ibid., 1:501, 502.

24. Ibid., 1:502. According to Turretin, those who hold that the "influx of the first cause" is "indifferent to this action or the contrary" do so "principally for two reasons: one is to vindicate God from the causality of sin; the other to establish the liberty and indifference *(adiaphoria)* of the human will in all acts (especially in conversion) and to reconcile it with divine providence" (ibid.).

observing what he has created but also by simultaneously working concurrently with created things "to cause them to act as they do,"[25] and governing their activity according to his wisdom to direct them to fulfill what Warfield calls "His all-determining will."[26] While Reformed believers concede that the modes of God's operation in preservation, in concurrence, and in government can be distinguished in one sense, they insist that these operations cannot be in another sense because they "are not parts or segments in which the work of providence is divided and which, being materially and temporally separate, succeed one another."[27] Rather, these operations "are always integrally connected; they intermesh at all times."[28] It is for this reason, then, that the providence of God involves, not a series of isolated and independent acts in which God works in one way and then in another with created things, but rather the organic and integrated means by which "the purposive will of the eternal God" is progressively realized.[29] "From the very beginning," Bavinck argues,

> preservation is also government, and government is concurrence, and concurrence is preservation. Preservation tells us that nothing exists, not only no substance, but also no power, no activity, no idea, unless it exists totally from, through, and to God. Concurrence makes known to us the same preservation as an activity such that, far from suspending the existence of creatures, it above all affirms and maintains it. And government describes the other two

---

25. Wayne Grudem, *Bible Doctrine: Essential Teachings of the Christian Faith* (Grand Rapids: Zondervan, 1999), 142. Bavinck concludes his discussion of concurrence with this helpful summary: "In relation to God the secondary causes can be compared to instruments (Isa. 10:15; 13:5; Jer. 50:25; Acts 9:15; Rom. 9:20–23); in relation to their effects and products they are causes in a true sense. And precisely because the primary and the secondary cause do not stand and function dualistically on separate tracks, but the primary works through the secondary, the effect that proceeds from the two is one and the product is one. There is no division of labor between God and his creature, but the same effect is totally the effect of the primary cause as well as totally the effect of the proximate cause. The product is also in the same sense totally the product of the primary as well as totally the product of the secondary cause. But because the primary cause and the secondary cause are not identical and differ essentially, the effect and product are *in reality* totally the effect and product of the two causes, to be sure, but *formally* they are only the effect and product of the secondary cause" (Bavinck, *Reformed Dogmatics*, 2:614–15).

26. Warfield, "Predestination," 62.

27. Bavinck, *Reformed Dogmatics*, 2:605.

28. Ibid.

29. Warfield, "Confessional Doctrine," 95.

as guiding all things in such a way that the final goal determined by God will be reached. And always, from beginning to end, providence is one simple, almighty, and omnipresent power.[30]

Providence as "Continuous Creation"

The Creator-Creature Relationship: Utterly Unique

At the formative center of this understanding of providence is the insistence that the universe was "freely created out of nothing, by a creator whose perfection is in no way enhanced by the act of creating, so that [the act of creation] must be thoroughly gratuitous."[31] When God spoke the universe into existence, advocates of this view of providence maintain, he created a universe that is simultaneously both distinct from and yet utterly dependent on him for its existence from one moment to the next. Unlike the gods of the various pagan religions, which are "never conceived as capable of being without the world," the God of Christian theism "could have been all that there is," these believers insist, because the world, quite simply, "does not have to be."[32] "In Christian belief," Robert Sokolowski argues, "we understand the world as that which might not have been, and correlatively we understand God as capable of existing, in undiminished goodness and greatness, even if the world had not been."[33]

Since the God of Christian theism is not like the gods of the pagan religions — in that he is not "established as God" by that which distinguishes him from "other things ... within the horizon of this world"[34] — it follows that the relationship between God and the universe ought not to be construed "as we construe [the relationship between] objects within the universe,"[35] for the relation "of the creator-of-all with all that is created" is utterly unique.[36] Indeed, it is the utterly unique nature of this relationship that establishes "the utterly gratuitous character of the

30. Bavinck, *Reformed Dogmatics*, 2:605.

31. David B. Burrell, "Creation, Metaphysics, and Ethics," *Faith and Philosophy* 18, no. 2 (April 2001): 207.

32. Robert Sokolowski, *The God of Faith and Reason: Foundations of Christian Theology* (Notre Dame: University of Notre Dame Press, 1982), 18, 19, 33.

33. Ibid., 19.

34. Ibid., 33.

35. Burrell, "Creation, Metaphysics, and Ethics," 206.

36. David B. Burrell, "Creator/Creatures Relation: 'The Distinction' vs. 'Onto-Theology,'" *Faith and Philosophy* 25, no. 2 (April 2008): 179.

act of creation,"[37] for since the world does not "have to be," it must be that it now *is* only because of "a choice. And if the choice was not motivated by the need for 'there' to be more perfection and greatness, then the world is there through an incomparable generosity," a generosity "that has no parallel in what we experience in the world."[38] What this suggests, then, is that the world we live in is radically contingent[39] and ultimately exists from one moment to the next, not for the benefit of human beings or anything else that is found within the horizon of this world, but "simply for the glory of God. The glory of God," Sokolowski argues, "is seen not only in particularly splendid parts of the world but in the very existence of the world and everything in it."[40]

Absolute Dependence and "Continuous Creation"

For those who conceive of the Creator-creature relationship in this fashion, it follows that the created order is utterly dependent on the providential activity of the Creator for its moment-to-moment existence, because it does not have the power of existence in itself. It has, in other words, "no independent existence," for from one moment to the next it exists "only in and through and unto God (Neh. 9:6; Ps. 104:30; Acts 17:28; Rom. 11:36; Col. 1:15ff.; Heb. 1:3; Rev. 4:11)," despite what those with deistic tendencies would have us believe.[41] While those with deistic tendencies presume that God is a more or less passive agent to whom the world is related much like a machine is related to the person who made it, Reformed believers insist that "the relation to the creation sustained by God, and that sustained by man to the work of his hand," are entirely distinct.[42] Indeed, as Archibald Alexander Hodge makes clear in his response to those who represent the Creator "as exterior to his creation in the same manner in which a mechanician is exterior to the machine he has made and set in motion," whereas "a man

---

37. Ibid., 184.

38. Sokolowski, *God of Faith and Reason*, 34.

39. Burrell, "Creation, Metaphysics, and Ethics," 205.

40. Sokolowski, *God of Faith and Reason*, 34.

41. Bavinck, *Reformed Dogmatics*, 2:592. Those with deistic tendencies presume that God endows secondary causes with certain capacities and then grants them a measure of autonomy, that is, the capacity to govern themselves.

42. Archibald Alexander Hodge, *Outlines of Theology* (1860; repr., Edinburgh: Banner of Truth Trust, 1991), 259.

is necessarily *exterior* to his work, and even when present capable of directing his attention only to one point [of his handiwork] at a time ... God is omnipresent, not as to his essence only, but as to his infinite knowledge, wisdom, love, righteousness, and power, with every atom of creation for every instant of duration."[43] What this suggests, then, is that for Reformed believers, the world of secondary causes is never "separated from the primary cause and ... [therefore] independent,"[44] but it "is always interpenetrated as well as embraced in the divine thought and will, and ever is what it is and as it is because of God."[45]

Among those who insist that the universe is both radically contingent and utterly dependent are those Reformed thinkers who embrace the doctrine of concurrence, in part because they recognize that, given what the notion of utter dependence entails, the very idea of an "independent creature" is nonsense.[46] Whereas some Reformed thinkers repudiate concurrence because they are persuaded that "the power to originate our own acts" is compatible with the fact of creaturely dependence,[47] others maintain that since "the world has no existence in itself," independence of any kind—including the kind that is presup-

---

43. Ibid., 259, 260.

44. Bavinck, *Reformed Dogmatics*, 2:613.

45. A. A. Hodge, *Outlines of Theology*, 260. According to Bavinck, "Just as providence is a power and an act, so it is also an almighty and everywhere present power. God is immanently present with his being in all creatures. His providence extends to all creatures; all things exist in him" (Bavinck, *Reformed Dogmatics*, 2:606).

46. Bavinck, *Reformed Dogmatics*, 2:592. It is also, Bavinck notes, "an oxymoron" (ibid.).

47. Charles Hodge, *Systematic Theology*, 1:605, 604. Denying that created beings have the ability to "originate action" is founded, thinkers like Charles Hodge curiously maintain, on the "arbitrary and false assumption" that "the power of spontaneous action" must be denied if "the absolute control of God over created beings" is to be maintained (ibid., 1:604). Hodge's repudiation of concurrence is "curious" because it seems uncharacteristically confused and confusing. While Hodge repudiates concurrence on the one hand because he wants to maintain that we "originate our own acts," he insists on the other hand that the power to "originate our own acts" is "not ... inconsistent" with being "moved and induced to exert our ability to act by considerations addressed to our reason or inclinations, or by the grace of God" (ibid.). But how, one wonders, is this all that different from Reformed thinkers who endorse the doctrine of concurrence? For example, Bavinck, as we have seen, embraces the doctrine of concurrence, yet he rejects the notion that secondary causes "are ... merely instruments, organs, inanimate automata, but they are genuine causes with a nature, vitality, spontaneity, manner of working, and law of their own" (Bavinck, *Reformed Dogmatics*, 2:614). Given my work elsewhere on the Princeton theologians, it pains me to say that this might be one place where Scottish realism got the better of Hodge, for his repudiation of concurrence, while informed by a number of measured considerations, is also informed by an appeal to the principles of common sense: the "arbitrary and false assumption" that informs the doctrine of concurrence—namely, that creatures cannot "originate action"—is false, Hodge argues, because it "contradicts the consciousness of men" (Hodge, *Systematic Theology*, 1:604).

posed by those who insist that secondary causes have the capacity to act more or less independently of God, the primary cause—"is tantamount to nonexistence."[48] Indeed, as Bavinck insists, "A creature is, by definition, of itself a completely dependent being: that which does not exist *of* itself cannot for a moment exist *by* itself either. If God does not do anything," Bavinck contends, "then nothing exists and nothing happens."[49]

How, then, do Reformed believers conceive of the providence of God given the radically contingent nature of the creaturely condition? What does the fact of absolute dependence suggest, in other words, for how they understand the providential activity of the Creator? Reformed thinkers who embrace the doctrine of concurrence are persuaded that the answer is found in the intimate nature of the relationship between "the activity of God in creating the world" on the one hand and God's ongoing work of providence on the other.[50] According to Bavinck, although "it is the same omnipotent and omnipresent power of God that is at work both in creation and in providence," nevertheless the precise nature of God's work in creation and in providence is "essentially distinct" because in each case, "the relation that God assumes toward his creatures" is different.[51] Whereas in creation God "calls into being the things that are not, things that have no other existence than that of ideas and decrees in the being of God," in providence— which, like creation, "is a positive act, not a giving permission to exist but a causing to exist and working from moment to moment"—God actively sustains those things that have received "their own unique existence" and as a consequence are distinct from him.[52] In providence, in other words, the power of God yields not existence, as if "creatures or second causes have no real continuous existence but are reproduced every successive moment out of nothing, in their respective successive states, conditions, and actions by the perpetual efflux of the 'vis creatrix' of God."[53] Rather, it yields "persistence in existence"—the kind of

48. Bavinck, *Reformed Dogmatics*, 2:592.

49. Ibid., 2:605–6. According to Turretin, "As man depends upon God as to essence and life, so he must depend upon him as to the actions and movements of his soul.... For to pretend that man is independent in will and action is to make him independent in being because whatever he is in acting such he is in being" (Turretin, *Institutes of Elenctic Theology*, 1:500).

50. Bavinck, *Reformed Dogmatics*, 2:605.

51. Ibid., 2:607, 605, 607.

52. Ibid., 2:608, 605, 608.

53. A. A. Hodge, *Outlines of Theology*, 260.

"persistence in existence" that does not "nullify" but rather establishes the real existence of secondary causes—and this is why thinkers like Bavinck insist that the providential activity of the Creator ought to be regarded as a "continuous creation," that is, as "a form of preservation which presupposes creation."[54] Conceiving of the doctrine of providence in this fashion, Bavinck fittingly concludes, presents us with a "mystery" that far exceeds our capacity to understand, and this is why our minds are "always inclined to do less than justice" either to the fact of our absolute dependence on God or to the reality of our unique creaturely existence.[55] "It is this inclination," he notes,

> that underlies both pantheism and Deism. Both of these trends proceed from the same error and oppose God and the world to each other as two competing entities. The former sacrifices the world to God, creation to providence, and believes that God's existence can only be a divinely infinite existence if it denies the existence of the world, dissolves it into mere appearance, and allows it to be swallowed up by divine existence. The latter sacrifices God to the world, providence to creation, and believes that creatures come into their own to the extent that they become less dependent on God and distance themselves from God. The Christian, however, confesses that the world and every creature in it have received their own existence, but increase in reality, freedom, and authenticity to the extent that they are more dependent on God and exist from moment to moment from, through, and to God. A creature is the more perfect to the degree that God indwells it more and permeates it with his being. In that respect preservation is even greater than creation, for the latter only initiated the beginning of existence, but the former is the progressive and ever increasing self-communication of

---

54. Bavinck, *Reformed Dogmatics*, 2:608, 614, 607. Bavinck's understanding of "continuous creation" is not intended, he argues, "to erase the distinction between creation and providence, as [Charles] Hodge for one fears.... Creation and providence are not identical. If providence meant a creating anew every moment, creatures would also have to be produced out of nothing every moment. In that case, the continuity, connectedness, and 'order of causes' would be totally lost, and there would be no development or history. All created beings would then exist in appearance only and be devoid of all independence, freedom, and responsibility. God himself would be the cause of sin. Although many theologians called providence a 'continuous creation,' they by no means meant to erase the difference between the two. They all regarded providence rather as simultaneously also an act of causing creatures to persist in their existence, as a form of preservation that presupposes creation" (ibid., 2:607).

55. Ibid., 2:608.

God to his creatures. Providence is "the progressive expression in the universe of his divine perfection, the progressive realization in it of the archetypal ideal of perfect wisdom and love."[56]

The "True View" of Providence Summarized

For classical Reformed thinkers, then, the "true view" of providence stands midway between the extremes of deism on the one hand and pantheism on the other,[57] for it affirms not just that secondary causes are and remain distinct from God, the primary cause, but also that the primary cause "confers reality" on secondary causes and that these causes continue to exist "solely as a result of the first."[58] Indeed, it is the primary cause, Reformed thinkers reason, that "is precisely the reason for the self-activity of the secondary causes, and these causes, sustained from beginning to end by God's power, work with a strength that is appropriate and natural to them."[59] As such, the classical Reformed view of providence can be summarized according to "the following propositions:

1. Created substances, both spiritual and material, possess real and permanent existence, i.e., they are real entities.
2. They possess all such active or passive properties as they have been severally endowed with by God.
3. The properties or active powers have a real, and not merely apparent, efficiency as second causes in producing the effects proper to them; and the phenomena alike of consciousness and of the outward world are really produced by the efficient agency of second causes, as we are informed by our native and necessary intuitions.
4. But these created substances are not self-existent, i.e., the ground of their continued existence is in God and not in themselves.
5. They continue to exist not merely in virtue of a negative act of God, whereby he merely does not will their destruction, but in virtue of a positive, continued exercise of divine power, whereby

---

56. Ibid.
57. A. A. Hodge, *Outlines of Theology*, 261.
58. Bavinck, *Reformed Dogmatics*, 2:614.
59. Ibid.

they are sustained in being, and in the possession of all their properties and powers with which God has endowed them.

6. The precise nature of the divine action concerned in upholding all things in being and action is, like every mode of the intercourse of the infinite with the finite, inscrutable—but not more mysterious in this case than in every other."[60]

Perceived Weaknesses of Divine Omnicausality

Divine Omnicausality and the Pagan Context

So what are we to make of the doctrine of providence that I have attempted to outline in the preceding pages? In my estimation, the primary difficulty with the doctrine is found not in the doctrine itself but in the increasingly pagan milieu that makes the doctrine sound almost completely implausible to contemporary listeners. It perhaps goes without saying that the doctrine itself commends a vision of God and of his providence that is growing more and more foreign in a culture that is increasingly beholden to pagan assumptions about God and the self. As scholars like David Wells, Peter Jones, and Ann Douglas have argued, we live in a culture in which more "classical" forms of spirituality are slowly being eclipsed by one form or another of "pagan spirituality,"[61] the heart of which is always found in the repudiation of what J. Gresham Machen calls "the awful transcendence of God."[62] As a consequence of this accommodation, it is becoming increasingly difficult for those who are and are not members of the church even to consider the possibility that, as created beings, we are, as Warfield puts it, "wholly at the disposal of another."[63] In short, the doctrine of divine omnicausality is growing more and more difficult for many of our con-

---

60. A. A. Hodge, *Outlines of Theology*, 261–62. Obviously, the phrase "upholding all things in being and action" in proposition six above is loaded. For Hodge and Reformed believers generally, it entails "the universal, efficient control of God, whereby ... he determines and disposes of all actions and events according to his sovereign purpose" (ibid., 268).

61. See, e.g., David Wells, *Losing Our Virtue: Why the Church Must Recover Its Moral Vision* (Grand Rapids: Eerdmans, 1998); Peter Jones, *Spirit Wars: Pagan Revival in Christian America* (Mukilteo, Wash.: WinePress; Escondido, Calif.: Main Entry Editions, 1997); Ann Douglas, *The Feminization of American Culture* (1977; repr., New York: Noonday Press, 1998).

62. J. Gresham Machen, *Christianity and Liberalism* (1923; repr., Grand Rapids: Eerdmans, 1990), 62. See also idem, "My Idea of God," in *My Idea of God* (Boston: Little, Brown and Co., 1927), 39–50.

63. Warfield, "Predestination," 103.

temporaries to take seriously because we think increasingly little of God and progressively more of ourselves and of our capacities. Indeed, to one degree or another, we have accommodated the paganism of the age and in the process have "gone soft" on the Creator/creature distinction, and as a consequence, as Warfield provocatively notes, "we wish 'to belong to ourselves,' and we resent belonging, especially belonging absolutely, to anybody else, even if that anybody else be God."[64]

Moral Responsibility and Determinism

It goes without saying, however, that many who reject the doctrine of divine omnicausality do so, not because they are eager to embrace one form of pagan spirituality or another, but because they are persuaded that rejecting omnicausality is what faithfulness to the God of the Bible requires them to do. The determinism entailed in the notion that God is the primary cause of all things must be repudiated, these scholars reason, not only because it is inconsistent "with the moral responsibility that is essential to the Christian understanding of reality,"[65] but more importantly because it commends a vision of God that they find revolting.

The determinism that is entailed in the doctrine of divine omni-causality must be repudiated in the first place, these scholars reason, because it undermines the genuineness of human freedom. According to these scholars, we should embrace ways of telling the Christian story that are grounded in the conviction that the providence of God is occupied not with the "operation" of all things generally but, as Turretin

---

64. Ibid. Note that both pantheism and deism magnify the importance of the self. While deism's magnification is more obvious [Bavinck insists that for deists, "the salvation of humanity consists not in communion with God but in separation from him.... In principle, Deism is always the same; it deactivates God, but one Deist will walk that road further than another. A Deist is a person who in his short life has not found the time to become an atheist," (*Reformed Dogmatics*, 2:603)], pantheism's magnification is subtler. According to Warfield, pantheists regard God as "a universal force acting uniformly" ("Confessional Doctrine," 94). God, in other words, acts not as a personal being but as "an amorphic force by a uniform pressure made effectual here, there, or elsewhere by differences in the object on which it impinges" (ibid.). As such, given the uniform nature of this "divine influence," the magnification of the self is found in the role the self plays in responding to the influence: "What happens to the individual ... is determined, not by the 'divine influence' which plays alike on all, but by something in himself which makes him respond more or less to the 'divine influence' common to all" (B. B. Warfield, "What Fatalism Is," in *Shorter Writings*, 1:394).

65. Thomas H. McCall, "We Believe in God's Sovereign Goodness: A Rejoinder to John Piper," *Trinity Journal*, 29 ns, no. 2 (Fall 2008): 246.

summarizes their position, "only with the conservation of things."[66] We should think of "the divine concurrence or continuing ontological support" of the world that God has made, in other words, as "flow[ing] not into the activity of the will," as those who embrace the doctrine of divine omnicausality maintain, but, as Richard Muller describes their view, "into its effect, leaving the will entirely free while at the same time providentially supporting its result."[67]

Reformed believers typically respond to the suggestion that "there are moments in the framework of volitional contingency that arise entirely from the creature"[68] by arguing along two different lines. According to the first line of argument, they grant that although the question of how "the concourse of God can be reconciled with the contingency and liberty of second causes — especially of the will of man" — is difficult and "incapable of being sufficiently explained" by those who are contingent beings themselves,[69] nevertheless the question is principally a theological rather than a philosophical question. The question that should guide our attempts to formulate a Christian understanding of providence, they argue, is not the philosophical question of whether it is logically possible for God to create contingent beings that have the ability to act independently of his all-determining will, but the theological question of what the Scriptures teach regarding the relationship between the providence of God and human freedom in this world.[70] When our consideration of the question is "religiously restrain[ed] ... within the bounds prescribed by [Scripture]," Reformed believers insist, it becomes immediately clear that in this world, God "concurs with all

66. Turretin, *Institutes of Elenctic Theology*, 1:503.

67. Richard A. Muller, "Grace, Election, and Contingent Choice: Arminius's Gambit and the Reformed Response," in *The Grace of God, the Bondage of the Will*, vol. 2 of *Historical and Theological Perspectives on Calvinism*, ed. Thomas A. Schreiner and Bruce A. Ware (Grand Rapids: Baker, 1995), 265.

68. Ibid.

69. Turretin, *Institutes of Elenctic Theology*, 1:511.

70. In other words, the methodological starting point for our consideration should be revelation rather than reason. Scott Oliphint and Lane Tipton wisely note that "if one wants to know about God's omniscience or his eternity, if one wants to think deeply about God and his relationship to the world, if one wants to do apologetics, the first place to look is to Scripture, and then to those theologians who faithfully articulate its teachings. Philosophy, even Christian philosophy, has a long and resolute history of turning its back on a consistent Reformed theology. It, therefore, has not fared well with regard to theological (or philosophical-theological) discussions" (Introduction to *Revelation and Reason: New Essays in Reformed Apologetics*, ed. K. Scott Oliphint and Lane G. Tipton [Phillipsburg, N.J.: P&R, 2007], 2–3).

second causes and especially with the human will" while simultaneously leaving the "contingency and liberty of the will … unimpaired."[71] Scripture presumes that determinism and genuine human freedom are compatible, in other words, even though it does not explain the mechanics of how this is possible, and "the method of this reconciliation cannot in this life be clearly and perfectly explained by us."[72] As Turretin summarizes the matter, when we eschew eisegesis and begin with the data of Scripture, the careful analysis of the text yields two "indubitable" conclusions, both of which must be held in tension without allowing either one to cancel the other out:

> that God on the one hand by his providence not only decreed but most certainly secures the event of all things, whether free or contingent; on the other hand, however, man is always free in acting and many effects are contingent. Although I cannot understand how these can be mutually connected together, yet (on account of ignorance of the mode) the thing itself is (which is certain from another source, i.e., from the word) not either to be called in question or wholly denied.[73]

According to the second line of argument, Reformed believers suggest not only that libertarian freedom is impossible to reconcile with many of the things that Scripture explicitly teaches about God's relationship to the things that "hold together" (Col. 1:17) and have their "being" (Acts 17:28) in him,[74] but also that the concept of libertarian freedom is itself extremely problematic, for it presumes that "some things existed prior to and apart from the creative work of God and continue to exist outside of God's providence."[75] This presumption, Richard Muller argues, is seen most clearly in the Molinist and Arminian

---

71. Turretin, *Institutes of Elenctic Theology*, 1:511.

72. Ibid. Note that for Turretin, this mystery is an occasion for praise: "But how these two things can consist with each other, no mortal can in this life perfectly understand. Nor should it seem a cause for wonder, since he has a thousand ways (to us incomprehensible) of concurring with our will, insinuating himself into us and turning our hearts, so that by acting freely as we will, we still do nothing besides the will and determination of God. Thus here deservedly, if anywhere else, we may exclaim: 'O the depth … how unsearchable are his judgments, and his ways past finding out!' (Rom. 11:33 KJV)" (ibid.).

73. Ibid., 1:512.

74. For an extended discussion of the biblical data that establishes "that God controls nature, history, and individuals (including their free decisions) in minute detail" (Frame, *Doctrine of God*, 287), see Frame, *The Doctrine of God*, 47–79.

75. Muller, "Grace, Election, and Contingent Choice," 266–67.

view of divine concurrence: Molina and Arminius after him argue that the divine action or concurrence that supports the existence of works or effects brought about by contingent agents enters the finite order of events in the effect, not in the secondary or finite cause. God thus supports the effect and gives it actuality while not strictly bringing it about or willing it. The finite agent acts independently in bringing about the action or effect.[76]

While Reformed believers acknowledge that theories of providence that are grounded in a commitment to libertarian freedom can in some sense account for the "effects" of secondary causes, nevertheless they insist that these theories fall "into ontological absurdity" because they cannot account "for the ... action" of the secondary causes themselves.[77] Though they affirm both the doctrine of creation *ex nihilo* and the fact of creaturely dependence on the one hand, they simultaneously presume that human beings with libertarian freedom are sources of primary causality on the other, and thus they reveal a Manichaean tendency[78] that,

---

76. Ibid., 267.

77. Ibid.

78. I am indebted to Walter Schultz for characterizing in this fashion the problem with libertarian freedom. Note that Schultz does *not* suggest that libertarian freedom *is* Manichaean (indeed, he argues for the conceptual possibility of a restricted form of libertarianism himself), but that the way it is advocated can exhibit a Manichaean *tendency*. In personal correspondence that is cited with permission, Schultz clarifies: "It goes without saying that most Protestants and Catholics believe that God is sovereign and good, that creation is *ex nihilo* and that agents will be held responsible by God. The challenge for those who equate genuine freedom with libertarian freedom is to logically and scripturally give an account of how creatures that are ontologically dependent on God from one moment to the next can at the same time possess a measure of functional autonomy. That is, the challenge is to give an *explanation*—not merely an *assertion*, and not merely a *description* of a libertarian free action—but an explanation of *how* a created agent, who is ontologically dependent on God at every moment of its existence (if neurological correlates count and if Planck physics is correct, then every *moment* must be a Planck moment 10^{-43} seconds), can *ever* be functionally independent. Reformed thinkers who claim that the relationship between God's sovereignty and human responsibility is 'inscrutable' don't think that such an explanation *can* be given. Of course, this is not because they think that these notions are contradictory. The set of notions, *sovereignty, goodness, creation ex nihilo*, and *responsibility*, while paradoxical, is consistent, they believe, provided that the content of each notion is grounded in the clear teaching of scripture.

"Here is the main point: some Christian theists, including most Reformed thinkers, would rather live with inscrutability and emphasize God's sovereignty and goodness than to diminish its content in ways apparently contrary to scripture. By contrast, when some advocates of libertarianism—because of their commitment to libertarianism—seem willing to *diminish* the scriptural content of the notion of God's sovereignty and its scripturally explicit implications, they seem (in effect) to treat created agents as ontologically independent sources of causality, and they do this despite the fact that they lack an account of the *mechanism* of libertarian free choice. One feature of the Manichaeism opposed by Augustine was its commitment to more than one ontologically independent source of causality. While our semi-Pelagian and Arminian brothers and sisters would reject Manichaeism, some of them seem to exhibit a

in addition to being essentially unintelligible,[79] subverts the *solas* of the Reformation as well as the essential tenets of a biblical metaphysic. Indeed, the "power to do otherwise"[80] that is essential to these theories of providence not only "assaults the doctrine of salvation by grace" by regarding human beings with libertarian freedom as "the first and effective agent[s] in salvation."[81] More importantly, it challenges "the assumption that God alone is original, self-existent, and necessary and that the entire contingent order depends on God for its existence," for it presumes — without so much as a shred of explicit biblical support — that finite agents have the capacity to bring themselves and other things "from potency to actuality without the divine concurrence."[82]

The Revulsion Factor: Confusing God and Satan

The determinism entailed in the doctrine of divine omnicausality must be repudiated in the second place, these scholars reason, because it is grounded in a vision of God that they believe is nothing less than revolting. A particularly disturbing example of this sentiment is found in Gregory Boyd's none-too-subtle suggestion that there are legitimate grounds for confusing the God of Reformed believers with Satan. In his book *Satan and the Problem of Evil: Constructing a Trinitarian Warfare Theodicy*, Boyd notes:

---

tendency to prefer one of its essential components in place of a more robust biblical view of God's sovereignty" (Walter J. Schultz in an email to Paul Kjoss Helseth, November 1, 2010).

79. For a brief summary of what is called "the intelligibility question," see Robert Kane, "Introduction: The Contours of Contemporary Free Will Debates," in *The Oxford Handbook of Free Will*, ed. Robert Kane (New York: Oxford University Press, 2002), 22–23.

80. For a helpful discussion of the "power to do otherwise," see Gregory A. Boyd, *Satan and the Problem of Evil: Constructing a Trinitarian Warfare Theodicy* (Downers Grove, Ill.: InterVarsity Press, 2001), 56–57.

81. Muller, "Grace, Election, and Contingent Choice," 266.

82. Ibid., 266, 267. If the "scandal" of the Reformed worldview "is that ultimately the logical problems posed cannot be fully resolved," the dirty little secret of the Arminian worldview is that the independence that the Arminian system requires "cannot be exegetically vindicated" (Thomas R. Schreiner, "Does Scripture Teach Prevenient Grace in the Wesleyan Sense?" in Schreiner and Ware, *Grace of God, Bondage of the Will*, 2:381, 382). While the recognition that those who are dead in sin and without the ability to pursue Christ apart from regenerating grace is essential to the Reformed worldview and explicitly taught throughout Scripture (see, e.g., 1 Cor. 1 and 2), the prevenient grace that rescues Arminianism from Pelagianism and makes the system work "is a philosophical imposition of a certain world view upon the Scriptures" (ibid., 2:381).

If God, not Satan, is behind all the nightmares of the world, then far from trusting God we should rather follow the advice of W. Robert McClelland and consider it our moral obligation to "rage" against God as our "enemy." ... He agrees that we should not accept all things as coming from God's hand. In his view, we should *revolt* against God *because* all things come from his hand. From the blue-print [i.e., the omnicausal] model of providence McClelland draws the logical conclusion that God can only be understood in the midst of suffering as "the enemy." In my estimation, all of McClelland's instincts are right except for the fact that he confuses God and Satan. If one grants McClelland's omni-controlling view of God, however, everything that he says about God follows.[83]

While Reformed believers usually respond to a polemic like this by commending the critic for his candor even while challenging the critic for a lack of nuance that is appalling, they also insist that the Reformed view of providence is the only view that can unambiguously affirm what Scripture affirms with respect to particular evils. Indeed, not only can the Reformed view affirm that God does in fact work in some mysterious way through pain and suffering and evil for the good of his children and the glory of his name (there is no better example of this, they suggest, than the cross, which happened according to "the definite plan and foreknowledge of God," Acts 2:23 ESV; cf. Acts 2 and 4), but it can also salvage purpose and meaning in the midst of suffering precisely because it affirms that "all the paths of the LORD are steadfast love and faithfulness, for those who keep his covenant and his testimonies" (Ps. 25:10 ESV). In short, Reformed believers are persuaded that particular evils happen not merely because "God chose to actualize a possible world in which those evils would obtain," nor because "he — for one arbitrary reason or another — chose not to coercively intervene in human history in order to prevent such evils from happening in this world." Rather, particular evils happen because he ordained that they would, and he did so for reasons that, while ultimately inscrutable, nevertheless serve to conform believers more and more to the image of Christ (Rom. 8:28 – 30) and, in the process, to cultivate in them the Christian virtues of perseverance, proven character, and hope (Rom. 5:1 – 5). This

---

83. Boyd, *Satan and the Problem of Evil*, 163 n. 27.

is why Reformed believers conclude with Calvin, in his commentary on 1 Thessalonians 5:18, that "even in our afflictions we have large occasion of thanksgiving. For what is fitter or more suitable for pacifying us, than when we learn that God embraces us in Christ so tenderly, that he turns to our advantage and welfare everything that befalls us?"[84]

Speaking of Contemptible Beings

In response to Dr. Boyd's none-too-subtle suggestion, then, many Reformed believers insist that although there is a viable candidate for a truly contemptible deity within the orbit of contemporary evangelicalism, it is not the God "who works all things" — including evil things — "according to the counsel of his will" (Eph. 1:11 ESV). Rather, it is the God of open theism, for that God, as I have demonstrated elsewhere, is a capricious being who cannot be trusted to work in every situation in a way that maximizes good and minimizes evil for his creatures.[85] The justification for this contention is found in the arbitrary role that "select determinism" plays in the open view of providence.[86] As Dr. Boyd's

84. John Calvin, *Commentaries on the Epistles of Paul the Apostle to the Philippians, Colossians, and Thessalonians*, vol. 21 of *Calvin's Commentaries*, trans. and ed. John Pringle (Grand Rapids: Baker, 1996), 297.

85. For a much fuller exposition of the polemic in the forthcoming paragraphs, see Paul Kjoss Helseth, "On Divine Ambivalence: Open Theism and the Problem of Particular Evils," *JETS* 44 (September 2001): 493–511; idem, "What Is at Stake in the Openness Debate? The Trustworthiness of God and the Foundation of Hope," in *Beyond the Bounds: Open Theism and the Undermining of Biblical Christianity*, ed. John Piper, Justin Taylor, and Paul Kjoss Helseth (Wheaton, Ill.: Crossway, 2003), 275–307; idem, "Neo-Molinism: A Traditional-Openness Rapprochement?" *Southern Baptist Journal of Theology* 7, no. 3 (Fall 2003): 56–73. While I suspect that Dr. Boyd will want to challenge my characterization of his views for, if nothing else, "a lack of nuance that is appalling," I must confess that I do not see how he can gainsay the substance of my critique, for I do not see how everything that I have argued about the God of open theism does not follow from Dr. Boyd's writings in general and his treatment of Peter in particular. Obviously, Dr. Boyd does not owe me an explanation, but I would appreciate knowing how I am misrepresenting his views, if in fact I am.

86. Jason A. Nicholls, "Openness and Inerrancy: Can They Be Compatible?" *JETS* 45 (December 2002): 640. According to Nicholls, the standard critiques of the open view of providence tend to presume that openness theologians cannot affirm that God is the sovereign Lord of history because their commitment to the concept of libertarian freedom is unlimited. This presumption, Nicholls argues, is based on "a misconception about the openness view," namely, that openness theologians are unwilling "to make room in their system for the possibility of periodic instances of divine intervention . . . , perhaps even to the point of controlling, overwhelming or overriding libertarian freedom on occasion" (ibid., 631, 647). The God of open theism in fact retains providential control over the unfolding course of cosmic history, Nicholls contends, because he is willing "to control the final outcome of a partly unforeseen future by means of specific, periodic, unilateral intervention, something that might be called his *select determinism*" (ibid., 640).

treatment of Peter's denial of Jesus makes clear, the God of open theism "can and does at times unilaterally intervene and work in a coercive way to bring about a certain state of affairs,"[87] yet he does so without "an all-encompassing divine blueprint."[88] Indeed, he retains providential control over a future that is partly settled and partly open, in part by acting in ways that violate the self-determining freedom of responsible moral agents, yet he does so without an exhaustive plan that determines when he will act unilaterally and when he will not, thus suggesting that his unilateral activity is governed by nothing more than the passing whims of one particular moment or the next.

This willingness to sanction coercion—particularly coercion that is entirely arbitrary because it does not take place according to an "overarching divine purpose"[89] and plan—poses an insurmountable problem for the open view of providence, I would argue, for at least two reasons. First, it demonstrates that the foundational assumptions of the openness program cannot be consistently applied to the analysis of the flow of history. Openness theologians would have us believe that the future is open to God as well as to human beings because the "ultimate purpose [of God] includes having free agents"[90] whose libertarian freedom is "irrevocable."[91] The willingness of openness theologians to allow for God to work in a fashion that violates the self-determining freedom of responsible moral agents jettisons the coherence of the openness program, then, for it establishes that the God of open theism cannot accomplish his ultimate purpose without violating an essential component of that purpose. Indeed, it establishes that the God of open theism is not just an arbitrary being but a conflicted being as well.

Second, the willingness of openness theologians to sanction coercion makes it much more difficult—if not altogether impossible—to rescue the God of open theism from being tarnished by the problem of evil. Why? Before I suggest an answer to this question, note that open-

87. Gregory A. Boyd, "A Response to John Piper," May 4, 1998. www.bgc.bethel. edu/4know/response.htm. Accessed September 3, 1999.

88. Gregory A. Boyd, *God at War: The Bible and Spiritual Conflict* (Downers Grove, Ill.: InterVarsity Press, 1997), 302 n. 18.

89. Gregory A. Boyd, *God of the Possible: A Biblical Introduction to the Open View of God* (Grand Rapids: Baker, 2000), 153.

90. Gregory A. Boyd and Edward K. Boyd, *Letters from a Skeptic* (Wheaton, Ill.: Victor, 1994), 47.

91. Boyd, *Satan and the Problem of Evil*, 181–84.

ness theologians would have us believe that their view of evil is superior to the Reformed view, not only because it helps us understand that evil in general and specific evils in particular are simply the unfortunate consequences of free decisions to reject the love of God, but also because it helps us understand why "the all-powerful Creator of the world" does not prevent certain events "he wishes would not take place."[92] Whereas Reformed believers insist that there is "a *specific* divine reason for each *specific* evil in the world,"[93] advocates of the open view are persuaded that certain evils occur because God—in order to preserve his integrity—simply cannot prevent them without revoking the irrevocable gift of self-determining freedom that is necessary to love. But if the God of open theism in fact *is* willing—as he was in the case of Peter's denial of Jesus—to revoke the gift of self-determining freedom in order to bring about states of affairs that he really wants to bring about, then what becomes of this defense? In other words, what becomes of the attempt to get God "off the hook" for the problem of evil if he in fact *is* willing to violate the gift of self-determining freedom that he has given to moral agents, the gift that openness theologians insist is not just "irrevocable" but "the key to morally responsible personhood"?[94] What becomes of it, in short, is that it is destroyed, for if God can and does work unilaterally from time to time to bring about states of affairs that he really wants to bring about, and if this coercive involvement can and does involve—as it did in the case of Peter—real violations of the gift of self-determining freedom given to responsible moral agents, then we simply cannot account for *particular* evils by appealing to the self-determining freedom of wicked moral agents.

This willingness to sanction coercion is the kiss of death to the open view of providence, then, because it establishes that the God of open theism is a capricious being who cannot be trusted to do what is best in every circumstance for those he claims to love. Indeed, while the God of open theism is clearly able to intervene in the course of human history to prevent the pain and suffering that are associated with particular evils, he nevertheless often does not, not because his nonintervention is governed by an overarching purpose or plan that determines when his intervening

---

92. Ibid., 16.
93. Ibid., 429.
94. Ibid., 232–33.

mercies will be extended and when they will be withheld, but because, in the end, he just does not feel like intervening in a particular circumstance. What this suggests, then, is that when push comes to shove, people suffer in the open view neither because the self-determining freedom of wicked moral agents is irrevocable, nor because their suffering was ordained for a greater good, but because God was simply not inclined to intervene coercively on their behalf at some point in the historical past or present, and this is why their suffering is entirely pointless. While openness theologians would have us believe that they have a viable solution to the problem of evil in *general*, in fact they can only hope that those who have been traumatized by *particular* evils do not find out that their suffering could have been prevented if God had simply been inclined to act in their cases as he does from time to time in others, namely, coercively.

Concluding Reflections on Divine Omnicausality
The Meaning of the World

There are a number of reasons why I would argue that the doctrine of divine omnicausality merits a fresh appraisal in the contemporary context, particularly by those who are eager to maintain the methodological priority of Scripture in their thinking about these matters. The first has to do with how it encourages us to think about what it means really to understand the world in which we live. Given that every aspect of the created order is utterly dependent on the providential activity of the Creator for its moment-to-moment existence, it follows that the ultimate explanation for everything that *is*, is found in the will of the one who wills to sustain what is from moment to moment to moment. As Scott Oliphint argues, "A thing is what it is by virtue of the plan and activity of God. A thing holds relationships to other things and to all things generally because of, and only because of, that all-sufficient plan. To attempt to know some 'thing,' therefore, without knowing it as having its being and meaning by virtue of God's plan is, in some important sense, not to know it truly at all."[95] What this suggests, then, is that the doctrine of divine omnicausality merits a fresh appraisal because it

---

95. K. Scott Oliphint, "Jonathan Edwards on Apologetics: Reason and the Noetic Effects of Sin," in *The Legacy of Jonathan Edwards: American Religion and the Evangelical Tradition*, ed. D. G. Hart, Sean Michael Lucas, and Stephen J. Nichols (Grand Rapids: Baker, 2003), 138–39.

encourages us to think about the meaning of the world and everything in it in overtly theocentric, as opposed to covertly anthropocentric, terms. It reminds us, in other words, that no aspect of created reality can be understood rightly outside of the context of the Creator's good, sovereign, and sustaining will, for without that will, absolutely nothing would exist, and nothing would transpire. "What is true with respect to the existence of the whole space-time world," Cornelius Van Til argues,

> is equally true with respect to the *meaning* of it. As the absolute and independent existence of God determines the derivative existence of the universe, so the absolute meaning that God has for himself implies that the meaning of every fact in the universe must be related to God. Scripture says constantly that the world has its whole meaning in the fact that it was created for the glory of God. This appears most beautifully in Revelation 4:11, where the redeemed creation joins in one grand Hallelujah chorus in praise of the Creator: "Worthy art thou, our Lord and our God, to receive the glory and the honor and the power: for thou didst create all things, and because of thy will they are, and were created." ... If we hold with Paul (Romans 11:36 KJV) that "of him, and through him, and to him, are all things: to whom be glory for ever," we see clearly that the existence and meaning of every fact in this universe must in the last analysis be related to the self-conscious and eternally self-subsistent God of the Scriptures.[96]

A Sacramental Universe

Another reason that I believe the doctrine of divine omnicausality merits a fresh appraisal has to do with how this doctrine encourages us to view the world in which we live. If the Creator/creature distinction as interpreted by those who endorse the doctrine of divine omnicausality holds any water, then we should view the world in which we live in a "sacramental" as opposed to a "secular" sense, because the world in which we live is itself not neutral. Every aspect of the world in which we live, and thus "every element of man's experience," has a kind of sacred

---

96. Cornelius Van Til, *An Introduction to Systematic Theology*, 2nd ed., ed. William Edgar (Phillipsburg, N.J.: P&R, 2007), 58.

significance, in other words, not because it is sacred in itself but because it is "an object of cognition that ... leads ultimately to God," who is both the cause of the whole creation and the end "to which the whole creation inexorably and teleologically strives."[97] Viewing created things as objective testimonies to the "glorious qualities"[98] of their Maker, then, gives fresh momentum to the efforts of Christian scholars to integrate faith and learning, for it reminds us that there are, as Warfield argues, "two ways of looking at the world."[99] "We may see the world and absorb ourselves in the wonders of nature," he suggests. "That is the scientific way. Or we may look right through the world and see God behind it. That is the religious way."[100] "The scientific way of looking at the world is not wrong," Warfield reminds us,

> any more than the glass manufacturer's way of looking at the window. This way of looking at things has its very important uses. Nevertheless the window was placed there not to be looked at but to be looked through; and the world has failed of its purpose unless it too is looked through and the eye rests not on it but on its God. Yes, its God; for it is of the essence of the religious view of things that God is seen in all that is and in all that occurs. The universe is his, and in all its movements speaks of him, because it does only his will.[101]

The Free-Will Defense and the Problem of Evil Reconsidered

Finally, and in conclusion, the doctrine of divine omnicausality merits a fresh appraisal because it calls believers not primarily to philosophical speculation but to humble faith, particularly with respect to the two "riddles" that continue to perplex Christian thinkers.[102] The first of these has to do with the understanding of human freedom that the Christian worldview presupposes. The doctrine of divine omnicausality

---

97. Herschel Baker, *The Wars of Truth: Studies in the Decay of Christian Humanism in the Earlier Seventeenth Century* (Cambridge, Mass.: Harvard University Press, 1952), 305, 5.

98. Richard Pratt Jr., *Every Thought Captive: A Study Manual for the Defense of Christian Truth* (Phillipsburg, N.J.: P&R, 1979), 14.

99. Warfield, "Predestination," 108.

100. Ibid.

101. Ibid.

102. Bavinck, *Reformed Dogmatics*, 2:594.

does not trade in an understanding of human freedom that is familiar yet unintelligible. Rather, it encourages believers to embrace an understanding of freedom that, although ultimately inscrutable, emphatically affirms our status as contingent beings while attempting to do justice to the kinds of tensions that are found in the overarching covenantal framework of Scripture, as well as in particular texts like Isaiah 10, Daniel 4, Acts 2 and 4, 1 Corinthians 1 and 2, and Philippians 2.

The second riddle has to do with the related issue of the problem of evil. Given Walter Schultz's recent critique of the role of libertarian freedom in the free-will defense, we now know that "it *is* possible for God to achieve his purposes (as libertarian free-will theists describe them) and to prevent every moral evil."[103] We now know, in other words, that despite what the proponents of the free-will defense would have us believe, "apparently pointless or excessive suffering as a result of the actions of others is *not* an unavoidable consequence of granting libertarian freedom."[104] What this suggests, then, is that the doctrine of divine omnicausality merits a fresh appraisal because we can no longer pretend that the concept of libertarian freedom has the explanatory power that many have presumed it to have with respect to the problem of evil. It is now clear, in other words, that even if we grant the existence and coherence of libertarian freedom, evil must be regarded as something that is not contrary to, but an essential component of, God's will, something that advances rather than frustrates his good purposes and plans. This, of course, is how Reformed believers have always thought about the problem of evil, for it is only in this way of thinking, they argue, that we can salvage purpose and meaning in the midst of pain

---

103. Walter J. Schultz, "'No-Risk' Libertarian Freedom: A Refutation of the Free-Will Defense," *Philosophia Christi* 10, no. 1 (2008): 165–66, emphasis added.

104. Ibid., emphasis added. According to Schultz, "Christians are divided over how to understand apparently pointless suffering at the hands of others. Was it because God *couldn't* prevent it or God *wouldn't* prevent it? The *Free Will Defense* and related theodicies take the first view, postulating that such sufferings are the unavoidable consequences of creature-freedom. They hold that in order to achieve his purposes in creation, God had to grant libertarian free will, because such purposes involve a creature's freely choosing to do good. The idea is that were God always to prevent every creature from choosing to do evil he could not achieve his purposes. '"No-Risk" Libertarian Freedom' shows how it is *possible* for God to achieve his purposes so described while preventing every moral evil. Such a possibility is a refutation of the *Free Will Defense* and related theodicies. However, it demands an account of God's goodness that would justify God's not preventing moral evil when he could have" (Walter J. Schultz in an email to Paul Kjoss Helseth, November 12, 2009).

and suffering. Indeed, as Warfield argues, it is in this way of thinking, and in this way of thinking alone, that

> the plummet is let down to the bottom of the Christian's confidence and hope. It is because we cannot be robbed of God's providence that we know, amid whatever encircling gloom, that all things shall work together for good to those that love him. It is because we cannot be robbed of God's providence that we know that nothing can separate us from the love of Christ—not tribulation, nor anguish, nor persecution, nor famine, nor nakedness, nor peril, nor sword.... Were not God's providence over all, could trouble come without his sending, were Christians the possible prey of this or the other fiendish enemy, when perchance God was musing, or gone aside, or on a journey, or sleeping, what certainty of hope could be ours? "Does God send trouble?" Surely, surely. He and he only. To the sinner in punishment, to his children in chastisement. To suggest that it does not always come from his hands is to take away all our comfort.[105]

In the end, then, the doctrine of divine omnicausality merits a fresh appraisal not because it imagines that we can scrutinize that which is "inscrutable" (Rom. 11:33 ESV), but because it reminds us that we are called to place our confidence in the character and promises of our Father, even when we have no idea precisely what he is doing as he works out the particulars of his sovereign will. This is why Reformed believers conclude that the doctrine of providence is properly understood not as "a philosophical system but," as Bavinck puts it, "a confession of faith, the confession that, notwithstanding appearances, neither Satan nor a human being nor any other creature, but God and he alone—by his almighty and everywhere present power—preserves and governs all things."[106]

---

105. B. B. Warfield, "God's Providence Over All," in *Shorter Writings*, 1:110.

106. Bavinck, *Reformed Dogmatics*, 2:618–19. I would like to thank Walter Schultz for his thoughtful comments on earlier drafts of this essay. Whatever shortcomings remain are, of course, entirely my own.

WILLIAM LANE CRAIG

A A. Hodge's six-point summary of the classical Reformed view of divine providence, quoted by Paul Kjoss Helseth under "The 'True View' of Providence Summarized," falls short of expressing the radical distinctives of the Reformed position that Helseth defends. The Molinist would affirm all of these points—except, perhaps, the sixth, which punts to inscrutability rather than provides an account of the nature of divine action in the world. Helseth's own characterization, "divine omnicausality," is a more forthright description of his view but still not entirely adequate, since a Molinist doctrine of simultaneous concurrence could also be so characterized. Rather, what truly distinguishes Helseth's view is that it is a form of divine, causal determinism. Helseth thinks that God causally determines everything that happens.

Now, certainly God has the power to create a world characterized by universal, causal determinism. He could have created a world operating according to deterministic natural laws and containing no sentient creatures at all. Perhaps he could have even created a world containing sentient, self-conscious beings who have the illusion of indeterministic freedom of the will, just as he could have created vats containing brains that have the illusion of bodies acting in some external world. But why should we think that he has done so? Why should we think that our experience of indeterministic freedom is illusory?

Helseth seems to provide two grounds for embracing universal, divine, causal determinism. The first and foremost consideration is that Scripture requires it. But is that really the case? It needs to be kept in mind that universal, divine determinism is an *interpretation* of Scripture, an interpretation that some Reformed divines themselves regard as *irreconcilable* with other clear teachings of Scripture. The scriptural worldview involves a very strong conception not only of divine sovereignty over the world and human affairs but also of human freedom and responsibility.

While too numerous to list here, biblical passages affirming God's sovereignty have been grouped by D. A. Carson under four main heads: (1) God is the creator, ruler, and possessor of all things, (2) God is the ultimate personal cause of all that happens, (3) God elects his people, and (4) God is the unacknowledged source of good fortune or success.[107] No one who takes these passages seriously can embrace open theism, which denies God's sovereignty over the contingent events of history. On the other hand, the conviction that human beings are free moral agents also permeates the Hebrew way of thinking, as is evident from passages that Carson lists under nine heads: (1) people face a multitude of divine exhortations and commands, (2) people are said to obey, believe, and choose God, (3) people sin and rebel against God, (4) people's sins are judged by God, (5) people are tested by God, (6) people receive divine rewards, (7) the elect are responsible to respond to God's initiative, (8) prayers are not mere showpieces scripted by God, and (9) God literally pleads with sinners to repent and be saved.[108] These passages rule out a deterministic understanding of divine providence, which precludes human freedom.

Turretin recognizes these two streams of competing texts. Helseth writes:

> As Turretin summarizes the matter, when we eschew eisegesis and begin with the data of Scripture, the careful analysis of the text yields two "indubitable" conclusions, both of which must be held in tension without allowing either one to cancel the other out:
>
> "that God on the one hand by his providence not only decreed but most certainly secures the event of all things, whether free or contingent; on the other hand, however, man is always free in acting and many effects are contingent. Although I cannot understand how these can be mutually connected together, yet (on account of ignorance of the mode) the thing itself is (which is certain from another source, i.e., from the word) not either to be called in question or wholly denied."[109]

---

107. D. A. Carson, *Divine Sovereignty and Human Responsibility: Biblical Perspectives in Tension*, New Foundations Theological Library (Atlanta: John Knox, 1981), 24–35.

108. Carson, *Sovereignty and Responsibility*, 18–22. One should mention also the striking passages that speak of God's repenting in reaction to a change in human behavior (e.g., Gen. 6:6; 1 Sam. 15:11, 35 KJV).

109. Turretin, *Institutes of Elenctic Theology*, 1:512, cited by Helseth on p. 40.

When one's interpretation of Scripture leads one into this sort of cul de sac, it is a good idea to reassess whether one has, indeed, rightly interpreted Scripture.

Molinism provides a different interpretation of the same scriptural data. It affirms God's decreeing and securing the event of all things, along with human freedom and contingency, and moreover, provides the means of their reconciliation through the doctrine of divine middle knowledge. Middle knowledge enables us to explain how God brings all things to pass (which is the affirmation of Scripture), but not by means of universal, causal, determinism (which is Helseth's interpretation of Scripture), thereby preserving contingency and indeterminism. Helseth thinks that God brings all things to pass by *strongly actualizing* (causally determining) various states of affairs, whereas the Molinist thinks that God *weakly actualizes* certain states of affairs (by bringing about the nondetermining circumstances in which he knew persons would freely choose something). Given the distinction between strong and weak actualization, I think it would be quite difficult to show that a Molinist interpretation of the scriptural data is exegetically untenable.[110] On the contrary, it enjoys the considerable advantage of being coherent.

Curiously, Helseth does *not*, as Turretin advises, hold these truths in tension without allowing either one to cancel out the other. By affirming universal, divine determinism and a compatibilistic view of freedom, he abolishes the mystery. Understanding how determinism and a compatibilistic view of freedom can be mutually connected is not difficult. Ultimately, there is no contingency in the world, and everything we think and do is causally determined by God. The problem is that such an interpretation of Scripture is lopsided in that it must run roughshod over all the texts that seem to imply indeterminism with respect to human choices and actions. It denies what Scripture repeatedly and variously affirms: human beings are not totally determined by God.

Consider, for example, Paul's promise in 1 Corinthians 10:13: "No temptation has overtaken you that is not common to man. God is faithful, and he will not let you be tempted beyond your strength, but with the temptation will also provide the way of escape, that you may be able

---

110. A point that my former student and assistant Shaun McNaughton has emphasized in personal conversation.

to endure it"(RSV). Imagine, then, a situation in which a Christian succumbs to temptation. According to this passage, there was available to him at the time of temptation an escape route that he could have taken; he did not have to yield. He had the power to act otherwise than he did. To say that he was causally determined to succumb and so was unable to do otherwise is to deny this promise of Scripture.

Helseth's response to the failure of his view to provide a coherent interpretation of scriptural texts is odd. He says, citing Schreiner, "If the 'scandal' of the Reformed worldview 'is that ultimately the logical problems posed cannot be fully resolved,' the dirty little secret of the Arminian worldview is that the independence that the Arminian system requires 'cannot be exegetically vindicated.'" I am puzzled by this retort. Reformed thinkers themselves recognize the broad stream of texts that justify the Arminian postulate of indeterministic human free will. The question, then, seems to be whether the doctrine of middle knowledge will enable the Arminian to offer a plausible interpretation of those texts which affirm that God brings all things to pass. Helseth does not address this question, so far as I can see, in his contribution.

Universal, divine determinism cannot, as the classical Reformed divines cited by Helseth frankly acknowledge, do justice to the full data of Scripture, and that is why the Reformed view holds that the reconciliation of these texts is inscrutable. By contrast, Molinism, I am convinced, can reconcile these texts and so offers us a coherent interpretation of Scripture. Helseth has offered no scriptural arguments against Molinism. So the argument from Scripture fails to support Helseth's doctrine of universal, divine determinism.

The second argument Helseth gives in support of determinism is that libertarian freedom is theologically and philosophically problematic. Unfortunately, Helseth does not develop these arguments at any length but refers to the work of others. With respect to the theological problems, Helseth cites Muller's objection to the Molinist/Arminian doctrine of simultaneous concurrence. The objection, as I understand it, seems to be this: according to Molina, God does not act on the human will to produce its effect but rather acts along with the human will to produce its effect. This is alleged to be ontologically absurd, however, because no finite being can bring anything, including its own will, from potency to actuality without God's concurrence.

It is not clear to me that the Molinist is guilty of doing anything more than simply disagreeing with the Thomistic/Reformed view of divine concurrence. It is not the case, as Muller alleges, that according to Molina, "God thus supports the effect and gives it actuality while not strictly bringing it about or willing it."[111] On the contrary, in Molina's view, God not only conserves both the secondary agent and its effect in being; he also wills specifically that the effect be produced, and he concurs with the agent by causing the intended effect. Without such concurrence, the effect would not be produced. The difference between Molina's view and the Thomistic/Reformed view is that God does not cause the secondary agent's will to choose one way or the other; he just concurs with the agent's choice by causing the intended effect. (This is, by the way, why the Molinist view holds that God is not the author of sin. While he concurs with the sinful will in producing its effect, God does not move the agent's will to sin. By contrast, in the Thomistic/Reformed view, God causes the agent to sin by moving his will to choose evil, which makes the allegation that God is the author of sin difficult to deny.)

So what is the problem here supposed to be? In the Molinist/Arminian view, secondary free agents are capable of willing one thing or another without being caused to do so by God. It is not as though some potency actualizes itself. Rather, the soul, which is an actual entity, actualizes it own potency to will this or that. This is right in line with the traditional understanding of the soul as a self-mover. Perhaps the problem is supposed to be that in this case the secondary agent is causing something, namely, the motion of its own will, but is doing so without divine concurrence, which contradicts the doctrine of divine concurrence. But libertarians do not consider an agent's freely choosing something to be an instance of an agent's causing its own choice, for that would lead to an infinite regress of causes.[112] Rather, an agent's freely willing something is just an action of the agent, not an effect of the agent. So it is not as though some effect is produced by a secondary cause without God's concurring. I do not, then, see that any insuperable problem exists here; on the contrary, the Molinist doctrine of simultaneous concurrence enjoys the considerable advantage of not making God the author of sin.

---

111. Muller, "Grace, Election, and Contingent Choice," 267.

112. Helseth's own source, Walter Schultz, recognizes this point (Walter J. Schultz, "'No-Risk' Libertarian Freedom: A Refutation of the Free Will Defense," *Philosophia Christi* 10, no. 1 (2008): 187. As Schultz puts it, "Agents do not decide to decide."

Helseth also charges that allowing that human beings endowed with libertarian freedom are sources of primary causality "reveal[s] a Manichaean tendency that ... subverts the *solas* of the Reformation as well as the essential tenets of a biblical metaphysic." The attempt to impugn Molinism/Arminianism through guilt by association with Manichaeism is just silly and unworthy of a serious scholar. One may as well try to impugn Helseth's theory by associating it with Spinozism because of its universal determinism!

Is regarding human agents as primary causes theologically subversive? Helseth again has recourse to Muller, whose full statement is as follows: "If the salvation of human beings rests on divine foreknowledge, the human being is clearly regarded as the first and effective agent in salvation, and God is understood simply as the one who responds to an independent human action."[113] This charge seems to rest on a failure to distinguish carefully between simple foreknowledge and middle knowledge. If we think that God looks into the future and sees who will receive his grace and so, foreknowing this, ordains that it should happen, one *could* think that God is responding to an independent human action (though even that seems a stretch, since what he sees is a human response to his grace). But in a Molinist view, none of what God knows via middle knowledge actually exists. Such knowledge is purely hypothetical. God knows that if he were to offer some person *S* his grace under such-and-such circumstances, *S* would (or would not) respond. God would have such hypothetical knowledge even if he never created anything! So God is not responding to an independent human action, since no such action exists. In fact, theoretically, one could say that God looked at all the worlds of free creatures that were feasible for him to create, decided that they were all a bad lot, and so chose instead to create a deterministic world such as Helseth imagines, in which God's grace is unilaterally and irresistibly imparted. How would that subvert *sola gratia*? The Reformed theologian must take *sola gratia* to entail that God's knowledge of counterfactuals of creaturely freedom is part of his free knowledge, a claim far removed from anything that could be justified by biblical exegesis. In that case, the only thing being subverted is the Reformed view.

The charge that essential tenets of biblical metaphysics would be subverted by regarding human agents as sources of primary causality

---

113. Muller, "Grace, Election, and Contingent Choice," 266.

appears to be merely a reiteration of Muller's previous charge of onto-logical absurdity. But, as we have seen, Molinism affirms *creatio ex nihilo* ("creation out of nothing"), divine conservation, and concurrence. So what is the problem? I should have thought that turning human agents into mere instrumental causes, as Helseth does, rather than primary causes created and conserved by God subverts the biblical metaphysics of personhood and agency. I am pleased to learn that Charles Hodge repudiated the denial of primary causality to human persons that Helseth imagines to be essential to a biblical worldview.

In addition to these objections to a Molinist doctrine of concurrence, Helseth makes the passing claim that assuming human beings to be endowed with libertarian freedom is "essentially unintelligible," citing an introductory essay by Robert Kane. The so-called intelligibility problem concerns how to distinguish libertarian choices from mere random or chance events. Helseth does not consider any of the several libertarian proposals, including Kane's own solution, such as agent causation or noncausal reasons for action. Helseth's verdict that libertarian free will is essentially unintelligible would be more impressive were it based on a considered weighing of these proposed solutions. I could not help but be somewhat amused when Helseth assures us that the doctrine of divine, causal determinism "does not trade in an understanding of human freedom that is familiar yet unintelligible" (like libertarian free will). "Rather, it encourages believers to embrace an understanding of freedom that is ultimately inscrutable." This is supposed to be an advantage? Helseth's view sacrifices familiarity with no gain in intelligibility.

Helseth's scriptural and theologico-philosophical arguments for determinism are therefore inconclusive at best. What objections, then, might be raised against universal, divine, causal determinism? At least five come immediately to mind.

1. Universal, divine, causal determinism cannot offer a coherent interpretation of Scripture. The classical Reformed divines recognize this. They acknowledge that the reconciliation of scriptural texts affirming human freedom and contingency with scriptural texts affirming divine sovereignty is inscrutable. Now, Helseth does manage to reconcile universal, divine, causal determinism with human freedom by interpreting

freedom in compatibilistic terms. Compatibilism entails determinism. The problem is that adopting compatibilism achieves reconciliation only at the expense of denying what these scriptural texts seem clearly to affirm: genuine indeterminacy and contingency. It is the mirror image of the open theist's "reconciliation" of these two textual traditions by his denial of God's meticulous providence.

2. Universal causal determinism cannot be rationally affirmed. There is a sort of dizzying, self-defeating character to determinism. For if one comes to believe that determinism is true, one has to believe that the reason he has come to believe it is simply that he was determined to do so. One has not in fact been able to weigh the arguments pro and con and freely make up one's mind on that basis. The difference between the person who weighs the arguments for determinism and rejects them and the person who weighs them and accepts them is wholly that one was determined by causal factors outside himself to believe, and the other not to believe. When you come to realize that your decision to believe in determinism was itself determined and that even your present realization of that fact right now is likewise determined, a sort of vertigo sets in, for everything that you think, even this very thought itself, is outside your control. Determinism could be true, but it is very hard to see how it could ever be rationally affirmed, since its affirmation undermines the rationality of its affirmation.

3. Universal, divine determinism makes God the author of sin and denies human responsibility. Curiously, Bavinck admits that if we construe divine conservation in terms of continual re-creation, "All created beings would then exist in appearance only and be devoid of all independence, freedom, and responsibility. God himself would be the cause of sin."[114] But there is no more independence, freedom, and responsibility on the deterministic view than on the re-creation view. For in contrast to the Molinist view of simultaneous concurrence, the deterministic view holds that even the movement of the human will

114. Quoted by Helseth on p. 36, note 97.

is caused by God. God moves people to choose evil, and they cannot do otherwise. God determines their choices and makes them do wrong. If it is evil to make another person do wrong, then in this view God not only is the cause of sin and evil, but he becomes evil himself, which is absurd. By the same token, all human responsibility for sin has been removed, for our choices are not really up to us: God causes us to make them. We cannot be responsible for our actions, for nothing we think or do is up to us. Helseth's response? "The mechanics of how God can be the efficient cause of sin without actually doing, and thus being culpable for, sin is inscrutable."

4. Universal, divine determinism nullifies human agency. Since our choices are not up to us but are caused by God, human beings cannot be said to be real agents. They are mere instruments by means of which God acts to produce some effect, much like a man using a stick to move a stone. Of course, secondary causes retain all their properties and powers as intermediate causes, as the Reformed divines remind us, just as a stick retains its properties and powers that make it suitable for the purposes of the one who uses it. Reformed thinkers need not be occasionalists like Malebranche. But these intermediate causes are not agents themselves but mere instrumental causes, for they have no power to initiate action. Hence, Yandell's claim that it is dubious that in divine determinism there really is more than one agent in the world seems quite justified. Helseth's response that "Reformed believers are not persuaded that 'omnicausality' necessarily entails 'monocausality'" tells us merely about the psychology of Reformed believers rather than the shortcomings of Yandell's objection and in any case misconstrues the objection by conflating "monocausality" (which need not follow from divine determinism) and "monoagency" (which does follow). Helseth's lengthy quotation from Warfield affirms "the reality and real efficiency of all second causes ... as the proximate producers of the effects that take place in the world" but does not answer the objection that in a deterministic world there is but one agent: God. I suspect that since Helseth believes that there really is only one primary cause in

reality, he would at the end of the day agree that there is but one agent in reality. This conclusion not only goes against our knowledge of ourselves as agents but also makes it inexplicable why God then treats us as agents, holding us responsible for what he caused us and used us to do.

5. Universal, divine determinism makes reality into a farce. The whole world becomes a vain and empty spectacle. There are no free agents in rebellion against God, whom God seeks to win through his love, and no one who freely responds to that love and freely gives his love and praise to God in return. The whole spectacle is a charade whose only real actor is God Himself. Far from glorifying God, Helseth's view, I am convinced, denigrates God for engaging in such a farcical charade. It is deeply insulting to God to think that he would create beings that are in every respect causally determined by him and then treat them as though they were free agents, punishing them for the wrong actions he made them do or loving them as though they were freely responding agents. God would be like a child who sets up his toy soldiers and moves them about his play world, pretending that they are real persons whose every motion is not in fact of his own doing and pretending that they merit praise or blame. I am certain that Helseth will bristle at such a comparison. But why it is inapt for the doctrine of universal, divine, causal determinism remains for me inscrutable.

Paul Kjoss Helseth presents the case for God's omnicausality with grace and defends it with acumen. Rather than voicing his private philosophical opinions, he speaks as a representative of the Reformed tradition or simply in the name of "Reformed believers." He draws on the magisterial Reformed confessions of faith and catechisms and relies on well-respected representatives of this tradition, especially Herman Bavinck. Though Helseth's essay by no means lacks creativity and individuality, it resonates with a confessional tone, supported by a chorus of the venerable dead. Helseth's willingness to acknowledge that he stands on the shoulders of others imparts to his chapter a winsome quality quite unlike the other chapters in this volume. Helseth's heavy reliance on the Reformed tradition reinforces his essay with all the strengths and weaknesses of that tradition.

All Things Serve Him

As careful readers of Helseth's and my essays will discern, our views are closer to each other than they are to either of the other two essays in this volume. Hence, I owe it to the reader to clarify this agreement and point out the differences. I anticipate that some critics will dismiss Helseth's essay with a wave of the hand as just one more example of "Calvinism." Every fair-minded theologian should admit, however, that caricature and insult do not suffice for analysis and criticism. One danger of speaking in the name of a tradition is that one can easily be dismissed with a label that has come to characterize that tradition in the popular mind. What is forgotten by the critics of "Calvinism" is that almost everything about God and providence preserved in the Reformed tradition goes back through the middle ages to Augustine, who studied the apostle Paul intensely. Calvin preserved but did not originate it. Though Roman Catholics of the Dominican order differentiate their views from Calvin in certain respects (e.g., the universal presence of sufficient grace), on the subject of providence they are almost of one mind.[115] Hence, we cannot simply pass over Helseth's essay as "Calvinist" boilerplate without displaying appalling ignorance of and shocking arrogance toward the tradition in which almost the entire Western church lived out its faith for centuries.

My fundamental agreement with Helseth's view of providence does not derive from mutual loyalty to Calvin, much less to my intention to hew to the line of a confession of faith. As I see it, it is due to my being persuaded that the tradition of thinking about God's providence that stretches back from Barth and Bavinck through Johann Heidegger, Calvin, Aquinas, and Bernard of Clairvaux to Augustine best preserves the biblical teaching about the greatness and goodness of God as manifested in Jesus Christ. The strength of Helseth's essay derives from his reliance on this tradition. He correctly begins with the gratuitous character of God's act of creation and the radically contingent nature of the creation. He rightly points to the intimate union between creation and providence, thereby showing the inconsistency of deism and its close relative, open theism. It is unthinkable that a world created from nothing escapes dependence on God at any point. And why would we want such "freedom" anyway? It is the glory and joy of a creature to depend on its creator and an even greater glory for that creature to will freely its dependence on its creator. I agree with Helseth that nothing escapes the will of God or defeats his power. His power, glory, and will are manifested in all creation, in everything that transpires. All things serve him. God is not limited to responding to what might happen as it happens, so that he must work toward a general end unknown in detail. Nor must God choose from the range of feasible worlds determined by what free creatures would do in every situation. No. As Helseth argues, we should believe that God simply does what he wills: no constraints, no trade-offs, and no defeats. If we find reconciling this faith with our own experience and reason difficult, we should not be surprised or disheartened. God is greater than our reason and "greater than our hearts" (1 John 3:20).

---

115. See Fr. Reginald Garrigou-Lagrange, *Predestination: The Meaning of Predestination in Scripture and the Church*, trans. Dom Bede Rose (Rockford, Ill.: TAN Books, 1998), 117–22. For a Dominican view of providence, see idem, *Providence*, trans. Dom Bede Rose (Rockford, Ill.: TAN Books, 1998).

Finally, I agree with Helseth's criticism of the notion of libertarian freedom. Despite all Molinist, Arminian, and open theist attempts to thwart its innate logical tendency, the idea of libertarian freedom implies that the "free agent" who enjoys it is an unmoved mover: a self-originating god. In this theory, God has nothing to do with the decisive act of the free agent. Moreover, the theory of libertarian freedom cannot be confined to matters of general providence. It relates directly to the debate about grace and justification that raged in the sixteenth century. This theory transforms God's will to save into a mere offer subject to human validation. How ironic that some evangelical heirs of the Protestant Reformation would outdo their Roman Catholic contemporaries in making a sleepy church comfortable with the Semipelagianism that the Reformers risked life and limb to expose!

Critical Thoughts of a Christocentric Trinitarian

Despite my fundamental agreement with Helseth and the Reformed tradition on the theme of providence, I harbor a few reservations and perhaps some disagreements. Theologians in the Reformed tradition have sometimes given ammunition to their enemies by expressing themselves in infelicitous ways. Their use of such terms as "decree," "determination," and "cause" can give the impression of fatalism to those who do not understand what fatalism really is.[116] It needs to be made clear that when used in reference to God these terms do not mean the same as when used of a human decree or determination or a worldly cause. Unlike God's decree and its execution, a human decree and its execution are two different things and resonate with overtones of authoritarianism and coercion. Imagining a divine decree being given and then executed in time through means gives plausibility to the charge of fatalism. If, however, we understand the "decree" as the intentionality and final meaning of the gracious act of the loving God in creation, providence, and salvation, the impression of fatalism is replaced by a feeling of gratitude. How can one think of God's loving gift as an impersonal fate?

The way we ordinarily use the word "cause" makes it almost impossible to think of God as "causing" freedom and free action. The results of

---

116. Fatalism is the theory that each and every event is completely determined by an impersonal necessity embedded in the impersonal events that precede it.

an impersonal worldly cause are of like nature to the cause: impersonal. We do not usually speak of human beings causing things, except when the relation is indirect. For example, we do not say the builder caused the house to be built, or I caused my hand to wave, or John caused the cake to be baked. We say, rather, that Sam's neglect caused the accident — an indirect relation. Persons *do* things, *build* things, or *bake* things. Hence, we should not say that God causes us to come into being, brings it about that we are cared for, causes us to be loved, or brings it about that we attain salvation. Instead, we should say that God creates us, cares for us, loves us, and saves us. Likewise, we should not say that God *causes* us to act.[117] We should say that his presence in us gives us life, and his free activity in us activates our freedom. God's action differs greatly from human action. Just as his love for us evokes our love in return, his righteousness in us becomes ours in him, and the touch of his holiness sanctifies us for his service; his freedom frees us for genuine freedom.

It is unfortunate that Reformed thinkers could contrive no better way to speak of God's relation to sinful acts than to say that God is the "efficient" but "remote" cause of sin. Sin possesses no substance and, hence, can have no cause. It would be much better to differentiate clearly among the actor, the act, and the defectiveness of the act, so that we can affirm with confidence that God does not "cause" sin in *any sense of the word*. God gives no affirmation to the defects in the actor's will and no being to the defects in the act. As I argue in my chapter, God gives being to everything good in the human act and brings it to its final result, at which point all defects are overcome and its final meaning is achieved.

In dealing with the problem of evil, Helseth falls into the standard pattern of terminology about evil. He says, "Particular evils happen because he [God] ordained that they would." Helseth uses the expression "particular evils" here to mean painful events that contradict our natural desires rather than reserving the word "evil" for things God does not will.[118] This ambiguity makes the Reformed view vulnerable

---

117. Even the distinction between primary and secondary causality falls victim to this problem. How does the primary cause move the secondary cause without compromising its freedom?

118. See my chapter in this volume for my discussion of this ambiguity and the confusion it fosters in discussions of providence and evil.

to the criticism that God does things that "ought not to be done" or that God is the "author of sin." To say that God ordains all events differs greatly from saying that God ordains all particular evils. It should be axiomatic for Christian theology that God does not ordain evil and *never* uses evil as a means to an end. The very notion of a "particular" event isolated from other events in creation and the one event of divine creation imposes a human perspective on divine action. Divine action, like the divine Actor, is one and simple. The history of providence and salvation is the unfolding history of God's eternal "no" to evil, and the resurrection of Christ is the loudest expression of that "no." The eschatological resurrection of the dead, furthermore, will be the final and definitive revelation of that divine "no," and this final negation will be retroactive, applying to the whole history of creation. From the perspective of eternity, God's negation of evil has never been mixed with "yes" or "maybe." To pronounce a particular event "evil" is to usurp God's role as Judge and to pronounce final judgment before the time (1 Cor. 4:5).

Finally, I think that the Reformed view of divine providence is insufficiently christocentric and Trinitarian, a characteristic it shares with much Western theology written since the Middle Ages.[119] Helseth argues that divine omnicausality deserves careful examination because "it encourages us to think about the meaning of the world and everything in it in overtly theocentric, as opposed to covertly anthropocentric, terms." Helseth here sets theocentric theology in opposition to anthropocentric theology in a way that fails to take into account the reconciliation of God and humanity in Christ. Theologizing about God as the all-determining reality or the primary cause or the world sovereign tends toward abstraction and speculation. Speaking about the divine decree or creation or predestination or providence without constant reference to Christ does not allow us to differentiate sufficiently the Christian view from pagan variants of these ideas. Asserting merely that God does everything for his own glory might lead us to believe that divine glory could as easily be manifested by damning as by saving, by destroying as by creating, by harming as by healing. Such abstract theocentrism neglects the crucial fact that God showed us the true nature

---

119. Let me make it clear that I believe Reformed (and medieval) Christology and Trinitarian teaching are orthodox. My point is that they treated these doctrines as topics rather than thinking every doctrine through christologically.

of his glory by sending his Son to die on a cross for us sinners. On the cross, God's infinite dignity emerged as the self-giving love that binds the Father, Son, and Holy Spirit together. And the creature's dignity and freedom come to light in the divine and human self-giving of the Son to the Father in utter trust. Here God's glory, sovereignty, justice, freedom, and love are reconciled; indeed, it is revealed that they were never in tension and that God is eternally like Jesus Christ. Christian theology should think from a center in Christ back to creation and the decree and forward to the *eschaton*. Because of the revelation of God in Christ, we confess that God *is* Father, Son, and Spirit and that everything that comes from God is accomplished from the Father, through the Son, and in the Spirit. This conviction should animate and permeate all Christian theology, including the doctrine of providence.

GREGORY A. BOYD

I appreciate Helseth's clear presentation of the classical Reformed perspective on divine providence. I especially admire the integrity of Helseth's essay. While some contemporary Reformed writers attempt to soften the doctrine of divine determinism by saying that God merely "permits" or "allows" sin and evil, Helseth is forthright in acknowledging his belief in divine "omnicausality." With Bavinck, Helseth believes that every single thing that exists, including evil, does so "totally from, through, and to God." He courageously concedes, "The ultimate explanation for everything that *is*, is found in the will of the one who wills to sustain what is from moment to moment to moment." God thus actively wills, ordains, and, in some mysterious sense, even causes all that comes to pass, including sin and evil. I appreciate such candor.

Having said this, I must candidly state that Helseth's beliefs about the nature of God and divine providence are about as antithetical to my own as I can imagine any views being. I will cluster my responses to Helseth's essay around four issues: his critique of the open view, his understanding of God's greatness, the mysterious "in such a way" clause, and the problem of evil.[120]

Critique of the Open View

Helseth believes the open view is "truly contemptible," because this God "is a capricious being who cannot be trusted to work in every situation in a way that maximizes good and minimizes evil for his creatures." He concludes this because he believes that the God of open theism is able

---

120. Space does not permit me to delve into the myriad of exegetical issues that separate Helseth's position from my own. For my interpretation of the classical proof texts for divine determinism, see Boyd, *Satan and the Problem of Evil*, 394–416; idem, *Is God to Blame?* (Downers Grove, Ill.: InterVarsity Press, 2003), 177–94; as well as www.gregboyd.org/category/qa/predestination-free-will/scriptures-dealing-with-determinism/.

to intervene to override free will and prevent evil whenever he wants to; he simply chooses not to much of the time. He alleges that in the open view when God refrains from intervening, it is not "because [he has] an overarching purpose or plan," nor "because the self-determining freedom of wicked moral agents is irrevocable, nor because their suffering was ordained for a greater good." It is rather "because God was simply not inclined to intervene coercively on their behalf ... and this is why their suffering is entirely pointless."

I completely agree with Helseth that the view of God he just ascribed to open theists is "truly contemptible" (though perhaps less so than the view that God *ordains* all evil). Unfortunately, this portrait of a capricious God has nothing in common with the actual view that open theists espouse. For starters, it's not at all clear to me why Helseth would claim that I and other open theists believe that God is "clearly able" to intervene to prevent evil whenever he wants to. While I and most other advocates of the open view grant that God has the *sheer power* to do whatever he wants, we nevertheless argue that he *cannot* do whatever he wants given the fact that he chose to create a cosmos populated with free agents. To the extent that God gives humans and angels say-so, he by definition limits his own unilateral say-so.

Because the open view holds that God gives agents genuine say-so, it can make better sense of the urgency and power associated with prayer in Scripture than alternative views can. Things *really do* hang in the balance on whether or not people pray, and prayer *really does* change things. By God's own sovereign design, he *needs* humans to align their hearts with his to see aspects of his will being done "on earth as it is in heaven."[121] Conversely, when God fails to intervene, it is precisely *because* "the self-determining freedom of wicked moral agents is irrevocable." I am puzzled as to how Helseth overlooked this fundamental point, especially since he several times cites the work in which I most thoroughly develop my thoughts on the irrevocability of free will (*Satan and the Problem of Evil*).

Along similar lines, Helseth clearly has not understood the open view when he imagines that we deny that God has "an overarching purpose or plan," which is why he concludes that for open theists "suffering

---

121. For an excellent discussion along these lines, see R. Ellis, *Answering God* (Waynesboro, Ga.: Paternoster, 2005). See also Boyd, *Is God to Blame?* 125–51.

is entirely pointless." Just because God faces a future partly comprised of possibilities does not mean that he has no "overarching purpose or plan." The truth is that open theists absolutely affirm that God has an overarching plan; we simply deny that God needs to ordain or foreknow as a certainty the future free decisions of agents in order to have a plan as to how he will weave every one of our possible free decisions into his "overarching plan." Helseth's charge that suffering is pointless in the open view is thus without merit.

Also without merit is Helseth's caricature of the God of open theism making moment-by-moment decisions whether he will honor or override free will to prevent a person's suffering based on nothing more than whether he feels "inclined to intervene coercively on their behalf." As I shall argue more fully in my contributing chapter, we can think of the open model of providence along the lines of a "Choose Your Own Adventure" children's book.[122] As the author of the Choose Your Own Adventure creation, God determined the scope of what would be settled and the scope of what would remain open for each of the possible story lines comprising creation. God also decided, prior to creation, what his response would be to each possible event within each possible story line, thereby determining how he would weave each possible event into his overarching plan should the possible event come to pass. On top of this, God is lovingly at work, moment to moment, to maximize good and minimize evil as much as possible given that he must work around the irrevocable free will of humans and angels. While the God of open theism obviously does not microcontrol all that comes to pass, it is also obvious that he is miles removed from the "contemptible" and "capricious being who cannot be trusted to work in every situation in a way that maximizes good and minimizes evil for his creatures" in whom Helseth imagines open theists believe.

The Greatness of God

Along with the classical Calvinistic tradition, Helseth defines God's greatness largely in terms of his control. To the extent that one views

---

122. The "Choose Your Own Adventure" series of children's books was very popular in the 1980s and 1990s. Readers are at various points allowed to decide which among several possible storylines a character in the book follows.

others as having a measure of say-so *over and against God*, therefore, one diminishes God's greatness, according to this view. Hence, for example, Helseth (quoting Warfield) insists that God would be a little "godling" if he were "subject to forces acting 'independently ... and outside of his teleological control.'" Again citing Warfield, Helseth argues that any conception of God granting freedom to creatures makes God "govern himself by the course of events," and this "actually overthrow[s] the whole theistic conception, and enthrone[s] the 'course of events' as the real ruler of the world." Two points may be made in response.

First, I confess I am unable to grasp the remarkable leap in logic from God granting some measure of autonomous power to agents, on the one hand, to God being "govern[ed] ... by the course of events" and the "course of events" becoming "the real ruler of the world," on the other. How does *that* follow? Why would God's lordship be threatened if he gave some measure of say-so to independent agents? What warrants this sort of all-or-nothing thinking?[123] To the contrary, everything in our own experience as well as all that we have learned about the world from science over the last century suggests that reality is *a balance* between order and chaos, stable structures and dynamic processes, predictable and spontaneous events, settled realities and freedom.[124] In this light, there is simply no reason to assume that God must control *everything* in the world for him to remain in *overall* control of the world.

So far as I can see, this is precisely the sort of control that Scripture ascribes to God. Yes, angels and humans can sin by rejecting God's plans and, to some extent, by thwarting his will for themselves and others. Yet God remains the sovereign Lord of history who confidently works toward his creational objectives, using even the evil actions of

---

123. One of the clearest and most entertaining expressions of this all-or-nothing way of thinking was provided by R. C. Sproul, who argued that "if there is one single molecule in the universe running around loose ..., perhaps that one maverick molecule will lay waste all the grand and glorious plans that God has made and promised to us" (*Chosen by God* [Wheaton, Ill.: Tyndale House, 1986], 26–27). While Sproul offered this argument as a defense of God's absolute (viz., all-controlling) sovereignty, I frankly have trouble imagining a more impotent and insecure deity than one whose plans are threatened by a single maverick molecule!

124. For an excellent, readable discussion of how aspects of contemporary science have illustrated this balance, see Giuseppe Del Re, *The Cosmic Dance: Science Discovers the Mysterious Harmony of the Universe* (Philadelphia: Templeton Foundation, 2000). For several interesting reflections on the concept of chance in science and providence, see Ian Stewart, *Does God Play Dice?* (1989; repr., Cambridge, Mass., and Oxford: Blackwell, 1995), and Keith Ward, *God, Chance and Necessity* (Oxford: Oneworld, 1996).

rebels to accomplish his purposes. And because he is infinitely intelligent and can anticipate possible events as effectively as predetermined events, he does not need to ordain evil events in order effectively to use them in this fashion.

Second, and most important, while I do not find it at all surprising that pagans typically define a deity's greatness by his or her level of control over others—humans, after all, have worshiped power since the dawn of history—I am nonplussed as to why followers of Jesus would ever think this way. At the center of the New Testament is the shockingly beautiful revelation that Jesus, the crucified Son of God, reveals what God is *really* like. Jesus is the very "radiance of God's glory" and the one and only "exact representation of his being" (*hypostasis*) (Heb. 1:3). To understand the true nature of God, we are to look nowhere else but to Jesus (John 14:7–9). If our thinking about God was unwaveringly fixed on Jesus, I honestly cannot see how we could ever conclude that God's greatness is primarily about how much control he exerts over others. To the contrary, in Jesus we discover that God's greatness is most clearly revealed in the foolishness and the weakness of the cross (1 Cor. 1:18–25). God's greatness is most magnificently displayed in Jesus' willingness *not* to use his power and authority to defeat his enemies but instead, out of love, to allow them to crucify him (Matt. 26:53). God's greatness is most profoundly revealed in his relentless, other-oriented, self-sacrificial, humble love (1 John 3:16; 4:8). Next to this breathtakingly beautiful revelation of the unfathomable greatness of the God who is love, I submit that the portrait of a God who needs or desires to microcontrol everything to preserve or manifest his lordship is the real "godling."

The Mysterious "In Such a Way" Clause

As is uniformly the case with Christian divine determinists, Helseth appeals to the mysterious "in such a way" clause to which I allude in my contributing chapter. He says, for example, that God "determines all things *in such a way* that 'the real activity of second causes' is both affirmed and maintained, and for this reason [God] is neither the 'sole cause' of everything that transpires in the universe that he has made, nor is he the author of evil."[125] He repeatedly declares (usually quoting

---

125. The quotes within this quotation are from Warfield, "Confessional Doctrine," 98.

others) that, though God is the ultimate cause of all that is, God "'concurs with all second causes and especially with the human will' while simultaneously leaving the 'contingency and liberty of the will ... unimpaired.'"[126] Hence, everything happens in strict accordance with God's predestined plan, yet *in such a way* that God remains all-holy for predestining evil, while agents are morally responsible for carrying out the evil God predestined them to do.

To his credit, Helseth acknowledges that this is "ultimately inscrutable," yet he justifies embracing this impervious "mystery" by contending that the God-creation relationship is *sui generis*. Since it is utterly unique, Helseth concludes, there is nothing to which we can compare this relationship, and thus we must simply accept it for the incomprehensible mystery that it is. The primary problem with this argument, however, is that words have meaning only insofar as they have some connection, if only analogically, with our experience. Hence, if the God-creation relationship were *utterly* unique, to the point that no analogy for it could be found, we could say nothing meaningful about it. Yet while all orthodox theologians throughout history have agreed that the God-world relationship is unique, none has denied the meaningfulness of *analogically* speaking about it. And Helseth seems to agree with this consensus, since he does, after all, have a good bit to say about the God-creation relationship.

This brings us to a problem at the heart of Helseth's deterministic theology. Neither Helseth nor any other advocate of divine determinism of whom I am aware has provided an analogy that renders meaningful *the kind of* God-creation relationship divine determinists want to defend. And until they do, I honestly cannot see how we can ascribe meaning to, let alone grant the truthfulness of, the mysterious "in such a way" clause. So far as I can see, the phrase amounts to nothing more than a restatement of the unintelligibility of the position being defended.[127]

---

126. The quotes within this quotation are from Turretin, *Institutes of Elenctic Theology*, 1:511.

127. This unintelligibility is succinctly illustrated in D. A. Carson, *How Long, O Lord? Reflections on Suffering and Evil* (Grand Rapids: Baker, 2006), 189. He writes, "God stands behind evil *in such a way* that not even evil takes place outside the bounds of his sovereignty, yet the evil is not morally chargeable to him; it is always chargeable to secondary agents, to secondary causes. On the other hand, God stands behind good *in such a way* that it not only takes place within the bounds of his sovereignty, but it is always chargeable to him, and only

Determinists can passionately stress the reality of "secondary causes" and the importance of "concurrence" all they like, but until we are given some means of ascribing coherent meaning to the "in such a way" clause, these "explanations" simply reexpress the unintelligibility of this view.

For this reason, I frankly had trouble ascribing meaning to most of Helseth's deterministic explanations. For example, Helseth notes that God is always "working concurrently with created things 'to cause them to act as they do.'"[128] But what can this possibly mean if God is already exhaustively controlling all "created things"? What is there left for God to work "concurrently with" in order to "cause them to act as they do"? Unless there is some over-and-against aspect to "created things" prior to God's working concurrently with them—which there is *not* if all "created things" are exhaustively determined by God from the start—then there is no "*con*currence"; there is simply an "occurrence," and *it is all God's*.

Similarly, Helseth insists, "Secondary causes are and remain distinct from God, the primary cause." We are confidently informed that this happens in such a way that "the primary cause 'confers reality' on secondary causes" such that the secondary causes "exist 'solely as a result of the first.'" But what can it possibly mean to claim that secondary causes "remain distinct" from the primary cause when we are also told that the primary cause that "confers reality" on the secondary cause *exhaustively determines* it? If y (secondary cause) is 100 percent determined by x (primary cause), how is y not simply another name for x? Unless there is some over-and-against quality of y in relation to x, then, so far as I can determine, the claim that y "remains distinct" from x is merely verbal.

Related to this, Helseth contends that the "true view" of providence stands midway between the Scylla of deism and the Charybdis of pantheism. I agree with him, but despite his sincere desire to avoid it, I cannot see how Helseth's own view can logically keep from being sucked

---

derivatively to secondary agents" (emphasis added). Yet, as with all theological determinists, Carson affirms that God controls evil no less than he controls good. This means that the "in such a way" clause *serves opposite purposes* when used to "explain" how God is *not responsible* for the evil he controls, on the one hand, and how God is *exclusively responsible* for the good he controls, on the other. Whatever the mysterious phrase might mean, therefore, I can only conclude that it can also, at the same time, mean its exact opposite. And this, to my way of thinking, forces the conclusion that the "in such a way" clause means *nothing*. Remove it from the above sentences, and the meaning of the sentences is not altered. Retain it in these sentences, and their intelligibility is not increased.

128. The quote within this quotation is from Grudem, *Bible Doctrine*, 142.

into the Charybdis. If the world is 100 percent determined by God, its "primary cause," then, so far as I can see, the distinction between God and the world is merely verbal.[129] Of course, I am certain Helseth and others will emphatically, and with complete sincerity, insist that God exhaustively determines the world *in such a way* that the world remains ontologically distinct from God and pantheism is altogether avoided. And at this point I can only mutter, once again, *What does that mysterious phrase mean?*

The Problem of Evil

As I noted above, I applaud Helseth's candor in frankly confessing his belief that "particular evils happen because [God] ordained that they would" and that "the ultimate explanation for everything that *is*, is found in the will of the one who wills to sustain what is from moment to moment to moment." Yet my respect for Helseth's integrity does not lessen how profoundly disturbing I find his position.

We need to think concretely about the implications of this teaching. Imagine for a moment: The innocent, happy world of a charming and witty nine-year-old girl is instantly transformed into an unthinkable nightmare when she is kidnapped by a demented, sadistic pedophile. For years she is imprisoned in a dark cell while being tortured and raped daily. The psychological hell her parents descend into as they for years ponder their beloved daughter's unknown fate is as diabolically dark as the hell experienced by their daughter.

Based on Helseth's account, this is all exactly as God ordained it to be! Every single perverted impulse the sadistic pedophile has, every sadistic action he afflicts on his tortured victim, every sobbing plea and terrified scream that comes out of this abused child's mouth, and every

---

129. I first began to suspect that strict Calvinism logically implied pantheism while reading Jonathan Edwards in graduate school. Edwards, always a stickler for consistency, comes very close to inferring pantheism from his own view of divine omnicausality. In his private notebooks he makes statements such as, "Speaking most strictly there is no proper substance but God Himself"; "Properly it may be said that God is and ... there is none else"; and "[God] is an infinite being. Therefore all others must necessarily be considered as nothing ... in metaphysical strictness and propriety, [God] is and there is none else." H. Townsend, ed., *Philosophy of Jonathan Edwards from His Private Notebooks* (Westport, Conn: Greenwood Press, 1955), 17, 33, 48. For theological reasons, Edwards of course adamantly wanted to avoid pantheism, but he seems to have realized privately that the logic of deterministic theology at least pointed in this direction.

anguished speculation of what might be happening to their daughter that slowly erodes the sanity of this child's tormented parents—*all of this* is *exactly* as God wills it to be, "moment to moment to moment." And as is the case with all evil, we are told that every horrific detail of this macabre episode is willed by God "for the good of his children and the glory of his name." The suggestion frankly leaves me dumbfounded.

On top of this, Helseth insists that God is always at work to maximize good and minimize evil. Given that everything is from the start exactly as God wills it to be, it is not clear what it means to claim that God *works at* maximizing or minimizing anything. The more important point, however, is that, when combined with an omnicausal understanding of providence, this conviction forces the awkward conclusion that every single horrific detail of this macabre episode *is maximally good*! Indeed, since the all-good God is at every moment maximizing the good while exhaustively determining every detail of this episode, we must accept the ghoulish conclusion that God's glory as well as maximal goodness would have been *shortchanged* if the pedophile had tortured this girl less viciously and less frequently than he did, and if this victim had shed one less tear and uttered one less scream than she did.

At this point, it seems to me that the concepts of "good" and "evil" have lost all meaning. I am left wondering, If this is what an *all-good* God ordains, what would an *evil* god ordain? The very fact that the divine omnicausal model of providence makes this a plausible question is perhaps the most fatal objection against it.

GOD DIRECTS ALL THINGS
ON BEHALF OF A MOLINIST VIEW OF PROVIDENCE

WILLIAM LANE CRAIG

Christian theologians have traditionally affirmed that in virtue of his omniscience God possesses hypothetical knowledge of conditional future contingents. He knows, for example, what would have happened if he had spared the Canaanites from destruction, what Napoleon would have done had he won the Battle of Waterloo, how your neighbor would respond if you were to share the gospel with him. Not until F. D. E. Schleiermacher and the advent of modern theology did theologians think to deny God such hypothetical knowledge. Every orthodox thinker who considered the issue agreed that God has such knowledge.

Such hypothetical knowledge is knowledge of what philosophers call *counterfactual conditionals*, or simply *counterfactuals*. Counterfactuals are conditional statements in the subjunctive mood. For example: "If I were rich, I would buy a Mercedes"; "If Goldwater had been elected president, he would have won the Vietnam War"; "If you were to ask her, she would say yes." Counterfactuals are so called because the antecedent and/or consequent clause is typically contrary to fact: I am not rich; Goldwater was not elected president; the U.S. did not win the Vietnam War. Nevertheless, sometimes the antecedent and/or consequent clause is true. For example, your friend, emboldened by your assurance that "if you were to ask her, she would say yes," does ask the girl of his dreams for a date, and she does say yes.

Counterfactual statements constitute a significant part of our ordinary language and are an indispensable part of our decision making. "If I pulled out into traffic now, I wouldn't make it"; "If I were to ask J. B.

for a raise, with his mood, he'd tear my head off"; "If we sent the Third Army around the enemy's right flank, we would prevail." Clearly, life-and-death decisions are made daily on the basis of the presumed truth of counterfactual statements.

Historical Background

Christian theologians have traditionally not disputed that God has knowledge of true counterfactuals and, hence, of the conditional future contingent events they describe. What theologians did dispute, however, was, so to speak, *when* God has such hypothetical knowledge. The question here did not have to do with the moment of time at which God acquired his hypothetical knowledge. For whether God is timeless or everlasting throughout time, in neither case are there truths that are unknown to God until some moment at which he discovers them. As an omniscient being, God must know every truth there is and so can never exist in a state of ignorance. Rather, the "when" mentioned above refers to the point in the *logical* order concerning God's creative decree at which God has hypothetical knowledge.

This idea of a logical order with regard to God's decrees is a familiar one to Reformed theologians. For although all God's decrees occur at once rather than sequentially, there is a logical order among the decrees. For example, so-called infralapsarians say that God's decree to create human beings and to permit them to fall into sin logically preceded his decree to save some and condemn others. Although God predestined some to condemnation, infralapsarians claim, he did not create them in order to condemn them. The decree to condemn is logically subsequent to God's decree to permit human beings to fall into sin. Supralapsarians, by contrast, say that God did create some human beings in order to condemn them. God's decree to save some human beings and condemn others, in their view, thus logically preceded his decree to create them and allow their fall into sin. Even though it was agreed on all hands that God's decrees occur all at once, theologians debated how they were to be logically arranged.

A similar dispute existed among post-Reformation theologians with respect to the place of God's hypothetical knowledge. Everybody agreed that logically prior to God's decree to create a world, God had knowledge of all necessary truths, including all the possible worlds he might create. This was called God's *natural knowledge*. It gives him knowledge of what *could* be. Moreover, everyone agreed that logically subsequent to his decree to create a particular world, God knows all the contingent truths about the actual world, including its past, present, and future. This was called God's *free knowledge*. It involves knowledge of what *will* be. The disputed question was where one should place God's hypothetical knowledge of what *would* be. Is it logically prior or posterior to the divine decree?

Catholic theologians of the Dominican order held that God's hypothetical knowledge is logically *subsequent* to his decree to create a certain world. They maintained that in decreeing that a particular world exist, God also decreed which counterfactual statements are true. Logically prior to the divine decree, there are no counterfactual truths to be known. All God knows at that logical moment are the necessary truths, including all the various possibilities.

At that logically prior moment, God knows, for example, that there is a possible world in which Peter denies Christ three times and another possible world in which Peter affirms Christ in precisely the same circumstances. God picks one of these worlds to be actual, and thus subsequent to his decree, it is true that Peter will deny Christ three times. Moreover, God knows this truth because he knows which world he has decreed. Not only so, but in decreeing a particular world to be real, God also decrees which counterfactuals are true. Thus, he decrees, for example, that if Peter had instead been in such-and-such circumstances, he would have denied Christ two times. God's hypothetical knowledge, like his foreknowledge, is logically posterior to the divine creative decree.

By contrast, inspired by Luis de Molina, Catholic theologians of the Jesuit order maintained that God's hypothetical knowledge of creaturely free decisions is logically *prior* to his creative decree. This difference between the Jesuit Molinists and the Dominicans was no mere matter of theological hairsplitting! The Molinists charged that the Dominicans had in effect obliterated human freedom by making counterfactual truths about creaturely choices a consequence of God's decree. For it is God who determines what a person would choose in whatever circumstances he finds himself. By contrast, the Molinists, by placing God's hypothetical knowledge of creaturely free decisions prior to the divine decree, made room for creaturely freedom by exempting counterfactual truths about creaturely choices from God's decree. In the same way that necessary truths like 2 + 2 = 4 are prior to and therefore independent of God's decree, so counterfactual truths about how creatures would freely choose under various circumstances are prior to and independent of God's decree.

Not only does this view make room for human freedom, but it affords God a means of choosing which world of free creatures to create. For by knowing how persons would freely choose in whatever circumstances they might be, God can, by decreeing to place just those persons in just those circumstances, bring about his ultimate purposes *through* free creaturely decisions. Thus, by employing his hypothetical knowledge, God can plan a world down to the last detail and yet do so without annihilating creaturely freedom, since God has already factored into the equation what people would do freely under various circumstances. Since God's hypothetical knowledge lies logically in between his natural knowledge and his free knowledge, Molinists called it God's *middle knowledge*.[1]

In the Dominican view, there is one logical moment prior to the divine creative decree, at which God knows the range of possible worlds that he might create, and then he chooses one of these to be actual. In the Molinist view, there are two logical moments prior to the divine decree: first, the moment at which God has natural knowledge of the range of possible worlds and, second, the moment at which he has knowledge of the proper subset of possible worlds that, given the

---

1. Notice that we are speaking thus far solely about God's hypothetical knowledge of *creaturely* free decisions. In a Molinist scheme, God does not have middle knowledge of how he himself would freely choose to act in any set of circumstances. For that would obliterate God's freedom, since the truth of such so-called counterfactuals of divine freedom would be prior to and, hence, independent of God's decree. Rather, according to Molina, in decreeing which world is to be actual, God also decrees how he would freely act in any set of circumstances, so that counterfactuals of divine freedom acquire a truth-value simultaneously with the divine decree. So, for example, God knows via his middle knowledge that if Adam and Eve were in the garden, they would freely fall into sin, but at this stage, he does not yet know how he would respond to such a circumstance. In decreeing to create Adam and Eve in the garden, however, knowing that they would freely sin, God also decided that he would expel them from the garden, so that the counterfactual of divine freedom "If God were to find that Adam and Eve had fallen into sin, he would expel them from the garden" becomes true at that moment. Middle knowledge thus comprises knowledge of counterfactuals of creaturely freedom, but not of counterfactuals of divine freedom. A final caveat: if quantum indeterminacy is ontic rather than merely epistemic, then there are also counterfactuals of quantum indeterminacy that are known by God as part of his middle knowledge.

counterfactual propositions true at that moment, are feasible for him to create. The counterfactuals which are true at that moment thus serve to delimit the range of possible worlds to worlds feasible for God.

For example, there is a possible world in which Peter affirms Christ in precisely the same circumstances in which he in fact denied him. But given the counterfactual truth that if Peter were in precisely those circumstances, he would freely deny Christ, then the possible world in which Peter freely affirms Christ in those circumstances is not feasible for God. God could *make* Peter affirm Christ in those circumstances, but then Peter's confession would not be free.

Thus, based on the Molinist scheme, we have the following logical order (letting the circles represent possible worlds):

Moment 1: ... ○○○○○○○○○ ...
Natural Knowledge: God knows the range of possible worlds

Moment 2: ... ○ ○○   ○○○○ ...
Middle Knowledge: God knows the range of feasible worlds

Divine Creative Decree

Moment 3   ○
Free Knowledge: God knows the actual world

Arguments for Molinism

Why think that the Molinist scheme is correct? Basically, three lines of argument present themselves: biblical, theological, and philosophical.

Biblical Arguments

Biblically speaking, it is not difficult to show that God possesses hypothetical knowledge. For example, Jesus affirms before Pilate the counterfactual conditional "If my kingship were of this world, my servants would fight, that I might not be handed over to the Jews" (John 18:36 RSV). The Scriptures abound with examples of such counterfactual conditionals concerning creaturely choices and actions. Unfortunately, this fact does not settle the matter of whether God has middle knowledge. For the scriptural passages show only that God possesses knowledge of counterfactual propositions, and, as I have said, until modern times all theologians agreed that God possesses such hypothetical knowledge. The question remains, when in the logical order of things does this knowledge come? Is it before or after the divine decree? Since Scripture does not reflect on this question, no amount of proof texting concerning God's hypothetical knowledge can prove that such knowledge is possessed logically prior to God's creative decree. This is a matter for theologico-philosophical reflection, not biblical exegesis. Thus, while it is clearly unbiblical to deny that God has hypothetical knowledge, those who deny middle knowledge while affirming God's hypothetical knowledge cannot be accused of being unbiblical.

Theological Arguments

The strongest arguments for the Molinist perspective are theological. Once one grasps the concept of middle knowledge, one will find it astonishing in its subtlety and power. Indeed, I should venture to say that it is one of the most fruitful theological concepts ever conceived. Recent studies have applied it to the issues of Christian particularism,[2] perseverance of the saints,[3] biblical inspiration,[4] infallibility,[5] Christology,[6] the fall and natural evil,[7] and evolutionary theory.[8] An article begs to be written on a Molinist view of quantum indeterminacy and divine sovereignty. Here, however, we are interested in how the doctrine of

---

2. William Lane Craig, "'No Other Name': A Middle Knowledge Perspective on the Exclusivity of Salvation through Christ," *Faith and Philosophy* 6 (1989): 172–88; reprinted in *The Philosophical Challenge of Religious Diversity*, ed. Philip L. Quinn and Kevin Meeker (Oxford: Oxford University Press, 2000), 38–53.

3. William Lane Craig, "'Lest Anyone Should Fall': A Middle Knowledge Perspective on Perseverance and Apostolic Warnings," *International Journal for Philosophy of Religion* 29 (1991): 65–74.

4. William Lane Craig, "'Men Moved by the Holy Spirit Spoke from God' (2 Peter 1:2): A Middle Knowledge Perspective on Biblical Inspiration," *Philosophia Christi* 1 (1999): 45–82.

5. Thomas Flint, "Middle Knowledge and the Doctrine of Infallibility," *Philosophical Perspectives*, vol. 5, *Philosophy of Religion*, ed. James E. Tomberlin (Atascadero, Calif.: Ridgeview, 1991), 373–93.

6. Thomas P. Flint, "'A Death He Freely Accepted': Molinist Reflections on the Incarnation," *Faith and Philosophy* 18 (2001): 3–20.

7. Unwittingly by William Dembski, *The End of Christianity* (Nashville: Broadman & Holman, 2009).

8. Del Ratzsch, "Design, Chance, and Theistic Evolution," in *Mere Creation*, ed. William Dembski (Downers Grove, Ill.: InterVarsity Press, 1998), 289–312.

middle knowledge provides an illuminating account of divine foreknowledge and providence.

Divine Foreknowledge. First, middle knowledge can help us to understand the basis of divine foreknowledge of future contingents. Divine foreknowledge is based on (1) God's middle knowledge of what every creature would freely do under any circumstances and (2) his knowledge of the divine decree to create certain sets of circumstances and to place certain creatures in them. Given middle knowledge of counterfactuals of creaturely freedom and the divine decree, foreknowledge follows automatically as a result, without any need of God's peering into the future, as detractors of divine foreknowledge imagine.

Divine middle knowledge thus offers what has been called a *conceptualist* model of divine cognition as opposed to a *perceptualist* model. The perceptualist model construes divine knowledge on the analogy of sense perception. God "looks" and "sees" what is there. Such a model is implicitly assumed when people speak of God's "foreseeing" the future or having "foresight" of future events. The perceptualist model of divine cognition runs into real problems when it comes to God's knowledge of the future, for, given that future events do not exist, there is nothing there to perceive.[9] By contrast, on a conceptualist model of divine knowledge, God does not acquire his knowledge of the world by anything like perception. His knowledge of the future is not based on his "looking" ahead and "seeing" what lies in the future (a terribly anthropomorphic notion in any case). Rather, God's knowledge is self-contained; it is more like a mind's knowledge of innate ideas. It is based wholly in God's middle knowledge and knowledge of his own decree.

Divine Providence. Second, the Molinist account of divine providence is even more stunning than its account of divine foreknowledge. Consider the following biblical passages:

> "This Jesus, delivered up according to the definite plan and foreknowledge of God, you crucified and killed by the hands of lawless men" (Acts 2:23 ESV).

---

9. Notice, however, that if we think of propositions as being within God's purview, then even on a perceptualist model, God can know the future. For he perceives which future-tense propositions presently have the property of being true. Thus, by means of his perception of presently existing realities, he knows the truth about the future.

"For truly in this city there were gathered together against your holy servant Jesus, whom you anointed, both Herod and Pontius Pilate, along with the Gentiles and the peoples of Israel, to do whatever your hand and your plan had predestined to take place" (Acts 4:27–28).[10]

Here we have a staggering assertion of divine sovereignty over the affairs of men. The conspiracy to crucify Jesus, involving not only the Romans and the Jews in Jerusalem at that time but more particularly Pilate and Herod, who tried Jesus, is said to have happened by God's plan based on his foreknowledge and foreordination. How are we to understand such a far-reaching providence as this?

Molinist Account. If we take the biblical word "foreknowledge" to encompass middle knowledge, then we can make perfect sense of God's providential control over a world of free agents. For via his middle knowledge, God knew exactly which persons, if members of the Sanhedrin, would freely vote for Jesus' condemnation; which persons, if in Jerusalem, would freely demand Christ's death, favoring the release of Barabbas; what Herod, if king, would freely do in reaction to Jesus and to Pilate's plea to judge him; and what Pilate himself, if holding the prefecture of Palestine in AD 30, would freely do under the pressure of the Jewish leaders and the crowd. Knowing all the possible circumstances, persons, and permutations of these, God decreed to create just those circumstances and just those people who would freely do what God willed to happen. Thus, the whole scenario, as Luke insists, unfolded according to *God's plan.* This is truly mind-boggling. When one reflects that the existence of the various circumstances and persons involved was itself the result of myriads of prior free choices on the part of these and other agents, and these in turn of yet other prior contingencies, and so on, then we see that only an omniscient mind could providentially direct a world of free creatures toward his sovereignly established ends. In fact, Paul reflects that "none of the rulers of this age understood this, for if they had, they would not have crucified the Lord of glory" (1 Cor. 2:8). Once one grasps it, the doctrine of divine middle knowledge thus issues in adoration and praise of God for so breathtaking a sovereignty.

---

10. The verses here and in the remainder of this chapter are from the English Standard Version of the Bible.

Openness Account. What account of divine providence can be given in the absence of middle knowledge? Advocates of divine openness freely admit that without middle knowledge, a strong doctrine of divine providence becomes impossible. But such a viewpoint can make no sense whatsoever of scriptural passages such as those cited above. Consider the account of Saul's death in 1 Samuel 31:1–6 and 1 Chronicles 10:8–12. Both writers describe Saul's death at his own hand in lieu of surrender to the Philistines. But then the Chronicler adds the stunning comment: "Therefore the Lord slew him and turned the kingdom over to David" (1 Chron. 10:14 RSV). Now, how is the openness theologian to make sense of this assertion? Saul's suicide was considered a sinful and disgraceful deed and therefore could not have been causally determined by God. Yet Saul's suicide, says the Chronicler, was God's doing.

Or think of Joseph's statement to his brothers in Egypt: "Do not be grieved or angry with yourselves, because you sold me here, for God sent me before you to preserve life.... You meant evil against me, but God meant it for good in order to bring about this present result" (Gen. 45:5; 50:20 NASB). Again, the brothers' treachery and deceit could not have been caused by God, yet God sovereignly directed events toward his previsioned end of saving Israel from famine. Openness theology is at a loss to explain this coalescence of human freedom and divine sovereignty. Ironically, openness theology is forced to revert to Calvinistic determinism to account for God's providence and thus actually winds up destroying human freedom. By contrast, Molinism provides a perspicuous account of divine sovereignty and human freedom in terms of God's middle knowledge of counterfactuals of creaturely freedom.

Some openness theologians are fond of comparing God to a Grand Master in chess who is able, on the basis of his knowledge of his own prowess and his opponent's weakness, to predict exactly when and with what move he will checkmate his opponent. The analogy is an engaging one; unfortunately, in the openness view, God is not so brilliant a chess player as to be able to know that his plans will probably succeed. For he failed to achieve the universal salvation he desired and regretted having created man. Those are not the moves of a Grand Master! So how could he possibly know before the foundations of the world, for example, that his plan for Christ to be crucified through the free agency of Pilate and Herod would be fulfilled? By contrast, the Molinist can explain the absence of universal salvation in terms of the wrong counterfactuals being true. It may be that a world having more saved but less damned than the actual world was not feasible for God. But given his knowledge of true counterfactuals of creaturely freedom, God is certain that his plans will ultimately be achieved. He is thus like a Grand Master who is playing an opponent whom he knows so well that he knows every move his opponent would make in response to his own moves. Such a chess player could not actualize just any possible match, given his opponent's freedom, but he could actualize any feasible match.

The analogy also has relevance to the problem of suffering and evil. In the openness view, the Not-So-Grand Master will churn up a lot of unforeseen, unnecessary, and pointless suffering as he plays the game, but in the Molinist view, such suffering will be permitted only in light of the Master's ultimate purpose, namely, building the kingdom of God. Thus, we can rest assured that God has morally sufficient reasons for permitting the evils in the world, whereas on the openness view, it becomes inexplicable why God does not intervene to stop the suffering once it has begun. The cognitively limited deity of openness theology thus makes the problem of evil worse, not easier, for it becomes inexplicable why God just sits by wringing his hands while letting evils go on unchecked without any morally sufficient reason for not stopping them.

A few openness theologians have attempted to accommodate the insights of Molinism by affirming that God does have middle knowledge of "might" counterfactuals of creaturely freedom, even though he lacks middle knowledge of "would" counterfactuals of creaturely freedom. Thus, he knows logically prior to his decree what any person he could create might or might not do in any set of circumstances in which God should place him. By exploiting his middle knowledge of such "might" counterfactuals, God is able to plan how he himself would respond to any choice that any person might make in any set of circumstances. Thus, although God gambles, in that he knows neither how creatures *would* choose were he to create them, nor how they *will* choose in the actual world, nevertheless he is never caught off guard or unprepared for their choices, for he has already decided how he would respond to any action they *might* take. Moreover, he is so intelligent that he knows that however creatures might choose, he will so respond as to ensure the realization of his ultimate purposes.

Such a move appears at first blush to represent a significant step in the direction of Molinism, since there is a significant intuitive difference between what a person *might* do in a set of circumstances and what he *could* do. For example, when Adolf Hitler spoke to the Nazi rally at Nuremberg in 1937, he could have broken into an oration in praise of Winston Churchill, but doubtless this is not something that he might have done. Thus, there is an important difference between what a person could do and what he might do in any given set of circumstances.

If revisionary open theists mean to capture this intuitive sense of "might," then by admitting the truth of "might" counterfactuals logically prior to the divine decree, they seem to have quietly abandoned the most common and forceful objections to the doctrine of middle knowledge, namely, objections based on the lack of grounding of such propositions. In the revised view, there appear to be truths about what persons might or might not do under any set of circumstances, truths that seem to go beyond mere possibilities, which are known by God logically prior to his decree of which world should be actual.

But if "might" counterfactuals can be true logically prior to God's decree, then why not also "would" counterfactuals? It is important to understand that in the customary semantics for counterfactual conditionals, "would" counterfactuals logically imply "might" counterfactuals, so that in the Molinist view, *both* are true and known to God via his middle knowledge. Once the usual grounding objections to middle knowledge have been tacitly abandoned, what justification remains for denying the truth of "would" counterfactuals? If the revisionary open theist answers that "would" counterfactuals are incompatible with creaturely freedom, then he has forgotten the difference between what one *could* do and what one *might* do in any set of circumstances. *Freedom requires only that in a given set of circumstances one be in some sense capable of refraining from doing what one would do; it is not required that one might not do what one would do.* If revisionary open theists are willing to accept true "might" counterfactuals, then I see no reason remaining to deny the truth of "would" counterfactuals as well. But that gives you full-blown Molinism.

Unfortunately, by denying the truth of any "would" counterfactuals, the revised openness view seems to collapse the distinction between "might" and "could." So long as "might" counterfactuals are implied by true "would" counterfactuals, we can maintain the distinction between what someone might do and what he could do under any circumstances. It is true that Hitler might not give an oration in praise of Churchill because he would not, but still he could do so because there are possible worlds (less similar to the actual world than those in which he might not do such a thing) in which he does. But if all "would" counterfactuals are false, then it is false that he would not do such a thing, and so in the customary semantics, it is true by definition that he might do such a thing. No matter how outlandish an action we pick—like Hitler's delivering his oration while standing on his head—there will, in the absence of any true counterfactuals to the effect that he would not take such an action, be worlds among those most similar to the actual world in which he takes that action, and so it is true that he might do such a thing. Hence, the move of revised open theism toward Molinism turns out to be a mere feint. Since "might" counterfactuals collapse to counterfactuals about what someone could freely do, God knows nothing more than mere possibilities prior to his creative decree—which is exactly what traditional open theism claims!

Revisionary open theists, then, seem to face a fundamental dilemma: if "might" counterfactuals are distinct from statements about what one could do in any set of circumstances, then no reason remains for denying the truth of "would" counterfactuals as well; if they are not distinct, however, then revised open theism is only a trivial variation of the usual open theist view.

In the Molinist view, as in the revised openness view, God plans how he would react to any decisions that creatures could freely make. For when he decrees which world is to be actual, he simultaneously decrees the truth of counterfactuals of divine freedom, that is, counterfactuals concerning how God himself would freely act in any circumstances involving his creatures. In decreeing a world, God decrees not only how he will act in response to creatures but also how he would act were creatures to choose any differently. Thus, like the God of revised open theism, he is prepared for every contingency, but he exceeds the God of revised open theism in that he knows not only how creatures might (or could) choose in any set of circumstances but also how they would choose under any such circumstances.

In any case, as explained above, knowledge of mere "might" counterfactuals is insufficient to give God the sort of specific providential control described in the Bible. Nor is it clear that such knowledge is sufficient to bring about God's desired ends. If it were, then why has God not acted to secure universal salvation? The revised openness theologian seems forced to say that it is because God did not really desire it—which is, again, to collapse into Calvinism. Why does God not intervene to stop evil once it appears? In revised open theism, it cannot be that God permits it to persist because he knows that some justifying good will come out of it, for all he knows is that some justifying good might, with some inscrutable probability, come out of it. Thus, revised open theism fails to secure any of the advantages of Molinism.

Augustinian-Calvinist Account. The Augustinian-Calvinist perspective, on the other hand, interprets the biblical passages such as those quoted above to mean that foreknowledge is based on foreordination. God knows what will happen because he makes it happen. Knowing the intentions of his will and his almighty power, God knows that his purpose shall be accomplished. But this interpretation inevitably makes God the author of sin, since it is he who moved Judas, for example, to betray Christ, a sin that merits everlasting perdition for the hapless Judas. But how can a holy God move people to commit moral evil, and moreover, how can these people then be held morally responsible for acts over which they had no control? The Augustinian-Calvinist view seems, in effect, to turn God into the Devil.

The Reformed theologian might object that a Molinist theory of providence is *too* successful in showing how God could sovereignly control a world of free creatures, so that it ultimately becomes almost indistinguishable from the Reformed view. For given that the circumstances C in which persons are placed are nondetermining, it must be a brute, contingent fact how some person S would choose in C. But then it is plausible that there are an indefinite number of circumstances C^* that differ from C in imperceptible or causally irrelevant ways (for example, a different stellar event in Alpha Centauri at the time of S's decision), in which S would choose differently than in C. So by placing S in one of these circumstances C^*, God could bring it about that S chooses freely whatever God wishes without any deleterious impact on his providential plan. Thus, God can sovereignly bring about any creaturely decision he wants and, hence, any world that he wants.

We would do well to pause and ask ourselves what the import of this objection is even if it is successful. It would do nothing, I think, to undermine the Molinist account of providence as such. In particular, it would not in any way undermine the freedom of the creatures in whatever circumstances they find themselves, for their choices are in every case causally undetermined. If a choice is freely made in C, then it would be freely made in C^*, which includes some causally irrelevant event not included in C. If God places S in C, then S's freedom is not compromised by the mere fact that had God placed S in C^* instead, S would have chosen differently.

Rather, what the objection threatens to undermine, it seems, is the theological utility of the doctrine of middle knowledge. For if the objection is correct, the distinction between broadly logically possible worlds and feasible worlds becomes inconsequential, since God can bring about whatever free creaturely choices he desires without detriment to his providential plan. The Molinist account of providence would then be useless in explaining why apparently less-than-optimal states of affairs obtain; like the Augustinian-Calvinist, the Molinist would have to ascribe them to God's perfect will. But the Molinist account would still enjoy the considerable advantage of making room for creaturely freedom. It would just be of little help in explaining, for example, why evil exists.

The objection, in any case, is not successful, for it is predicated on a number of questionable assumptions. First, the objection seems to assume that one is dealing with events distributed across the various sets of circumstances by blind chance. But it is not by chance that S chooses a particular action A in C. So one must not think of S's free choices as randomly distributed across the various sets of circumstances. Quite the contrary, free choices are indeterministic events done for reasons. And that gives grounds for thinking that S's choices would not vary wildly in various C^*, namely, because the C^* are indistinguishable from C, one's reasons for choosing A in C also hold for C^*. (Empirical evidence for constancy across C^*: just ask the relevant person whether he would have chosen differently had C^* rather than C been his circumstances!)

Second, the objection assumes that the circumstances mentioned in the counterfactual's antecedent are unlimited. But this is far from obvious. It is universally agreed, for example, that events later than the time

t of S's choice ought not to be included in the circumstances. Why not? The most obvious answer is because events that are future at t can have no influence on S's situation at t and, hence, are irrelevant to S's decision. But events that are sufficiently distant from S are just as irrelevant as future events even if those events are simultaneous with or even earlier than t. Only events that are connectable via a light signal to the event of S's decision seem to be relevant to S's choice. Events having what is called "a spacelike separation" from the event of S's decision are as irrelevant as future events; indeed, special relativity theory holds that for some observers at S's location (those moving at near light speeds), these events *are* future at the time of S's choice. This suggests that only events in or on S's past light cone (that is, events from which a light signal could reach S at t) are properly part of C. Thus, the substitution of circumstances C^* for C, where C is a proper part of C^*, will not affect the truth of the counterfactual in question, since only C is relevant to its truth-value.

Third, the objection assumes that imperceptible events included in S's past light cone can be altered without significant effect on S's situation at t. But the lessons of both quantum theory and chaos theory have taught us that such an assumption is false. The imperceptible indeterminacy in the position of a cue ball on a billiard table is such that after only a dozen shots, the indeterminacy in the ball's location has been magnified to the size of the entire table. Chaotic systems vary unpredictably with the tiniest perturbation. Certainly some events, say, in the very recent past far from S's location, might be alterable without significant impact on S's situation at t; but these will be finite in number, and it will be pure speculation whether S would freely choose differently were one of them to be altered. The available alterations may fall far short of what is necessary for God's bringing about any desired free choice on S's part.

Finally, the objection assumes that God's concern is with S's choice alone. But God's concern is with a whole history of free creatures into eternity future. Even if substituting C^* for C were sufficient for bringing about any given free choice of S at t, that says nothing about the feasibility of actualizing a whole world of free creatures, a task that plausibly involves infinite complexity. It is, then, not at all implausible that the difference between broadly logically possible worlds and feasible worlds should become significant and dramatic.

So the objection at issue is predicated on a number of false assumptions, and even if successful, it would do nothing to rob Molinism of its chief ground for boasting: the successful reconciliation of divine sovereignty and human freedom.

Simple Foreknowledge Account. Finally, the proponent of simple foreknowledge can make no good sense of God's providential planning of a world of free creatures in the absence of middle knowledge. For on such a view God has, logically prior to the divine decree, only natural knowledge of all the possible scenarios but no knowledge of what would happen under any given circumstances. Thus, logically posterior to the divine decree, God must consider himself extraordinarily lucky to find that this world happened to exist. "What a break!" we can imagine God saying to himself. "Herod and Pilate and all those people each reacted just perfectly!" Actually, the situation is much worse than that, for God had no idea whether Herod, Pilate, the Israelite nation, or the Roman Empire would even exist posterior to the divine decree. Indeed, God must be astonished to find himself existing in a world, out of all the possible worlds he could have created, in which mankind falls into sin and God himself enters human history as a substitutionary sacrificial offering to rescue them! Of course, one is speaking anthropomorphically here, but the point remains that without middle knowledge, God cannot know prior to the creative decree what the world would be like. If the defender of simple foreknowledge goes on to say that God's foreordination of future events is based on his simple foreknowledge, this trivializes the doctrine of foreordination, making it a fifth wheel that carries no load, since the future by definition will be what it will be. Once God knows that an event really is future, there is nothing more left to do; foreordination becomes a redundancy. Surely there is more substance to the biblical doctrine of foreordination than the triviality that God decrees that what will happen will happen!

Thus, of the options available, the Molinist approach provides the most elucidating account of divine providence. It enables us to embrace divine sovereignty and human freedom without mysticism or mental reservation, thereby preserving faithfully the biblical text's affirmation of both these doctrines. We therefore have powerful theological motivation for adopting the doctrine of divine middle knowledge.

Philosophical Argument

Finally, we also have good philosophical grounds for thinking that a doctrine of middle knowledge is correct. For, as an omniscient being, God must know all truths. Since there are counterfactual truths, God must know these. Now, God knows such truths either explanatorily prior to his decree to create the world or only posterior to his creative decree. But they cannot be known only posterior to his creative decree, since in that case, it is God who decrees what choices agents shall make in whatever circumstances they find themselves, and human freedom is annihilated. Therefore, God must know counterfactuals of creaturely freedom logically prior to his creative decree, which is to say that God has middle knowledge.

We may formulate this argument as follows:

1. If there are true counterfactuals of creaturely freedom, then God knows these truths.
2. There are true counterfactuals of creaturely freedom.
3. If God knows true counterfactuals of creaturely freedom, God knows them either logically prior to the divine creative decree or only logically posterior to the divine creative decree.
4. Counterfactuals of creaturely freedom cannot be known only logically posterior to the divine creative decree.

From premises 1 and 2, it follows logically that

5. Therefore, God knows true counterfactuals of creaturely freedom.

From premises 3 and 5, it follows that

6. Therefore, God knows true counterfactuals of creaturely freedom either logically prior to the divine creative decree or only logically posterior to the divine creative decree.

And from premises 4 and 6, it follows that

7. Therefore, God knows true counterfactuals of creaturely freedom logically prior to the divine creative decree

—which is the essence of the doctrine of divine middle knowledge.

Let us now say a word in defense of each of the argument's premises. The truth of premise 1 is required by the standard definition of omniscience:

O S is omniscient = If any proposition p is true, then S knows
            that p and does not believe that not-p.

(O) entails that if there are counterfactual truths, then an omniscient being must know them. Openness theologians have suggested revisionary definitions of omniscience so as to be able to affirm that God is omniscient, even as they deny his knowledge of future contingents and counterfactuals of creaturely freedom. William Hasker's revisionist definition is typical:[11]

O'   God is omniscient = God knows all propositions which are
                such that God's knowing them is
                logically possible.

Openness thinkers then go on to claim that it is logically impossible to know propositions about future contingents, as shown by the argument for theological fatalism, and so God may count as omniscient despite his ignorance of an infinite number of true propositions.

As it stands, however, (O') is drastically flawed. It does not exclude that God believes false propositions as well as true ones. Worse, (O') actually requires God to know false propositions, which is incoherent as well as theologically unacceptable. For (O') requires that if it is logically possible for God to know some proposition p, then God knows p. But if p is a contingently false proposition, say, "There are seven planets in the sun's solar system," then there are possible worlds in which p is true and known by God. Therefore, since it is logically possible for God to know p, he must actually know p, which is absurd.

What the revisionist really wants to say is something like:

O''   God is omniscient = God knows only and all true
                propositions which are such that
                it is logically possible for God to
                know them.

---

11. For the following definition, see William Hasker, "A Philosophical Perspective," in Clark Pinnock, Richard Rice, John Sanders, William Hasker, and David Basinger, *The Openness of God: A Biblical Challenge to the Traditional Understanding of God* (Downers Grove, Ill: InterVarsity Press, 1994), 136.

Unlike (O'), (O'') limits God's knowledge to a certain subset of all true propositions. The fundamental problem with all such revisionary definitions of omniscience as (O'') is that any adequate definition of a concept must accord with our intuitive understanding of the concept. We are not at liberty to "cook" the definition in some desired way without thereby making the definition unacceptably contrived. (O'') is guilty of being "cooked" in this way. For, intuitively, omniscience involves knowing all truth, yet according to (O''), God could conceivably be ignorant of infinite realms of truth and yet still count as omniscient. The only reason someone would prefer (O'') to (O) is due to an ulterior motivation to salvage the attribute of omniscience for a cognitively limited deity rather than to deny outright that God is omniscient. (O'') is therefore unacceptably contrived.

A second problem with (O'') is that it construes omniscience in modal terms, speaking not of knowing all truth but of knowing all truth that is knowable. But omniscience, unlike omnipotence, is not a modal notion. Roughly speaking, omnipotence is the capability of actualizing any logically possible state of affairs. But omniscience is not merely the *capability* of knowing only and all truths; it *is* knowing only and all truths. Nor does omniscience mean knowing only and all knowable truths; it means knowing only and all truths, period. It is a categorical, not a modal, notion.

Third, the superiority of (O'') over (O) depends on there being a difference between a truth and a truth that is logically possible to know. If there is no difference, then (O'') collapses back to the general definition (O), and the revisionist has gained nothing. What is a sufficient condition for a proposition to be logically knowable? So far as I can see, the only condition is that the proposition be true. What more is needed? If the revisionist thinks that something more is needed, then we may ask him for an example of a proposition that could be true but logically impossible to know. Propositions like "Nothing exists" or "All agents have ceased to exist" come to mind, but on traditional theism, these propositions are not possibly true, since God is an agent whose nonexistence is impossible. Unless the revisionist can give us some reason to think that a proposition can be true yet unknowable, we have no reason to adopt (O''). It seems that the only intrinsic property that a proposition must possess to be logically knowable is truth.

The openness theologian will claim at this point that future contingent propositions are logically impossible for God to know, since if he knows them, then they are not contingent, as shown by the argument for fatalism. But here the openist thinker has committed a logical howler. He reasons that for any future-tense proposition p, it is impossible both that God knows p and that p is contingent; therefore, if p is contingent, it is not possible that God knows p. But such reasoning is logically fallacious, as is shown in the following:

A. Not-possibly (God knows p, and p is contingently true)
B. p is contingently true

These two premises do not logically imply that

C. Not-possibly (God knows p)

Rather, what follows logically from premises A and B is merely that

C'. Not (God knows p).

In other words, what follows from premises A and B is merely that God does not know p, not that it is impossible that God knows p. Thus, even *granted* the fatalist's premise A (which is moot) that it is impossible that God knows p and p is contingently true, it does not follow from the contingent truth of p that p is such that it is logically impossible for God to know p. Therefore, even based on the defective definition (O'') proposed by the revisionist, the open theologian's God turns out not to be omniscient, since p is a true proposition that, so far as we can see, is logically possible for God to know, yet God does not know p. Thus, the open theologian must deny divine omniscience and therefore reject God's perfection—a serious theological consequence indeed. Therefore, premise 1 cannot be easily denied.

Premise 2 asserts that there are true counterfactuals of creaturely freedom. This premise does not require us to believe that all counterfactuals about creatures' free acts are either true or false. But it does seem plausible that counterfactuals of the following form are either true or false (letting S be any person, A some action, and C any set of circumstances including the whole history of the world up until the time of decision):

CCF If S were in C, S would freely do A.

It is counterfactuals of this form that we dignify with the title "counterfactuals of creaturely freedom" (CCF).

We have every reason to think that there are true counterfactuals of creaturely freedom. First, it is plausible that counterfactuals of the form CCF are true or false. For since the circumstances mentioned in the antecedent in which S finds himself are fully specified, any ambiguity which might cause us to doubt that the counterfactual has a truth-value is removed. And it is plausible that in many cases S would freely do A in C, just as the counterfactual states. Second, we ourselves often know the truth of counterfactuals about how people would act or react under particular circumstances. While we may not know such truths with certainty, we constantly make decisions and act on the basis of which counterfactuals we think are probably true. A little reflection reveals how pervasive and indispensable such counterfactual truths are to rational conduct and planning. We sometimes base our very lives on their truth or falsity. Third, as pointed out above, Scripture itself gives examples of such true counterfactuals (think again about Paul's statement in 1 Cor. 2:8).

Premise 3 states logically exhaustive alternatives for an omniscient deity and so must be true: counterfactuals of creaturely freedom are known by God either prior to his decree or only after his decree.

Finally, premise 4 must be true because if counterfactuals of creaturely freedom were known only after the divine decree, then it is God who determined what every creature would do in every circumstance. Augustinian-Calvinist thinkers bear witness to the truth of this premise in their affirmation of compatibilist theories of creaturely freedom (according to which all our acts, though voluntary, are causally determined). They thereby testify that God's all-determining decree precludes libertarian freedom, which is the sort of freedom with which we are here concerned. Thus, if God knows counterfactual truths about us only posterior to his decree, then there really are no counterfactuals of creaturely freedom. If there are such counterfactuals, they must be true logically prior to the divine decree.

Given the truth of the premises, the conclusion follows that prior to his creative decree, God knows all true counterfactuals of creaturely freedom, which is to say that he has middle knowledge.

Conclusion

Via his middle knowledge, then, God can have complete knowledge of both conditional future contingents and absolute future contingents.

Such knowledge gives him sweeping sovereignty over the affairs of men. Yet such an account of God's knowledge is wholly compatible with human freedom, since the circumstances envisioned in counterfactuals of creaturely freedom are nondetermining and, hence, freedom-preserving. It is because of these advantages that I commend a Molinist account of divine providence for serious consideration.

PAUL KJOSS HELSETH

William Lane Craig is a brilliant scholar. He also writes beautifully. The substance of his chapter, however, is unworthy of his brilliance, for although it is beautifully written and descriptively superb, it does not argue a case as much as assert a position. Indeed, from beginning to end Dr. Craig offers, not an extended argument that carefully anticipates and answers the potential questions of those not already members of the Molinist camp, but a tendentious analysis that leaves the most difficult and important questions unaddressed.

Among these questions are the following: (1) What is the *ontological* status of counterfactuals of creaturely freedom for Molinists generally and for Dr. Craig specifically? Since counterfactual conditionals are logically "prior to and independent of God's decree," just how are they related to the will and providential activity of the Creator? Do they exist independently of God, and if so, how could anyone account for their existence without subverting the self-sufficiency of God "in *everything*: in his existence, in his attributes, in his decrees, and in his works"?[12] Or are they in fact dependent on God, and if they are, what is the nature of this dependence given the Molinist contention that counterfactual conditionals are neither caused nor determined by God?[13] (2) What are we

---

12. Herman Bavinck, *The Doctrine of God*, trans. and ed. William Hendrickson (Edinburgh: Banner of Truth Trust, 1991), 144–45.

13. According to Richard Muller, "For Molina's concept to function, the conditions standing prior to the contingent event must be understood as not merely possible, but as having some sort of actuality or quasi-actuality apart from the divine willing—inasmuch as the point is not that God knows various and sundry possible contingencies and knows what would result on condition of their occurrence (viz., given their actualization by him). That would, once again, press back into the divine necessary knowledge. Nor is the point that God knows certain conditions within the realm of actuality that he has willed and also knows what will result from them. That would point toward the divine voluntary knowledge. Rather the point is that God knows what will occur contingently upon certain conditions lying outside of his will: these conditions are not mere possibility nor divinely willed actuality, but foreknown

to make of the grounding objection? Dr. Craig commends the feasibility of Molinism in part by insisting that "counterfactual statements constitute a significant part of our ordinary language and are an indispensable part of our decision making." But how is our counterfactual knowledge of "how people would act or react under particular circumstances" like or not like God's middle knowledge of what creatures with libertarian freedom "would freely choose under various circumstances"? Is it possible that we, as those who are created in God's image, have a measure of middle knowledge as well? Or is our knowledge of counterfactual conditionals different from God's in that ours is inferential and therefore grounded yet fallible whereas his is noninferential and therefore not grounded yet infallible?[14] (3) Why, moreover, must we accommodate the assumption that libertarian freedom — "the sort of freedom with which [Dr. Craig is] ... concerned" in his essay — *just is* genuine freedom, particularly when the notion that human beings are genuinely free "is denied by no orthodox theology,"[15] and the intelligibility of libertarian freedom remains an open question? (4) How, finally, can Molinists escape the charge that they have embraced a form of fatalism that would make the most radical of hyper-Calvinists squeamish? According to Richard Muller:

---

conditions, foreknown as actual apart from the decree, at least for the sake of stating the contingency. Once again, the Reformed deny that there can be such knowledge: 'there can be no *scientia media*,' Cocceius wrote, 'because there can be no being independent of the divine will'" (Richard A. Muller, *Post-Reformation Reformed Dogmatics*, 3:421).

Note that the ontological status of "counterfactual conditionals" remains remarkably elusive even in Dr. Craig's "conceptualist model of divine knowledge." According to this model, "God's knowledge is self-contained; it is more like a mind's knowledge of innate ideas. It is based wholly in God's middle knowledge and knowledge of his own decrees."

14. Those who stand in the tradition of Reformed orthodoxy reject the Molinist account of counterfactual conditionals because they are persuaded that "there can be no real content to, because no referent for, abstract possibility; only possibility as a consequence of God's creative activity has any real content" (K. Scott Oliphint, *Reasons for Faith: Philosophy in the Service of Theology* [Phillipsburg, N.J.: P&R, 2006], 322). In his extended discussion of the Reformed insistence that "The triune God is in no way subject to possibility" (ibid., 323), Scott Oliphint cites Muller's contention that for those standing in the Reformed tradition, "there is nothing prior to the decree but pure possibility: God's decree establishes the order of things — it does not proceed from foreknowledge of the order.... The alternative view, that such an event (if this, then that) is not merely in the order of possibilities and must be known by a 'middle knowledge,' confers a quasi-actuality upon the possibility. Then, of course, the ground of the actuality once again becomes a matter of issue: from the Molinist, Arminian, and Socinian perspective, the contingency is known as an event prior to the divine willing — an event, which the Reformed contend, cannot be, inasmuch as all actuality is conferred by God" (Muller, *Post-Reformation Reformed Dogmatics*, 3:429; for a fuller discussion, see 3:417–32).

15. Oliphint, *Reasons for Faith*, 327.

If there is a middle knowledge in God, dependent on "external objects," then there is an eternal priority of these creatures and creaturely events over God and "creatures will not depend on God alone, but God will instead depend on creatures as his exemplars." This divine dependence, in turn, would argue the absolutely certain existence of future contingents "prior to all divine decrees" and, given the absolute certainty of such contingents, introduces a causal necessity into their effects—that is, the necessity of the consequent, which, from the perspective of the consequent act or thing itself is an absolute necessity. A radical conception of foreknowledge that insists on a divine foreknowledge of conditionals as conditional, in other words, reifies the conditionals, places events and things outside of the divine purpose, and hypothesizes an order of occurrences that, therefore, impinges negatively on the divine willing. Thus, those who "establish future events as prior to the decree of God, introduce Stoic fatalism, namely, an interconnection of things independent of God." This ... is the implication of the theory of middle knowledge, especially of the Socinian version. The attempt to gain freedom at the expense of the divine causality results, therefore, in a new fatalism, a replacement of the conception of overarching divine purpose with a model of blind natural necessity.[16]

In short, because Dr. Craig ignores these and other important questions, there is a hollowness to his presentation that renders his analysis unpersuasive not only to those who do not share his philosophical commitments but also to those who already do yet reject the Molinist proposal for one substantial reason or another.

According to the majority of those standing in the tradition of Reformed orthodoxy, this hollowness is particularly disturbing for two important reasons. First, it is disturbing because it discloses an aloofness that effectively ignores the categorical irrelevance of middle knowledge to accounts of divine providence that do not involve the libertarian view of human freedom. As Paul Helm has incisively argued, "The very notion of middle knowledge collapses if its underlying rationale and necessity are

---

16. Muller, *Post-Reformation Reformed Dogmatics*, 3:425. Note that the phrase "external objects" does not require us to embrace what Dr. Craig calls "a perceptualist model" of divine cognition.

changed. That rationale and necessity rest upon the Jesuit and Arminian commitment to the freedom of indifference. As it is impossible to have a soufflé without eggs, so it is impossible to have middle knowledge without the freedom of indifference."[17] Second, the hollowness of Dr. Craig's essay is disturbing because it encourages a kind of insolence that is not only entirely without justification but also, to put it charitably, entirely lacking in appropriate reverential caution. Dr. Craig brazenly opines that the Augustinian-Calvinist account of providence "seems ... to turn God into the Devil," because it "obliterate[s] human freedom" and "makes God the author of sin." While this statement and the assertions that support it will likely elicit squeals of delight from some quarters of an increasingly factious evangelical camp, it is theologically irresponsible—in fact, it is deserving of a stern rebuke—due in large measure to the magnitude of the questions that Dr. Craig ignores throughout his essay.

A Theological or Philosophical Account?

In my estimation, the tendentious nature of Dr. Craig's analysis is simply the inevitable manifestation of an approach to thinking about the providence of God that privileges philosophical speculation over the careful examination of what God has revealed in his Word. Indeed, Dr. Craig's analysis is grounded, not in the thoughtful investigation of what Scripture explicitly says about God's relationship to the world that he has made, but in a consideration of the text that has been compromised by a favored philosophical paradigm, in this case a cluster of assumptions surrounding the libertarian view of human freedom. According to Dr. Craig, genuine freedom *just is* libertarian freedom, and because "God must know all truths," he *just has* middle knowledge, and these are the assumptions that *just should* inform a Christian understanding of providence, despite the fact that even in "a *conceptualist* model of divine cognition," we cannot "adequately explain"[18] precisely how God could *just know* what creatures with libertarian freedom "would freely choose in whatever circumstances in which they might be."

---

17. Paul Helm, "Shunning Middle Knowledge," http://paulhelmsdeep.blogspot. com/2009/05/shunning-middle-knowledge.html; see also Paul Helm and Terrance L. Tiessen, "Does Calvinism Have Room for Middle Knowledge? A Conversation," *Westminster Theological Journal* 71 (2009): 437–54.

18. William Lane Craig, *The Only Wise God: The Compatibility of Divine Foreknowledge and Human Freedom* (Grand Rapids: Baker, 1987), 123.

While it is certainly true that we all have assumptions that in some sense affect the outcome of our theological analysis, it is also true that there is a significant difference between assumptions that are theologically justified and assumptions that are theologically reckless. Assumptions that are theologically justified, I would argue, emerge from the world of the Bible, and genuine mysteries—the riddles that we cannot "adequately explain" because they have to do with the inscrutable nature of the relationship between God and the world that he has made—are therefore those that have to do with what the text of Scripture more or less explicitly says. Isaiah 10:5–19, for example, presents us with a bona fide mystery, for it informs us that the Assyrians who were used by the Lord to trample the children of Israel down like "the mire of the streets" (Isa. 10:6)[19] were punished, not because they plundered the Israelites as they "so intend[ed]" (Isa. 10:7), but because they arrogantly presumed that they were able to do so *independently* of the Lord who was using them, i.e., "By the strength of [*their own*] hand" (Isa. 10:13): "Shall the axe boast over him who hews with it, or the saw magnify itself against him who wields it? As if a rod should wield him who lifts it, or as if a staff should lift him who is not wood!" (Isa. 10:15).

Assumptions that are theologically reckless, on the other hand, are more or less imposed on or read into the text of Scripture, and pseudo-mysteries—the riddles that will never be "adequately explained," not because they are inscrutable but because they have to do with scenarios that are simply foreign to the world of the Bible—are therefore those that trade in one way or another on philosophical contrivances that are unbiblical, and as such, more imagined than real.[20] When we conflate justified assumptions with reckless assumptions and as a consequence confound genuine mysteries with pseudo-mysteries, as I believe Dr.

---

19. Unless otherwise noted, all forthcoming Scripture quotations in this response are from the ESV.

20. I am reminded of a comment that Calvin makes in his response to Albert Pighius: "No plague is more hostile to the truth or a more deadly way of blinding someone completely than a false presupposition, especially when it is fixed obstinately in the mind" (John Calvin, *The Bondage and Liberation of the Will: A Defence of the Orthodox Doctrine of Human Choice against Pighius*, ed. A. N. S. Lane, trans. G. I. Davis [Grand Rapids: Baker, 1996], 198). For the record, I would suggest that an assumption is theologically reckless if it finds its genesis in the perceived need to rescue the Bible from a reading that, while exegetically sound, nevertheless is embarrassing or revolting to the interpreter. Such assumptions, it seems, are playing a formative role in the efforts of those who are introducing novel concepts to get God "off the hook" for the problem of evil.

Craig has done by insisting that God *just has* middle knowledge even though we cannot give an adequate account of precisely how he could infallibly foreknow the acts of creatures possessing libertarian freedom, we commit a serious methodological error, an error that, when all is said and done, does little more than sanction rank eisegesis. This, in short, is the danger of embracing a theological method that moves not from the text to philosophical speculation but from philosophical speculation to the text, a line of movement that Dr. Craig elsewhere suggests is the right way for "thinking Christians"[21] to come to an understanding of what Scott Oliphint and Lane Tipton rightly call "the deep things of God."[22]

Biblical Arguments? Regarding 1 Corinthians 2:8

At the beginning of his discussion of the "lines of argument" that he believes support the Molinist account of divine providence, Dr. Craig acknowledges that although the Bible is filled "with examples of ... counterfactual conditionals concerning creaturely choices and actions," this fact alone "does not settle the matter of whether God has middle knowledge." Scripture, he reasons, does not reflect on the question of whether God's knowledge of counterfactual propositions "is ... before or after the divine decree," and for this reason, the defenders of Molinism must concede that "no amount of proof texting concerning God's hypothetical knowledge can prove that such knowledge is possessed logically prior to God's creative decree. This is a matter for theologico-philosophical reflection, not biblical exegesis. Thus," Dr. Craig concludes, "while it is clearly unbiblical to deny that God has hypothetical knowledge, those who deny middle knowledge while affirming God's hypothetical knowledge cannot be accused of being unbiblical."

---

21. Craig, *The Only Wise God*, 11; see also William Lane Craig, *Time and Eternity: Exploring God's Relationship to Time* (Wheaton, Ill.: Crossway, 2001), 11.

22. Oliphint and Tipton, introduction to *Revelation and Reason*, 2. Oliphint and Tipton insist that Dr. Craig's line of movement "is most unfortunate. As happened in the medieval period, such thinking will inevitably lead to the need for a radical, biblical reformation of those ideas and concepts developed by philosophers. If one wants to know about God's omniscience or his eternity, if one wants to think deeply about God and his relationship to the world, if one wants to do apologetics, the first place to look is to Scripture, and then to those theologians who faithfully articulate its teachings" (ibid., 2–3).

For an outstanding example of an approach to thinking about "the deep things of God" that self-consciously moves from the text to philosophical speculation, see Oliphint, *Reasons for Faith*.

As a Reformed believer who is persuaded that God's knowledge of what moral agents would do in every possible world in which they exist is an essential component of his natural knowledge,[23] I must say that although I am gratified by Dr. Craig's willingness to acknowledge that one can reject middle knowledge without contravening the teaching of Scripture, I wonder if this concession somehow eclipses a more salient issue. The real question, it seems, is not whether those who deny middle knowledge are "being unbiblical" but whether Molinists like Dr. Craig can legitimately claim that there are biblical arguments "for" the Molinist account of divine providence if they cannot demonstrate that the essential commitments of Molinism are justified by the plain teaching of the Bible. To state the matter a bit differently, it seems that for Molinists like Dr. Craig to say that there are "biblical arguments" not just for God's knowledge of counterfactual conditionals but "for" the Molinist account of divine providence, they must be able to establish that Scripture unambiguously affirms, if not middle knowledge itself, then at least what middle knowledge presupposes, namely, the existence and biblical givenness of libertarian freedom. But can they? Apparently, Dr. Craig believes that they can, for he insists that "of the options available, the Molinist approach provides the most elucidating account of divine providence. It enables us to embrace divine sovereignty and human freedom without mysticism or mental reservation, thereby preserving faithfully *the biblical text's affirmation of both of these doctrines*" (emphasis added).

There is a sense, of course, in which no believing theologian would deny that the Bible affirms that God is sovereign and that human beings are genuinely free and responsible for what they do. I know of no consistently Reformed theologian, for example, who wants to argue that human beings are nothing more than automatons and therefore *not* genuinely free and responsible for the decisions that they make. What Dr. Craig means by "freedom" in the quotation above, however, is not freedom in

23. In his exchange with Terrance Tiessen, Paul Helm argues that "on the classic view of God's knowledge, God by his natural knowledge knows what A in all possible states of his mind could do in all possible sets of circumstances. The contents of all possible worlds containing A include propositions about what A would do if C were to be the case ... if D were to be the case, and so on. These are not so much counterfactual, as pre-factual. In the divine mind the states of mind and sets of circumstances of a possible agent A form elements in innumerable possible worlds, all of the possible worlds in which A exists" (Helm and Tiessen, "Does Calvinism Have Room for Middle Knowledge?" 441–42.)

general but libertarian freedom in particular, not only the kind of freedom that is essential to middle knowledge and the Molinist "scheme," but also the *only* kind of freedom that he believes is properly regarded as genuine freedom.[24] But does Scripture affirm that human beings have *this* kind of freedom? And if it does, may we plausibly conclude that, when Scripture's affirmation of this "doctrine" is combined with its clear affirmation of God's "sweeping sovereignty over the affairs of men," there are biblical grounds for believing not only that God has middle knowledge but also that Molinism provides the most compelling account of divine providence? Because he presupposes that libertarian freedom *just is* the "doctrine" of human freedom that Scripture affirms, Dr. Craig clearly believes that we not only may conclude that Molinism is both compelling and justified by the teaching of Scripture, but we must.

In this regard, Dr. Craig cites 1 Corinthians 2:8 as just one example in Scripture of God's middle knowledge of a "true" counterfactual, a true counterfactual that, like all true counterfactuals, points to the theological "subtlety and power" of the Molinist account of divine providence. When we consider the "mind-boggling" extent of God's providential control over the contingent events that both led up to and transpired during the week of Jesus' passion, "we see that only an omniscient mind could providentially direct a world of free creatures toward his sovereignly established ends. In fact, Paul reflects that 'none of the rulers of this age understood *this*, for if they had, they would not have crucified the Lord of glory' (1 Cor. 2:8). Once one grasps *it*, the doc-

---

24. Dr. Craig makes it clear throughout his essay that determinism is not only incompatible with genuine freedom; it actually "destroys" genuine freedom. One particularly concise statement of his position is found in the second half of his essay, in his assertion that counterfactual conditionals "cannot be known only posterior to his creative decree, since in that case, it is God who decrees what choices agents shall make in whatever circumstances they find themselves, and human freedom is annihilated." A more substantive statement of his position is found near the beginning of his essay, in his summary of the debate between the members of the Dominican and Jesuit orders over precisely "when" God has knowledge of counterfactual conditionals. Unlike the Catholic theologians of the Dominican order, he argues, "inspired by Luis de Molina, Catholic theologians of the Jesuit order maintained that God's hypothetical knowledge of creaturely free decisions is logically *prior* to his creative decree. This difference between the Jesuit Molinists and the Dominicans was no mere matter of theological hairsplitting! The Molinists charged that the Dominicans had in effect obliterated human freedom by making counterfactual truths about creaturely choices a consequence of God's decree. For it is God who determines what a person would choose in whatever circumstances in which he finds himself. By contrast, the Molinists, by placing God's hypothetical knowledge of creaturely free decisions prior to the divine decree, made room for creaturely freedom by exempting counterfactual truths about creaturely choices from God's decree."

trine of divine middle knowledge thus issues in adoration and praise of God for so breathtaking a sovereignty" (emphasis added).

While I appreciate and applaud Dr. Craig for his eagerness to praise the God of the Bible for his "breathtaking … sovereignty," I have yet to be persuaded that 1 Corinthians 2:8 comes anywhere close to supporting the case that Dr. Craig is trying to make for the biblical grounding of Molinism. In fact, I am quite certain that Dr. Craig's appeal to 1 Corinthians 2:8 does positive damage to his case, and it does so for two reasons. The first, which is admittedly not as consequential as the second, has to do with the ambiguity that is associated with the pronouns highlighted in the quotation above. Does Dr. Craig seriously believe that "the rulers of this age … would not have crucified the Lord of glory" if only they had understood as much as he and other Molinists claim to understand about "God's providential control over a world of free agents"? Surely, despite the plausibility of such an interpretation given the ambiguity associated with the pronouns "this" and "it," Dr. Craig *cannot* mean that, for if he did, it would suggest an arrogance that is almost superhuman. What he must mean, then, is that "the rulers of this age … crucified the Lord of glory" because they did not understand the "plan" that was being sovereignly accomplished in the life and ministry of Jesus. Had they understood that God was "providentially direct[ing] a world of free creatures toward his sovereignly established ends," and had they understood that these ends were being fulfilled in the person and work of Jesus, they would not have used their libertarian freedom to crucify the Lord of glory, but they would have embraced him as he is because they would have recognized that he *just is* "the power of God and the wisdom of God" (1 Cor. 1:24).

When we set grammatical ambiguities aside, however, there is a more compelling reason why Dr. Craig's appeal to 1 Corinthians 2:8 does positive damage to his case, and it has to do with the ultimate explanation for why "the rulers of this age" did not understand what God was doing before their eyes in the life and ministry of Jesus. The larger context of 1 Corinthians 2:8 suggests that "the rulers of this age … crucified the Lord of glory" neither because they were oblivious to the "mind-boggling" wonders of Molinism, nor because they did not have the intellectual ability to understand the propositional content of what the apostle Paul refers to as "the folly of what we preach" (1 Cor. 1:21).

Rather, they crucified the Lord of glory because, as Richard Gaffin has incisively argued, they were "devoid of the Spirit" and thus without the moral ability to understand "the age-to-come, eschatological wisdom of the gospel," the spiritual wisdom that "is not ultimately cognitive or merely intellectual,"[25] the kind of wisdom that is simultaneously revealed and concealed whenever "the word of the cross" (1 Cor. 1:18) is preached.[26] According to Gaffin, what Paul says about "the natural person" in 1 Corinthians 2:14

> must not be overlooked: "he cannot understand [the things of the Spirit]." It is not simply that such a person will not or refuses to accept what he right well knows to be true. No, he won't because he can't. Expressed here is a total cognitive inability, an incapacity that exists "because they [the things of the Spirit] are spiritually discerned," that is, they are properly appraised and assessed only through the Spirit's activity. Here, again, yawns the unbridgeable epistemological gulf between this age and the age to come, the nothing-less-than eschatological chasm between belief and unbelief. Calvin's pungent comment on [1 Corinthians] 1:20 comes to mind: faced with God's revelation, the unbeliever is like an ass at a concert.[27]

In the final analysis, then, the problem with Dr. Craig's appeal to 1 Corinthians 2:8 is that "the rulers of this age" did not possess what he insists moral agents must possess in every feasible world, namely, the freedom of indifference. Indeed, the context of 1 Corinthians 2:8 makes it clear that in this world, embracing Christ was simply not a viable option for them—*they could not do it*—neither because they did not have the ability to make real choices regarding the "secret and hidden wisdom" (1 Cor. 2:7) that was objectively present to their understanding, nor because they did not have the capacity to understand "the word of the cross" in any sense. Rather, they refused to embrace Christ because embracing Christ was—due to the "enervating and corrupting consequences [of sin] (1 Cor.

---

25. Richard B. Gaffin Jr., "Epistemological Reflections on 1 Corinthians 2:6–16," in Oliphint and Tipton, *Revelation and Reason*, 27, 23, 20.

26. For a particularly explicit discussion of how the preaching of the gospel simultaneously reveals and conceals, see Matthew 13:10–17 for Jesus' explanation of why he taught in parables.

27. Gaffin, "1 Corinthians 2:6–16," 28.

15:42–43; cf. vv. 21–22)"[28]—tantamount to embracing "folly" (1 Cor. 1:18). In short, "the rulers of this age ... crucified the Lord of glory" because they did not have the spiritual capacity to understand "the things of the Spirit of God" (1 Cor. 2:14), and thus they did not enjoy the kind of freedom that only those who have "the mind of Christ" (1 Cor. 2:16) enjoy, which *just is* the freedom to truly see and truly hear and freely act accordingly. "The rulers of this age" ultimately did what they did, then, *not* because they decided in this possible world to use their libertarian freedom in one way and not in another—again, they simply did not have this kind of freedom—but because they were without the moral ability "to attain to a true knowledge of God,"[29] an ability that they most certainly would have had if the Arminian doctrine of prevenient grace held just one drop of water.[30] It is this understanding of the relationship between moral character and moral activity and not that which is presupposed by the Molinist "scheme," I would suggest in closing, that is essential to understanding the "staggering assertion[s] of divine sovereignty over the affairs of men" that are found in passages like Acts 2 and 4. Indeed, it is this understanding alone that allows us to affirm without reservation that the God of the Bible is truly "the Lord of all the earth" (cf. Ps. 97:5).

---

28. Ibid., 27.

29. Ibid., 26.

30. The freedom to embrace Christ in saving faith presupposes the ability to discern that "the word of the cross" is "wisdom" (1 Cor. 1:18, 24). The ability to discern that "the word of the cross" is "wisdom" rather than "folly" (1 Cor. 1:18) presupposes, in turn, a measure of spiritual competence that is grounded in the life-giving work of the Spirit. It presupposes, in other words, precisely the kind of spiritual competence that those who are "natural" (1 Cor. 2:14)—that is, those who remain dead and in bondage to their sin—are entirely without. Since some human beings are spiritually incompetent because they remain dead in their sin, we may not conclude, Reformed believers insist, that the capacity to discern spiritual wisdom is a capacity that God has given to all human beings without exception. Thus, while all human beings have the ability to make real choices relating to Christ, not all human beings have the ability to make the kinds of choices that require spiritual discernment. For Reformed believers, then, what distinguishes the saved from the lost is not what particular moral agents do to actualize a capacity that God has allegedly given to all but rather what God does for particular moral agents to enable them to see, believe, and receive Christ. In short, while some freely reject Christ, because they regard "the word of the cross" as "folly," others freely embrace him in faith because God enables them to see that he *just is* "the power of God and the wisdom of God" (1 Cor. 1:18, 24). This is why those who have freely embraced Christ must "boast in the Lord" (1 Cor. 1:31) for their salvation, for he has given to them what he has not given to all, namely, the capacity to see "the light of the knowledge of the glory of God in the face of Jesus Christ" (2 Cor. 4:6). I would suggest that we will never make sense of what the apostle Paul is saying in 1 Corinthians 1 and 2 if we presume that all human beings have a measure of spiritual competence because the Spirit has poured out a kind of life-giving grace on all without exception. If God in fact has poured out this kind of life-giving grace on all, then why, one has to wonder, do any regard "the word of the cross" as "folly"?

Conclusion: "The Godness of God"

The majority of theologians standing in the tradition of Reformed orthodoxy typically respond to those who embrace the Molinist account of divine providence by insisting that there was only one and not two "logical moments prior to the divine creative decree." If we imagine that logically prior to the creative decree, the moment at which God had "knowledge of the range of possible worlds" was followed by a second moment "at which he [had] knowledge of the proper subset of possible worlds that, given the counterfactual propositions true at that moment, [were] feasible for him to create," then we are faced, Reformed believers reason, with a number of questions that suggest there are serious problems with the Molinist view of divine providence. Among these is the basic question of just what it means for God to be sovereign. To what extent can we say that a God whose decree is in some sense dependent on what free creatures would do in counterfactual circumstances really the sovereign Lord of the universe? To put it differently, in what sense can we say that a God whose rule is based, at least in some measure, on his discovery of feasibilities that are determined not by him but by things that in some sense are independent of him really reigning, particularly when those things have a real bearing on precisely *how* he reigns?[31] According to Reformed believers, the portrait of God that emerges from Scripture is of a God whose rule allows for genuine freedom but is in no sense dependent on or determined by things that are thought to be independent of his all-determining decree. The God of the Bible, they believe, is the God of Nebuchadnezzar and not of Molina, for God rules over all things not just in theory but in practice; indeed, it is he who determines what is feasible, he and nobody else. This is one reason why Reformed believers insist that God's dominion "is an everlasting dominion, and his kingdom endures from generation to generation; all the inhabitants of the earth are accounted as nothing, and he does according to his will among the host of heaven and among

---

31. In his response to Tiessen, Helm summarizes the nature of God's alleged dependence on what he discovers to be feasible like this: "The idea is that in decreeing what A in C would do, in rendering it actual, God utilizes the choices and actions that A in C would naturally make, make in an unforced or uncoerced [i.e., an undetermined] way.... God does this by (in a sense) 'finding' A in C. A in C is already 'there,' already 'present,' present as a possibility" (Helm and Tiessen, "Does Calvinism Have Room for Middle Knowledge?" 441).

the inhabitants of the earth; and none can stay his hand or say to him, 'What have you done?'" (Dan. 4:34–35).

While Reformed believers are persuaded that faithfulness to the God of the Bible requires us to affirm and really believe that God "works all things according to the counsel of his will" (Eph. 1:11), they acknowledge that many evangelicals find it difficult to swallow what Reformed theologians like Douglas Wilson call "the Godness of God"[32] for reasons having to do with something other than exegesis. Reformed believers recognize, in other words, that many reject the Augustinian-Calvinist account of divine providence because they have embraced a disjunction that leads them to conclude that any candidate for deity that does not conform to their standards or govern in a way that aligns with their moral sensibilities not only cannot be God but quite possibly might be Satan. In response to those who would reject the Augustinian-Calvinist view for this reason, Reformed believers solemnly warn that such individuals need to tread very carefully for at least two reasons. In the first place, they need to tread carefully because the antipathy that is manifest in such an attitude bears a striking—even if perhaps only incidental—resemblance to the antipathy that is essential to "*true* atheism," the two "fundamental tenets" of which are always, ironically, "One: There is no God. Two: I hate Him."[33] In the second place, they need to tread carefully lest, by moving from philosophy to the text rather than from the text to philosophy, they justify this attitude, and in the process arouse the wrath of God by suppressing—and encouraging others to suppress—the truth of God in unrighteousness (Rom. 1:18–32). In short, those who cannot stomach the God of the Augustinian-Calvinist tradition would be well advised to remember that God is no respecter of persons (Col. 3:25), not even of really smart philosophers.

---

32. Christopher Hitchens and Douglas Wilson, *Is Christianity Good for the World? A Debate* (Moscow, Ida.: Canon, 2008), 18.

33. Ibid., 58. Wilson is here clearly alluding to those who "suppress the truth" in unrighteousness in Romans 1:18–32.

RON HIGHFIELD

William Lane Craig has penned a clear and concise chapter on the concept of middle knowledge and has drawn out its implications for providence with characteristic rigor. His presentation will serve well our efforts to understand and evaluate this elegantly flawed theory. Craig's enthusiasm for the Molinist strategy shines through every line of his essay and, despite its logical form, imparts to it a poetic quality. Craig praises middle knowledge as "astonishing in its subtlety," "fruitful" in its results, and "stunning" in its effect, and indeed it is. I am saddened, therefore, that I cannot respond to every significant argument the essay contains. I will leave it to Greg Boyd and other open theists to assess Craig's criticisms of that view. And I will leave it to philosophers to assess Craig's philosophical case for the God of the philosophers. I will limit myself to three issues I consider decisive in judging whether a Molinist doctrine of providence can be incorporated into a genuinely Christian theology. My three concerns are these: Does the theory of middle knowledge do justice to the Christian conviction that God's greatness and glory tower beyond all we can think or imagine? Does the theory of middle knowledge attribute to God a level of sovereignty worthy of him? Does the middle knowledge answer to the problem of evil do justice to the way in which sin and evil are characterized in the New Testament?

The Middle Knowledge Picture of God

As Craig explains, middle knowledge lies in the logical space between God's knowledge of "necessary truths" (natural knowledge) and his knowledge of "what will be" (free knowledge). In his middle knowledge, God knows what any possible free creature would do in every possible circumstance, and this knowledge enables God to plan the world down to the last detail. As "fruitful" and "stunning" as this theory seems on the surface, however, I believe examination will show that it does not do justice to the Christian doctrine of God.[34] Notice, first, that Craig articulates all three forms of divine knowledge as conceptual knowledge of truths, which should not be surprising since Craig identifies himself as holding a "conceptualist" view of the operation of the divine mind. Instead of identifying God's natural knowledge as God's unmediated knowledge of himself (which includes knowledge of his power), Craig speaks of God's knowledge of "necessary truths."[35] Apparently, Craig holds that not all necessary truths refer to God's own being. Some truths, such as 2 +2 = 4, the laws of logic, and perhaps others, are necessary independently of God's being or *even of his existence*. Instead of speaking of God's free knowledge as God's knowledge of his will (again, divine self-knowledge), Craig speaks of God's knowledge of truths about "what will be." This "conceptualist" way of speaking allows Craig to insert middle knowledge into the logical sequence without glaring incongruity. But this terminological consistency hides the fact that middle knowledge cannot, like the other two, be articulated as a form of divine self-knowledge. The power of middle knowledge depends on its character as eternal knowledge of something other than God himself. It is knowledge of truths that in no way depend on God for their truth. They depend, rather, on what the free creature would do in the posited circumstances.

In this way, the "stunning" theory of middle knowledge wedges open the eternal being of God and inserts another eternal reality into its heart. With its concept of necessary truths, whose eternal truth and necessity stand independent of God, and counterfactual truths, whose truth depends not on God but on what free creatures would do, Craig's theory robs God of his essential divinity. The Molinist God does not possess absolute independence, or aseity. There exists a coeternal reality that is neither God nor God's creature; yet this quasi-divine reality determines and limits what God can be and do. Necessary truths

---

34. Craig's version of Molinism, like open theism, seems to presuppose the falsity of the doctrine of divine simplicity. For Craig, knowledge, like other divine attributes, appears to be something God *possesses* rather than something God *is*. See my response to Boyd on his rejection of divine simplicity — a response that applies equally to Craig.

35. Craig fails to make clear that Thomism and Reformed orthodoxy assert that God knows himself and all things by knowing himself. See Aquinas, *Summa Theologiae* I, q. 14, arts. 1–8. For Reformed orthodoxy, see Muller, *Post-Reformation Reformed Dogmatics*, 3:397–406.

determine what sort of divinity God can be, and the truths of middle knowledge determine what sort of world God can create. Christian theology must reject such metaphysical dualism under any name and in any guise, whether the coeternal reality is material, spiritual, or conceptual. Karl Barth is correct in stressing that God's power and will are "not subordinate and responsible to any higher power and independent idea of what is possible and impossible for Him either as concerns Himself or as concerns His works.... He is also the substance of everything that is possible."[36] The Zurich theologian Johann Heidegger (1633–1698) asserts this principle with impressive clarity:

> The object of divine power is ... the possible; not in itself, as though there were anything outside God, which has the cause of its possibility in itself, outside the power and will of God; but in the power and will of God, which alone is the foundation and root of all possibility. All things outside of God derive their essence and reality from the fact that, as God understands how to make them for His own glory, so He wills that they be and produces them.... Thus then that is possible, which God can will, order, call, do for His glory; impossible, which God cannot order, will, do for His glory.[37]

My second objection to the middle knowledge picture of God centers on its rationalism. Craig speaks of the logical distinctions we make in God's knowledge as if they indicate *real* differences in God. He seems to assume that God's being can be expressed adequately in the categories of our minds. Craig uses the language of knowledge and knowing, as far as I can tell, in the same sense when speaking of God as when referring to creatures. There is hardly a hint that our language, analogies, and definitions may need to be negated as well as affirmed. Craig's dismissive remark lumping together "mysticism" and "mental reservation," in contrast to his praise of Molinism as "elucidating," is another indication of a tendency toward rationalism. In disparaging "mysticism," Craig seems to be rejecting views that consider the being

36. Karl Barth, *Church Dogmatics* 2/1, eds. G. W. Bromiley and T. F. Torrance, trans. T. H. L. Parker and others (Edinburgh: T. & T. Clark, 1957), 535. Hereafter cited as *CD*.

37. Johann Heinrich Heidegger, *Corpus Theologiae Christianae* 3, quoted in Heinrich Heppe, *Reformed Dogmatics*, ed. Ernst Bizer, trans. G. T. Thomson (1950; repr., London: Wakeman Great Reprints, n.d.), 100–101.

of God as beyond the grasp of human language, logic, and reason. Is there no mystery in God? Is it merely fuzzy thought or empty words to think of God as transcending the polarities of necessity and freedom, person and nature, justice and mercy, and others?

Consider Craig's seemingly innocuous theory that middle knowledge serves God as a "means" of choosing a world to create. As I argue in my chapter in this volume, the notion that God needs a means or a "how" in order to create the world is deeply problematic. First, it projects into the life of God the human imperfection of needing means to act. We need means because we are not self-sufficient and, hence, cannot create things from nothing. Attributing to God the need for means contradicts the doctrine of creation from nothing; it sees God as needing a quasi-divine archetype for the feasible world he decides to create—an archetype that is equally eternal with God. But more seriously, Molinism's picture of God resembles Plato's demiurge (craftsman), who constructs the temporal, physical world according to eternal ideas that exist independently of him, more than it does the triune God of Christianity. In the New Testament and in patristic thought, however, the Word of God is the archetype, possibility, and *means* of creation. In Craig's chapter, middle knowledge, which is knowledge of *something other than* God, takes the place of the Word of God as the archetype of the world. Instead of understanding God's knowledge in a Trinitarian way, as the Father knowing his exact image in the Word/Son in the unity of the Spirit, Craig pictures a *monotheos* who thinks necessary truths and possible and feasible worlds! Instead of the Trinity of Scripture, who cannot be grasped by our thought, Craig substitutes the kind of God one reads about in philosophical journals, that is, an infinite Mind that contemplates eternal truths. From this rationalist presupposition flow all the other problems with Molinism, especially its inability to imagine that God creates and rules the world from a position so transcendent that the very same action by which he controls the world also liberates it into the freedom of the children of God.

A Feasible Kind of Sovereignty

According to Craig, the Molinist account of providence makes "perfect sense of God's providential control over a world of free agents." It is "truly mind-boggling" how middle knowledge allows God to unfold his plan "toward his sovereignly established ends." Indeed, "once one grasps it, the doctrine of divine middle knowledge thus issues in adoration and praise of God for so breathtaking a sovereignty." This is high praise, and there is a sense in which Craig is right. The Molinist account depicts an amazing Mind and a level of sovereign control over the world that stuns us into silent wonder. But does it rise to a doxological level worthy of the God of Scripture?

The Molinist theory begins with God's knowledge of all necessary truths and possible worlds. In the previous section, I objected to Craig's conceptualistic and dualistic scheme in which the necessity of necessary truths and the possibility of possible worlds are grounded in something other than God. In opposition to that view, I argued that possibility and necessity are grounded solely in God. In one sense, this distinction makes no difference for the doctrine of providence, since God possesses just as many "options" in one case as in the other; for I do not believe it makes sense to think it possible for God to declare the laws of logic invalid or to create worlds that possess incompatible properties.[38] Nevertheless, I believe that even in his discussion of natural knowledge Craig diminishes God's sovereignty. If God is not *absolutely* sovereign over his own being, knowledge, and eternal circumstances, how can God be absolutely sovereign over creation? As I will show, this primitive dependence will manifest itself in all of God's actions.

In the next "moment" of divine knowledge, middle knowledge, God knows what every free creature would do in every possible circumstance. This move narrows God's focus from the infinite set of possible worlds to the smaller but still virtually infinite subset of feasible worlds. What makes a possible world feasible? The deciding factor is creaturely freedom. Some possible worlds contain no free beings, while others contain beings capable of free action. Still other possible worlds contain free beings who actually exercise their freedom; only these worlds are feasible. Feasibility then applies only to worlds that are both possible and exhibit libertarian freedom. It is important to note that nothing God wills or does can make a possible world into a feasible one. The truth of a feasible world is eternal and independent of God. Middle knowledge,

---

38. This is so for the simple reason that in doing so, we would be attempting to conceive of God as negating, not the eternal laws of logic, but himself—an act as irreverent as it is inconceivable.

then, is completely passive in that God can see but cannot expand or contract the range of feasible worlds.

Only at the next logical "moment" (free knowledge) do God's will and power become relevant. Indeed, everything before this third stage would have been the same even if there were no creation. God could have contemplated necessary truths and possible and feasible worlds for all eternity without creating anything at all. Thankfully, however, God freely willed to create, to give being to something outside himself. Moreover, God willed to create a world with beings who can know and enjoy him and, through their libertarian freedom, participate in achieving their own identity and determining their eternal destiny. Because God wills the latter type of world, he will leave other possible worlds unrealized. But how does God select one from among the virtually infinite feasible worlds to make actual? It seems to me that Molinism faces a significant, even fatal, problem at this point. Does God possess an idea of his preferred world, the world he would realize if he faced no constraints? As infinitely wise, surely God possesses such an ideal standard; otherwise, what principle could God bring to bear to make the best decision about which feasible world to make actual?[39] Suppose that there happens to be a feasible world that conforms perfectly to God's ideal world. In this case, the fit between God's ideal world and this feasible world would be a lucky accident. It is like the couple who created a list of features characteristic of their ideal car. They anticipated a long search and did not dare hope for complete success, but to their amazement, when they arrived at the dealer's showroom, there stood their dream car down to the last detail. Now, no one would claim that the couple's amazing success demonstrates their wisdom or power. It simply shows their luck. In the same way, that there happens to be a feasible universe that conforms to God's ideal does not demonstrate God's "breathtaking ... sovereignty" but his good fortune.

In the Molinist theory, however, God does not get so lucky. Craig does not identify our world with the ideal that God would have preferred to actualize. To do so would render the problem of evil as unanswerable for Molinism as he thinks it is for determinism. According to Craig, God's decision to actualize our imperfect world rather than his ideal

---

39. Or is God's will constrained by the set of feasible worlds, so that God can will only what is feasible?

world can be accounted for by "the wrong counterfactuals being true."[40] Although there may be an infinite number of possible worlds without sin and evil, apparently there is no feasible world free of these ills. We can be sure, however, that "God has morally sufficient reasons for permitting the evils in the world." In other words, the good achieved is worth the evil endured. Perhaps this positive verdict characterizes many feasible worlds, but if so, this too would be accidental with reference to the will of God. Which one of the morally positive, feasible worlds should God actualize? Although Craig does not address this issue, the Molinist answer must be that God would actualize the best feasible world. Hence, our world, though not the best *possible* world, is the best *feasible* world.

Once the best feasible world is identified and God decides to actualize that world, God sovereignly executes this world plan down to the last subatomic event. Here, then, is where Craig breaks forth in praise for God's "breathtaking ... sovereignty." As I admitted above, I agree that such sovereignty is mind-boggling. The issue, however, is not whether divine sovereignty is stunning to the human mind but whether it is as great as we can conceive. I do not believe it rises to this height. For prior to God's sovereign actualization of the best feasible world, God is conditioned in two ways. First, God is not the ground of the possibility of possible worlds. God finds himself confronted and limited by the eternal laws of thought and being. Second, the availability of a feasible world that conforms to God's ideal will, or even of a feasible world in which good outweighs evil, is a lucky accident brought about by the fortuitous intersection of the set of feasible worlds and the set of worlds acceptable to God as candidates for actualization. It is logically possible that no feasible world exists in which good outweighs evil. That such worlds exist is a brute fact.

The irony in this situation is stunning. The theory of middle knowledge was supposed to rid the world of fate and chance while preserving human freedom. To accomplish this task, however, it limits *God's* freedom and subjects *him* to a kind of fate worse than the one from which it supposedly liberates human beings. If God determines our "fate," at least we can believe our destiny is determined by a free, loving, and just God. But if God is fated to be constrained eternally by

---

40. This is just a brute fact that God cannot change. It therefore exculpates God from all responsibility for evil.

impersonal laws and truths, we can take no such consolation. Indeed, it was against precisely this type of impersonal fate that the patristic theologians fought so hard! Craig correctly points out that in the Molinist doctrine of providence nothing happens by chance and God actualizes our world in every detail down to the leaf that trembles on the tree. Yet the very availability of a feasible world worth God's trouble to actualize is a lucky accident. However amazing when compared to human power, a divine sovereignty limited to the ability to actualize perfectly the best "feasible" world does not rise to the dignity of the God who is sovereign over all necessity and every "possible" and "feasible" world. Let the reader judge: Is it higher praise to say, "God is sovereign over all things, *except* the laws of thought and counterfactual truths," or "God is sovereign over all things, no exceptions"?

God, Freedom, and Evil

Molinism shares with open theism the theory of libertarian freedom. They both view freedom as a natural endowment that maintains its indifference between good and evil even after the fall. Open theism, in contrast to Molinism, insists that God cannot know with certainty the direction a libertarian free act will take before it actually happens, or to put it in middle knowledge terms, there are no eternal, counterfactual truths of creaturely freedom for God to know. In my chapter and in my response to Gregory Boyd, I make my position on freedom clear. There is no need to explain it in depth here. Suffice it to say that just as the God spoken about in Molinism is an abstraction only tangentially related to the gracious, triune God of Scripture, likewise the "free agent" who exercises libertarian freedom is only tangentially related to the created, fallen, blind, dying, enslaved sinner whom Jesus came to save. Of what use is it to reconcile two such abstractions? Indeed, it is only as abstractions that they need reconciling. The glorious freedom spoken of in the New Testament does not need reconciling with God's providence and grace. The question never arises, because genuine freedom is not a natural power undiminished by the fall but a gift bestowed by the gracious and liberating act of God the Father, through the Son, in the power of the Holy Spirit.

Craig argues that Molinism provides a satisfactory answer to the problem of evil, which is understood in his chapter as the problem of theodicy. His answer is twofold. First, God cannot be blamed for the unavailability of a feasible world untroubled by sin and evil. God has no control over this. Second, God would not choose to actualize a particular feasible world, thereby allowing some evil to be actualized, unless the total good achieved was worth the evil endured. This approach, as I indicated above, offers itself as a theodicy, a rational justification of God's ways with the world. The New Testament, however, does not approach sin and evil from this direction. The "problem" of evil is evil itself, its presence and effects in God's creation. Christianity's solution to the "problem" of evil is God's act of salvation in Christ, which culminates in the resurrection of the dead and the liberation of creation. Christ solves the problem of evil by eradicating evil in a total triumph. This eschatological victory is grasped by faith, anticipated in hope, and lived in love; it cannot be grasped by philosophical reason, which lives by sight alone. I do not see how Molinism can account for this confidence, since even on its premises, the best Molinism can guarantee is that good outweighs evil. It cannot assure us that even in the best feasible world, *all* evil will be turned eventually to the service of the good. If God cannot bring creation to definitive salvation and complete perfection because "the wrong counterfactuals" of creaturely freedom were true, it will be of little comfort to tell ourselves that it was not God's fault.

GREGORY A. BOYD

I want to applaud Craig for writing a stimulating and nicely argued essay. I found myself agreeing with a great deal of it. I concur with Craig that the Calvinist account of providence cannot avoid making God responsible for evil and that it "in effect ... turn[s] God into the Devil." I also agree with him that simple foreknowledge offers God no providential advantage and undermines the meaning of foreordination. I even agree with certain aspects of Craig's Molinist understanding of providence and with his criticisms of one version of open theism. Nevertheless, I found some of his arguments against the open view as well as many of his arguments supporting Molinism to be weak and in a few instances seriously flawed.

In what follows, I will first offer several miscellaneous critical observations regarding Craig's overall presentation and criticism of the open view. I will then turn to an issue I regard to be foundational in the debate between open theism and Molinism, namely, our different understandings of "would" and "might" counterfactuals. And I will end by interacting with Craig on the problem of evil.

Craig's Presentation and Critique of the Open View
How "Revisionary" Are the "Revisionary Open Theists"?

Certain aspects of Craig's presentation and critique of open theism were puzzling and/or inaccurate. To begin, Craig gives the label "revisionary open theists" to open theists such as myself who hold that God knows the truth-value of conjoined "might" counterfactuals prior to creation.[41]

---

41. For several defenses and applications of this view, see Alan R. Rhoda, Gregory A. Boyd, and Thomas G. Belt, "Open Theism, Omniscience, and the Nature of the Future," *Faith and Philosophy* 23 (2006): 432–59; Gregory A. Boyd, "Two Ancient (and Modern) Motivations for Ascribing Exhaustively Definite Foreknowledge to God: A Historic Overview and Critical Assessment," *Religious Studies* 46. No 1 (March 2010): 1–19; idem, "Neo-Molinism and the Infinite Intelligence of God," *Philosophia Christi* 5, no. 1 (2003): 187–204.

This label is quite misleading, however, for there has never been an established open-view position on God's pre-creational propositional knowledge. Hence, we who defend God's pre-creational knowledge of true conjoined "might" counterfactuals are not *revising* anything.

Along similar lines, Craig asserts that "revisionary open theists" differ from other open theists by holding that God is able to know more than logical possibilities prior to creation and is thus able to make contingency plans for possible forthcoming events. This is simply incorrect. While only a few of us open theists to date have expressed our view of God's pre-creational knowledge in terms of "might" counterfactuals, no open theist of whom I am aware has held that God knows only logical possibilities prior to creation. So too, every open theist of whom I am aware has affirmed that, at least to some extent, God was able to make contingency plans prior to the creation of the world.

Closely related to this, I was surprised to find Craig claiming that open theists deny the truth of all "would" counterfactuals prior to creation. I honestly have no idea why Craig would think any open theists (let alone every open theist) would embrace such a preposterous view. Every open theist of whom I am aware has at least held that God knew that *if* humans were to rebel, he *would* send his Son to save them. In fact, the only pre-creational "would" counterfactuals that we would argue are necessarily false are those that purport to express future libertarian free actions.

Yet another unusual aspect of Craig's presentation and critique of open theism was his claim that Hasker's revised definition of omniscience as the ability to know *all that is knowable* is "typical" for open theists. Craig thus argues that "openness thinkers ... claim that it is logically impossible to know propositions about future contingents," and he spends more than two pages refuting this view. In reality, Hasker's view is hardly typical among open theists. Many open theists hold that propositions about future contingents have *no* truth-value until agents resolve possibilities one way or another, while others, such as myself, argue that all propositions about future contingents, including "might" propositions, have a truth-value that God knows.[42]

---

42. See Alan R. Rhoda, "Generic Open Theism and Some Varieties Thereof," *Religious Studies* 44, no. 2 (June 2008): 225–34.

Oddly, even after discussing the view of "revisionary open theists," Craig continues to speak as if we not only accepted Hasker's view of omniscience but actually proposed it! The irony is that there was not one criticism Craig made against Hasker's view that I have not argued myself in other contexts. I think Craig's essay would have been significantly improved had he taken more care to differentiate between the views of his openness opponents.

Openness and Scripture

Craig alleges that open theists "can make no sense whatsoever" of certain passages of Scripture. He cites as an example Genesis 45:5 and 50:20, which speak of God sending Joseph into Egypt by means of his brothers' decision to sell him to some Ishmaelites (Gen. 37:27). What his brothers intended for evil, Joseph later said, "God intended ... for good." Craig asserts that "openness theology is at a loss to explain this coalescence of human freedom and divine sovereignty."

It is not clear why Craig thinks this passage is challenging for open theists. As I assert in my chapter in this book, I adamantly affirm that God has an eternally prepared plan as to how he will weave each and every future decision agents might make into his sovereign purposes. Hence, while evil things do not happen *for* a higher divine purpose, according to the open view, they always happen *with* a divine purpose.

The fact that Joseph's brothers did not *have* to choose to sell him into slavery, according to the open view, does not at all compromise the effectiveness with which God is able to weave their evil decision into his good sovereign plan. As I'll demonstrate in my chapter, only a "cognitively limited deity" would be able to weave future decisions that were certain into his sovereign plan more effectively than future decisions that were merely possible.

Another passage Craig alleges open theists can make no sense of is 1 Chronicles 10:8–14, in which the author says, "The Lord put [Saul] to death," even though, as a matter of fact, Saul took his own life. It seems to me that if this passage poses a problem for open theists, it does so for Craig as well. After all, Craig wants to affirm Saul's libertarian freedom in committing suicide as much as open theists do. Hence, Craig wants to deny that the Lord *caused* Saul to commit suicide as much as open theists do.

In reality, however, I do not believe this expression should be considered fatal for either of our positions. Old Testament authors frequently depict God as *bringing about* events he *merely allows* with a divine purpose. This way of speaking was in keeping with their conception of Yahweh as an ancient Near Eastern monarch and served to emphasize, over and against the polytheism of surrounding cultures, that the one and only Creator takes responsibility (though never the moral culpability) for all that comes to pass in his creation. Hence, for example, the Lord is spoken of as personally slaying the firstborn in houses that lacked the blood of a lamb on their doorpost (Ex. 12:12) even though, in reality, he simply did not protect these households from "the destroyer" (Ex. 12:23).[43] In any event, open theism has no more trouble reconciling compatibilistic-sounding Scriptures with libertarian freedom than does Molinism.

On "Might" and "Would" Counterfactuals[44]
The Independent Truth Status of Conjoined "Might"- Counterfactuals

The most important disagreement between Craig's view and my own concerns the logical status of "might" counterfactuals. I am aware that discussions on "might" and "would" counterfactuals may make some readers' eyes glaze over, but I encourage such readers to work through this material nevertheless. Though such discussions may sound pedantic, the truth is that a lot hangs in the balance in this discussion in terms of how we view God and understand his way of governing the world.

In Craig's view, "'would' counterfactuals logically imply 'might' counterfactuals." For example, if it is true that "Commander Karl *would* publicly praise Churchill if given a chance," then, in Craig's view, it must also be true that "Commander Karl *might* publicly praise Churchill if given a chance." In this view, "might" counterfactuals serve only to express the logical precondition of "would" counterfactuals and never independently serve as ultimate descriptors of a possible state of affairs.

---

43. I develop this theme at length in a forthcoming work tentatively titled *The Crucifixion of the Warrior God: Re-Interpreting Old Testament Violence in the Light of the Cross* (Downers Grove: InterVarsity, forthcoming).

44. I will restrict my comments in this section to conjoined "'might' counterfactuals" within God's pre-creational knowledge, though my arguments apply as well to conjoined "might" propositions describing the actual world. When "might" propositions describe actual states of affairs, they are not *counter*factual, but simply *factual*.

Hence, in this interpretation of "might" counterfactuals, God never knows the truth-value of "might" counterfactuals without also knowing the truth-value of corresponding "would" counterfactuals, and in knowing the latter, he already knows the former.

I believe this interpretation of "might" counterfactuals is flawed. As I discuss in my contributing chapter, its chief shortcoming is that it cannot adequately account for the fact that contrasting "might" counterfactuals can be conjointly true, while contrasting "would" counterfactuals cannot. It makes perfect sense to affirm as true the statement that "Commander Karl *might and might not* publicly praise Churchill if given a chance." But it is impossible to affirm as true the statement that "Commander Karl *would and would not* publicly praise Churchill if given a chance," for this statement is blatantly absurd. This suggests that the truth-value of the "might" counterfactuals in the first sentence is not logically implied by the truth-value of the "would" counterfactuals in the second.

Hence, while "might" and "might not" may serve merely as the logical precondition of "would" counterfactuals *when one or the other stands alone*, their truth-value cannot be viewed as derivative from "would" counterfactuals *when they are conjoined*. And this, in turn, suggests that conjoined "might" counterfactuals constitute a *distinct* category of counterfactuals, *alongside* "would" counterfactuals, that an omniscient God must know. There are, therefore, logically possible worlds in which God knows the future partly as a "maybe." Open theists simply believe that the actual world that God created is one such world.

I would go further and argue that not only is it false that the truth-value of conjoined "might" counterfactuals is logically *implied* by corresponding "would" counterfactuals, but the truth-value of conjoined "might" counterfactuals is actually *negated* by corresponding "would" counterfactuals. That is, if it is true that Karl *might* praise Churchill, then it is false that he *would not*, and if it is true that Karl *might not* praise Churchill, then it is false that he *would*. Craig must deny this, of course. He argues that "*freedom requires only that in a given set of circumstances one must be in some sense capable of refraining from doing what one would do; it is not required that one might not do what one would do*" [Craig's emphasis]. This sentence makes it clear that for Craig "would" does not contradict "might not" and "would not" does not contradict "might."

There are several problems with this account, however. First and foremost, it is not clear what it means to affirm that an agent is "capable" of refraining from activity *x* if one at the same time denies that that agent *might not* engage in activity *x*. Since Craig denies that it is historically possible for this agent actually to refrain from *x*, the only "sense" I can see that Craig can ascribe to this agent's capacity freely to refrain from *x* is that it is *logically possible* for the agent not to do *x*. But surely this is not adequate to account for the agent's freedom relative to *x*. Any compatibilist could say this much!

The fact is that a mere logical possibility does not come close to constituting a genuine capacity to act freely in a libertarian sense. If Commander Karl possesses libertarian freedom to praise Churchill or not, we need to say more than merely that either choice is logically possible. We need to affirm, rather, that given the totality of antecedent historical causes, it remains within Karl's power to choose to praise Churchill *or not*. And this means that, until Karl himself resolves the possibilities one way or another, the final truth about the matter is that Karl *might* and *might not* praise Churchill. Moreover, since the matter is yet open, we must regard it as false that Karl *certainly would* and false that he *certainly would not* praise Churchill.

"Would," "Could," and "Might"

At one point, Craig objects to the view that conjoined "might" counterfactuals have a truth-value independent of "would" counterfactuals by insisting that "we can maintain the distinction between what someone might do and what he could do under any circumstances" only when we view "'might' counterfactuals [as] implied by true 'would' counterfactuals." For example, Craig notes that "it is true that Hitler might not give an oration in praise of Churchill because he would not, but still he could do so because there are possible worlds ... in which he does." Craig insists that we open theists who argue for the independent truth status of conjoined "might" counterfactuals are forced to concede the outlandish claim that Hitler *might* praise Churchill, because, Craig presumes, we deny that Hitler *would* praise Churchill. "By denying the truth of any 'would' counterfactuals," he argues, "the revised openness view seems to collapse the distinction between 'might' and 'could.'" For "if all 'would' counterfactuals are false," he argues, "then it is false that

[Hitler] would not do such a thing, and so ... it is true by definition that he might do such a thing."

I am afraid this objection is significantly confused. As I noted earlier, Craig mistakenly assumes that we who affirm the independent truth status of conjoined "might" counterfactuals must commit ourselves to the ridiculous position that "all 'would' counterfactuals are false." In reality, we need regard as false only those "would" counterfactuals whose corresponding conjoined "might" counterfactuals are true.

In the case of Hitler, open theists have no trouble affirming the obvious truth that in 1937 Hitler *would not* praise Churchill. While Hitler *could* praise Churchill in the sense that it was logically possible for him to do so, the manner in which history unfolded up to this point in time, including the way Hitler had solidified his own character with his own free decisions, rendered it certain that he would not praise Churchill in 1937. And these same considerations rendered it false that Hitler "might and might not" praise Churchill in 1937. Craig's objection thus misses the mark.

In fact, it seems to me that this argument can be turned around and used against Craig, for his Molinist view collapses "would" and "might" in the same way he mistakenly thinks we "revisionary open theists" collapse "could" and "might." Consider that, while it is of course true that in 1937 Hitler and many other Nazi leaders *would not* praise Churchill under any circumstance, it is also true that there were a few in the upper echelons of Nazi power who had misgivings about Hitler and who were sympathetic to some of Churchill's concerns. Let us assume that the earlier mentioned Commander Karl was one of these Churchill sympathizers. Let us further suppose that Karl had become a candidate to deliver an important speech praising Hitler and condemning Churchill before a large Nazi audience. And, finally, let us assume for the sake of argument that Karl had not yet resolved whether he would courageously sacrifice his life and endanger his family by praising Churchill or whether he would play it safe and praise Hitler.

While Karl deliberated about what course of action he would take, we would naturally say, "Commander Karl *might and might not* praise Churchill if given a chance." And we would mean by this something very different than if someone were to say, "Commander Karl *would* praise Churchill if given a chance," or "Commander Karl *would not* praise Churchill if given a chance." The conjoined "might" proposition expresses the unresolved nature of Karl's deliberation in a way that the "would" propositions do not. Indeed, the "would" propositions *deny* the open-endedness we are trying to express with the conjoined "might" proposition. We would use the "might" proposition *precisely because* we believed his decision was not yet resolved to the point at which Karl either would or would not certainly praise Churchill if given the chance.

Because Craig collapses the truth of "might" counterfactuals into the truth of "would" counterfactuals, I do not see how he can account for this scenario. Not only this, but the very fact that a state of affairs could arise that is natural to describe with "might" propositions *instead of* "would" propositions argues against Craig's interpretation of "might" counterfactuals. So too, the very fact that we can coherently *intend* conjoined "might" propositions to serve as the ultimate descriptors of a state of affairs, *in contrast to* "would" propositions, is enough to demonstrate that there are possible worlds that are not exhaustively describable by "would" counterfactuals. And these facts imply that conjoined "might" counterfactuals constitute a distinct category of propositions alongside "would" counterfactuals, which an omniscient God must know prior to the creation of the world.

Hence, precisely because we affirm that God is omniscient and thus knows the truth-value of all meaningful propositions, we should affirm that God knows some of the future (at least of some possible worlds) as a "maybe." Ironically, while open theists are regularly accused of undermining divine omniscience, this argument suggests it is those who deny that God knows some of the future (at least of some possible worlds) as a domain of possibilities who are in fact undermining divine omniscience.

The Grounding Objection

While it plays a surprisingly minor role in Craig's essay, Craig made a comment about what is called "the grounding objection" that warrants a response. In essence, the grounding objection contends that it is implausible, if not incoherent, to suppose that there has existed from all eternity settled facts about what every conceivable libertarian free agent would do in every logically possible circumstance. The issue is this: What grounds, or makes true, the eternal "would" counterfactuals that comprise God's middle knowledge?

It cannot be God's will that grounds the eternal truth-value of "would" counterfactuals, for classical Molinism grants that this would undermine libertarian freedom. But neither can it be the libertarian free agents themselves, since these agents exist only as possibilities when God knows them in his pre-creational middle knowledge. In fact, it cannot even be the *future* actions of free agents, since all but one of the innumerable possible worlds including free agents will *never* exist. Hence, to embrace classical Molinism, one must accept that the facts about what every conceivable free agent would do in every conceivable circumstance *simply exist, from all eternity, as an ungrounded, metaphysical surd.* I and most other non-Molinists find this conclusion to be unacceptable if not completely incoherent.

Among other problems, it is a challenge to conceive of an eternal set of uncaused counterfactual truths pertaining to the behavior of nonexistent (and, in most cases, never-to-exist) free agents. We can readily understand how necessary truths and logical possibilities can be eternal, for these truths could not be otherwise and thus require nothing over and above their own definition to make them true. But God's middle knowledge is comprised of *contingent* truths that are *not self-explanatory.*[45]

On top of this, many of us find it hard to understand how agents can be said to possess libertarian freedom when the facts about every choice they will ever make eternally precede their making it. And, finally, I would argue that Molinism actually constitutes a form of metaphysical dualism, for it posits an eternal yet contingent reality alongside God that God neither chose nor created. This enormous body of uncreated and uncaused contingent facts has simply existed, alongside God, from all eternity as a brute metaphysical surd. To me, these objections are decisive against the Molinism Craig defends.

Craig does not address the grounding objection in his essay, though he concedes it is the most forceful argument against his view. What is interesting, however, is that he argues that we who believe God's

---

45. Craig's view that God knows all true propositions the way humans know "innate ideas" presupposes that truth is an *intrinsic* property of propositions. But unless we're speaking of propositions that are true by definition (e.g., tautologies), propositions are true only if they *correspond to reality,* which means "truth" is a *relational* rather than an *intrinsic* property. The grounding objection simply points out that there is no eternal reality that can serve as the "truth-maker" to "would" counterfactuals of creaturely freedom, since the creatures do not exist and in most cases never will exist.

pre-creational knowledge includes conjoined "might" counterfactuals as a distinct class of truths have "quietly abandoned" this objection. For in this version of the open view, he argues, "there appear to be truths about what persons might or might not do under any set of circumstances, truths that seem to go beyond mere possibilities, which are known by God logically prior to his decree of which world should be actual." I will now argue that Craig's claim is mistaken, and in the process of showing why it is so, I will highlight a fundamental advantage I believe open theism has over Molinism.

The reason Molinism is burdened with the grounding objection is because it rightly understands that "would" counterfactuals undermine libertarian freedom if God is their truth-maker but fails to grasp that "would" counterfactuals undermine libertarian freedom *regardless* of their truth-maker and *even (per impossibile) if they have no truth-maker.*[46] Curiously, Craig comes close to admitting as much when he denies that God has "middle knowledge of how he himself would freely choose to act in any set of circumstances." Were God to have such knowledge, Craig avers, it "would obliterate God's freedom, since the truth of such so-called counterfactuals of divine freedom would be prior to and, hence, independent of God's decree." But how is it that true "would" counterfactuals of *God's* free activity undermine God's freedom if known prior to his decree, while true "would" counterfactuals of *our* free activity do not undermine our freedom when known prior to our decree (that is, our decision)? The logic that undermines the freedom of the one undermines the freedom of the other as well.

In any case, the grounding objection can be completely avoided if we simply accept that libertarian freedom can be described only by conjoined "might" counterfactuals, not "would" counterfactuals, for now we need not deny that God's pre-creational knowledge is grounded in God's own nature and will. Prior to creation, God knows that to the extent that he confers on a possible agent in the context of a possible world a certain determinate nature, he grounds the true "would" counterfactuals

---

46. To be clear, "would" counterfactuals do not undermine *moral responsibility* when what the agent would do reflects a solidified (hence, predictable) character that was acquired by the exercise of the agent's own prior morally responsible libertarian free choices. Though it may be that an agent cannot *now* act otherwise, the agent is yet morally responsible for his action if (but only if) he *could have* acted otherwise had he in the past developed a different kind of solidified character through the exercise of his libertarian free will.

that describe that agent. To this extent, the being of an agent is *given to* him, not *chosen by* him. Yet to the extent that God confers on a possible agent in the context of a possible world libertarian free will, he grounds all true conjoined "might" counterfactuals that describe that agent. To this extent, the agent will acquire their being through the exercise of their free will. While eternally true "would" counterfactuals undermine libertarian freedom, eternally true conjoined "might" counterfactuals do not. To the contrary, conjoined "might" propositions express *what it means* to have libertarian freedom. Hence, there is no problem affirming that God's nature and will ground both true "would" counterfactuals and true conjoined "might" counterfactuals. Open theism's ability completely to avoid the grounding objection while affirming God's precreational knowledge of "would" and "might" counterfactuals gives it a distinct philosophical advantage over Molinism.

Helping God Bring About the Actual World

Before turning to Craig's critique of the open view's account of evil, there is one more important difference between open theism and Molinism that warrants mentioning. Because it excludes conjoined "might" counterfactuals as a distinct category of truths from God's middle knowledge, Molinism conceives of every possible world in terms of a single, exhaustively settled story line.[47] By contrast, in the open view, possible worlds that include conjoined "might" counterfactuals embody *multiple* possible story lines. To bring about a world that includes libertarian free will is to bring about a world that, by definition, is not exhaustively settled.[48] Whereas the Molinist account conceives of the actual world as well as every possible world as a traditional novel, the open view conceives of the actual world as well as every possible world that includes true conjoined "might" counterfactuals along the lines of a Choose Your Own Adventure storybook.

---

47. As I argue in my contributing chapter, this forces the implausible conclusion that the *very idea* of a world in which possibilities are ontologically real—that is, in which the future is partly open—must constitute *a contradiction*. So far as I am aware, no one has successfully argued this point. Indeed, very few in history have ever tried (e.g., Spinoza).

48. Molinists typically talk about God choosing to "actualize" a possible world. Since "actualizing possibilities" is ambiguous (does it mean transforming possibilities into actualities or actualizing a world that includes possibilities?), it seems more appropriate to speak of God *bringing about* or simply *creating* the world, just in case the world God chooses to create happens to include ontological possibilities, as open theists believe.

One significant practical implication of this difference is that, whereas in Molinism God unilaterally decided which single world story line would get actualized, in open theism free agents, making decisions in the actual flow of history, play an important role in deciding which world story line ends up getting actualized. Since all facts pertaining to the history of the world were settled in eternity before the world began, according to Molinism, the actual historical process decides nothing and contributes nothing. By contrast, because the open view holds that God created a world that contained true conjoined "might" counterfactuals, important matters still hang in the balance, depending on how free agents exercise their free will. In the open view, we do not *discover* what the future holds; we help *decide* what the future holds.

So far as I can see, this perspective best captures the biblical teaching that humans were created as God's viceroys and are designed to reign with him on the earth (2 Tim. 2:12; Rev. 5:10; 20:6; 22:5; cf. Gen. 1:26–28). Our job now is to serve as God's co-laborers who live and pray in a way that brings about God's will "on earth as it is in heaven" (Matt. 6:10; cf. 1 Cor. 3:9; 2 Cor. 6:1). In the open view, more so than in Molinism and far more so than in Calvinism, things *really* hang in the balance, *here and now*, and whether or not we live in accordance with God's will and whether or not we pray are decisive factors. Prayer *really* changes things! The significance and responsibility the open view places on us are, in my opinion, one of its distinct practical advantages.

The Problem of Evil

Which Chess Champion Is Most Praiseworthy?

In the final section of my response to Craig, I will consider his critique of the open view's account of evil. Much of Craig's critique centers on a chess analogy of providence to which open theists have frequently appealed. In this analogy, God is conceived of as a master chess champion who is assured of victory, not because he controls every move his opponents make (as in Calvinism), nor because he foresees every move his opponents will make (as in Arminianism), but because he can perfectly anticipate every move his opponents might make. In our estimation, the openness Master Chess Champion is more praiseworthy than the alternative Masters, because she alone wins *by virtue of her superior wisdom*. So too, open theists believe that the view of providence that most exalts God is one that envisions God confidently steering the creation toward his creational goals by means of his loving wisdom rather than only by means of his innate power or futuristic vision.

Craig attempts to critique the open view by turning the chess-master analogy around and using it against us. According to Molinism, Craig notes, "suffering will be permitted only in light of the Master's ultimate purpose, namely, building the kingdom of God." By contrast, Craig argues, "the Not-So-Grand Master" of the open view "will churn up a lot of unforeseen, unnecessary, and pointless suffering as he plays the game." In fact, Craig doubts that God's "knowledge of mere 'might' counterfactuals is ... sufficient to bring about God's desired ends." He even alleges that in the open view, "God is not so brilliant a chess player as to be able to know that his plans will probably [*sic*] succeed." The proof Craig offers of these allegations is that the God of open theism "failed to achieve the universal salvation he desired and regretted having created man. Those are not the moves of a Grand Master!" Craig argues. He thus concludes that the God of the open view is a "cognitively limited deity" who "just sits by wringing his hands while letting evils go on unchecked without any morally sufficient reason for not stopping them." None of the four distinct objections mentioned in this paragraph, however, carries any weight, as I will now argue.

It's Not about God's Cognitive Abilities!

First, as frequently as it is repeated among critics of the open view, the charge that the God of open theism is cognitively challenged is a non sequitur. It is true that the open view's Master Chess Champion is not certain of how his opponents would move in response to every conceivable circumstance, whereas the Molinist Master Chess Champion is. But this difference would imply a limitation on God's cognitive abilities only if *the facts about how agents would move in every conceivable circumstance existed for God to know*. Yet this is precisely what open theists deny.

Craig essentially presupposes the truth of his own ontology, including his conviction that the facts about what agents would do in every conceivable circumstance eternally exist, and then alleges that the God of open theism is cognitively challenged *for not knowing these facts*. This is as unfair as if I were to charge that Craig believes in a "cognitively limited deity" on the grounds that God is ignorant of what agents *might and might not* do in certain circumstances. The critique would be illegitimate, because I know full well that Craig affirms the perfection of God's cognitive abilities, just as I do. We simply disagree over the independent truth-value of "might" counterfactuals and thus over the precise content of God's perfect knowledge.

Remember God's Infinite Intelligence!

Second, according to Craig, "In the openness view, the Not-So-Grand Master will churn up a lot of unforeseen, unnecessary, and pointless suffering as he plays the game." Indeed, he is not smart enough "to know that his plans will probably succeed." Rather, he inexplicably "just sits by wringing his hands while letting evils go on unchecked without any morally sufficient reason for not stopping them."

In response, I concur with Craig that only a "cognitively limited deity" would fret in the manner Craig suggests because he faced a future partly comprised of possibilities. But the God of open theism does nothing of the sort! If we grant that God is infinitely intelligent, he can anticipate each and every one of any number of possibilities as though each was the only possibility he had to anticipate. We can hardly imagine this infinitely intelligent God "wringing his hands" as he confronted "unforeseen, unnecessary, and pointless suffering." An infinitely intelligent God can anticipate and prepare for events that *might* and *might not* take place just as effectively as for events that will *certainly* take place. Indeed, since he does not have to spread his unlimited intelligence thin to cover possibilities, God can anticipate each of the events that might and might not take place as if they were events that had to take place, and he can do this from all eternity.

Only a "cognitively limited deity" would be more prepared for *certain* events than for *possible* events. Hence, if Craig's understanding of the Master Chess Champion is such that he could not even "know that his plans will probably succeed" (let alone would *certainly* succeed) because he anticipates his opponents' moves as possibilities rather than certainties, I encourage Craig to consider the possibility that it is he, not I or any other open theist, who embraces a "cognitively limited deity."

Can God Secure His Desired Ends?

Third, Craig wonders if God's "knowledge of mere 'might' counterfactuals is ... sufficient to bring about God's desired ends. If it were," he continues, "then why has God not acted to secure universal salvation?" In response, I should first note that Craig's argument assumes that we who believe God's pre-creational knowledge *includes* true conjoined "might" counterfactuals must also hold that God's knowledge excludes all true "would" counterfactuals. As I stated earlier, however, there is absolutely no reason to think this.

More important, this argument strikes me as a bizarre one for Craig to make. If Craig is going to argue that God's knowledge in the open view is not sufficient to "bring about God's desired ends" on the grounds that God has not "acted to secure universal salvation," then Craig must either believe in universalism or accept that this argument counts as much against his own position as it does against open theism. All views that admit libertarian freedom must acknowledge that God could not "secure universal salvation," despite his desire for all to be saved. Only the Calvinist is able to ascribe to God an undefeatable will, though the bitter pill they must swallow for these bragging rights is the horrific belief that it was not God's will for all to be saved in the first place.

Fortunately for both Craig and myself, his argument carries no weight, since God's inability to secure universal salvation for a creation populated with free agents has *nothing to do with what God knows*. It rather has to do with the nature of free will. For both the Molinist and the open theist, God must *find out* how agents freely choose. God does not *make them* choose one way or the other. The only difference between the two views is that in Molinism God mysteriously discovers how agents freely choose prior to creation, whereas in the open view God discovers how agents freely choose in the actual flow of history. But this difference is inconsequential to the issue of whether God's desire to save all can be thwarted or not. We both grant that it can, as is demonstrated by the existence of sin, evil, and hell, none of which God wills. In both Molinism and open theism, therefore, God must do the best he can with the nonideal world (and with other possible worlds) as he finds it.

At the same time, the Molinist understanding of the nonideal situation that God must work with carries a significant burden from which the open view is free. The Molinist must accept that God actualized this particular world, down to the very last detail, after having evaluated every other possible world. Since God is all-good and always does the best thing, the Molinist must accept that, however nonideal this world may be, it nevertheless is *the best of all possible worlds*, down to the last detail.[49] In light of nightmarish horrors and incalculable suffering that have characterized human history, to say nothing of the eternal hell that most Christians (including traditional Molinists) believe awaits masses of humans after death, this is not an easy claim to accept. The fact that open theism does not require this conclusion is, to my mind, a distinct mark in its favor.

Why Doesn't God Stop Evil?

A final argument Craig raises against the open account of evil concerns why God does not "intervene to stop evil once it appears." Craig, like Helseth, is convinced the open view actually *worsens* the problem of evil since in this view it "becomes inexplicable why God just sits by wringing his hands while letting evils go on unchecked without any morally sufficient reason for not stopping them." In the Molinist account, by contrast, "suffering will be permitted only in light of the Master's ultimate purpose, namely, building the kingdom of God."

This frequently raised objection is frankly not hard to overcome. Craig and I agree that morally responsible libertarian free will entails that agents have, within limits, the capacity to choose good or evil. If God were to intervene unilaterally to stop an agent from choosing evil, as Craig's objection implies he should, then it would be false that God *gave* this agent the capacity to choose good *or evil*. As I have argued elsewhere and will flesh out in my contributing chapter, morally responsible libertarian free will must be, by definition, irrevocable.[50] On top of this, we must also take into serious consideration the biblical teaching that God wants to *use us* ultimately to vanquish evil, which is why we are depicted as God's coworkers, ambassadors, warriors, and viceroys.[51]

---

49. To be clear, the Molinist need not accept that this is the best *logically* possible world, simply the best possible world given God's knowledge of how all conceivable agents would act in every conceivable circumstance.

50. See Boyd, *Satan and the Problem of Evil*, 178–206.

51. See, e.g., 1 Cor. 3:9; 2 Cor. 5:20; 6:1; 2 Tim. 2:3–4, 12; Eph. 6:11–12; Rev. 5:10; 20:6; 22:5.

This purpose would not be accomplished if God unilaterally prevented all evil.

Once we understand the irrevocable nature of libertarian free will, the question is no longer "Why does God not intervene to stop it?" but "Why did God give free will to agents in the first place?" And to this question open theists and Molinists provide identical answers: *God deemed the value of free will worth the cost.* Hence, if the God of Molinism is morally justified in allowing evil, the God of the open view must be considered justified as well.

Nevertheless, as a final word, I want to note that there is an important difference in the particular way Molinists and open theists conceive of God's allowing evil. The Molinist must accept that each and every *particular* evil was *specifically* permitted by God for a *specific* good reason. While it is perhaps not ideal, the Molinist must accept that each and every one of the unthinkable atrocities that has ever befallen a human throughout history had God's specific stamp of approval. The open view has the distinct advantage of not requiring us to accept this difficult conclusion. In the open view, God has a morally justified reason for giving agents the capacity freely to engage in a certain range of *possible* behaviors but no specific reason for how agents use their freedom. While the ultimate rationale for why agents have freedom in the first place resides with God (it was necessary for love to be genuine), the ultimate rationale for how each agent chooses specifically to use that freedom resides with the agent, *not God.* Hence, while God wills that agents are free, there is no sense in which God wills the misuse of the freedom he gives.[52]

To be sure, because he is infinitely intelligent, God is always able to bring an eternally prepared good purpose *to* events that are brought about by our free will. But the open theist does not have to affirm that God specifically allowed any particular event *for* that good purpose. In light of the macabre nature of much of what comes to pass in this fallen, oppressed world, I believe this constitutes a significant advantage for the open view.

---

52. I have elsewhere argued that "natural" evil is ultimately the result of free choices as much as moral evil. See Boyd, *Satan and the Problem of Evil*, 242–318; idem, "Evolution as Cosmic Warfare: A Biblical Perspective on Satan and 'Natural' Evil," in *Creation Made Free: Open Theology Engaging Science*, ed. J. Oord (Eugene, Ore.: Pickwick, 2009), 125–45.

GOD CONTROLS BY LIBERATING[1]

RON HIGHFIELD

Our age is obsessed with freedom. We demand to make our own decisions, follow our own paths, and choose our own destinies. We stand vigilant, looking for encroaching oppression and rising tyranny. We hold it more in keeping with our dignity to make our own ruinous decisions than to be led like sheep to safe pastures by patronizing shepherds.[2] We want control, and we insist that controlling ourselves and our circumstances accompanies any meaningful liberty. The thought of being controlled by any other power, however benevolent, repels us as demeaning and enslaving. What hope, then, is there for a model of providence the heart of which is the thesis that God controls by liberating and liberates by controlling? Yes, it is counterintuitive and cuts against the grain of our autonomy-bewitched culture. But should it really surprise us that the God who created the world from nothing should act in paradoxical ways? Should we be taken aback upon learning that the gospel that proclaims a cross-shaped salvation should cut across the grain of our self-absorbed culture? If not, then I hope you will be open to hearing about the all-encompassing care of God, which begins with creation, reaches its stunning apex in Jesus Christ, and culminates in the glorious liberty of the children of God.

---

1. Unfortunately, the word "control" carries connotations of coercion, manipulation, and anxiety. None of these limitations characterizes God's action of accomplishing his will perfectly in all things.

2. In 1859 John Stuart Mill anticipated our own age when he laid down the principle that "the only purpose for which power can be rightfully exercised over any member of a civilized community, against his will, is to prevent harm to others. His own good, either physical or moral, is not a sufficient warrant" (*On Liberty* [Indianapolis: Bobbs-Merrill Co., 1956], 13).

The Decisive Issue

The Christian doctrine of providence touches on a bewildering array of issues: God's power, freedom, and mode of action in the world; human freedom, responsibility, and dignity; sin, grace, salvation, and many more. But no question is more decisive for a doctrine of providence than "Does God accomplish his will in all things?" The great divide among views of providence falls between those who answer yes and those who answer no to this question. Lately, theologians have begun to refer to the first as the "no-risk" view and the second as the "risk" view.[3] On one side stand those who affirm that God's eternal plan will be executed perfectly, because its fulfillment depends on him alone. Looking across from the other side of the chasm are those who assert that God jeopardizes his plan in the actual history of providence, because the plan's fulfillment requires the cooperation of some other reality.[4]

Whether we defend the risk or the no-risk view, we will not find an easy path in this discussion. The doctrine of providence deals with some of the knottiest problems of theology, and whatever alternative you choose, you will face mind-numbing difficulties. Those who deny that God's will is always done will be asked to explain how this denial squares with God's power and divinity and identity as the only Creator, Lord, and Savior. Those who affirm complete sovereignty of the divine will must face the charge that this assertion is irreconcilable with human freedom and responsibility and with the presence of evil in the world. As the title of my chapter makes clear, I stand on the no-risk side of this debate and will be offering my own distinctive defense of this view and criticisms of the risk view.

Since God's nature and his relationship to the world are ultimately incomprehensible by human reason, I think it is defensible, even if frus-

---

3. Terrance L. Tiessen, *Providence and Prayer: How Does God Work in the World?* (Downers Grove, Ill.: InterVarsity Press, 2000), 363–64. Tiessen relates eleven different models of providence on a sliding scale of how much control over the world they attribute to God. A decisive break occurs, however, between Molinism (model 6) and Thomism (model 7). In the first six models God risks failure, and in the last five God's will is assuredly done in all things.

4. I use the intentionally vague term "some other reality" because in Molinism, which Tiessen correctly numbers among the "risk" models *(Providence and Prayer,* 363), once God decides which possible and feasible world to realize, everything goes according to plan. However, God depends on there being such a possible and feasible world. God cannot make a world possible or feasible.

trating, for advocates of complete divine sovereignty to admit they do not know a way to bring belief in God's perfect lordship into complete harmony with human freedom.[5] And this position has much to commend it if the alternative is to allow biblically based theology to be overwhelmed by speculative metaphysics or logic or psychology or "passion for systematic consistency."[6] However, many writers, including me, believe it is possible to achieve some rational insight into this faith. Among these writers, some use metaphysical, logical, or psychological theories to show *how* God can be "perfectly provident" without compromising human freedom and incurring culpability for evil.[7] It seems to me that Molinism, Thomism, Scotism, and certain types of determinism take this route.

While I do not reject these approaches completely and feel more sympathy with some than with others, I would argue that they have too long dominated this discussion and have led to many fruitless impasses. I insist that before Christian theologians take up the role of metaphysicians or logicians or psychologists, they should exhaust the method evangelicals ought to hold nearest to their hearts: the analogy of the faith.[8] With this method, obscure elements of the faith are laid beside clearer parts. And each scriptural teaching is understood in the light of every other. Only after this method has been exhaustively applied should we feel free to make cautious use of speculative methods to probe the inherent rationality of the faith.[9]

---

5. This is the position that distinguished evangelical scholar J. I. Packer defends in his book *Evangelism and the Sovereignty of God* (Downers Grove, Ill.: InterVarsity Press, 1961), 18–24. David M. Ciocchi also adopts an "agnostic position" on the possibility of reconciling God's control and human freedom. See his "Reconciling Divine Sovereignty and Human Freedom," *Journal of the Evangelical Theological Society* 37, no. 3 (1994): 395–412. Ciocchi reasserts his agnostic position in a later article, "Suspending the Debate about Divine Sovereignty and Human Freedom," *Journal of the Evangelical Theological Society* 51, no. 3 (2008): 573–90.

6. Packer, *Evangelism and the Sovereignty of God*, 16.

7. Alfred J. Freddoso, introduction to *On Divine Foreknowledge (Part IV of the* Concordia*)*, by Luis de Molina, trans. Alfred J. Freddoso (Ithaca, N.Y.: Cornell University Press, 1988), 35.

8. See Muller, *Post-Reformation Reformed Dogmatics*, 2:493–97, for a discussion of the Reformed method of interpreting Scripture according to the analogy of faith. For Karl Barth's use of the analogy of faith, see *CD* 1/1, 243–47.

9. I should inform the reader that my ecclesiastical tradition, Churches of Christ (Stone-Campbell Movement), has always resisted committing itself to any creed, confession of faith, or extrabiblical theological system, such as Calvinism or Arminianism or any other. I believe it is very important to affirm every biblical truth even if one cannot explain fully how they all fit together, and I do not want to sacrifice even one biblical truth to make a theological system more internally consistent. I am not trying to be a good Calvinist or a good Arminian. So, in developing my understanding of providence, although I have considered many theories, I have tried to the best of my ability to conform my views to Scripture.

An Assertion of God's Comprehensive Control

Attempting to demonstrate that Scripture teaches God's comprehensive control of all things would require writing a large book. I cannot do justice to this task here; nevertheless, I cannot remain completely silent since Scripture is the material norm of theology. The following line of thought indicates how I think we should approach Scripture's teaching on providence. Scripture contains many confessional and doxological texts that generalize ideas of God's sovereign control or almighty power or unlimited knowledge. Typical are Job 42:2: "I know that you can do all things; no purpose of yours can be thwarted"; Isaiah 46:10–11: "I make known the end from the beginning, from ancient times, what is still to come. I say: 'My purpose will stand, and I will do all that I please'.... What I have said, that will I bring about; what I have planned, that will I do"; Ephesians 1:11: God "works out everything in conformity with the purpose of his will"; Philippians 3:20–21: "The Lord Jesus Christ, who, by the power that enables him to bring everything under his control, will transform our lowly bodies so that they will be like his glorious body"; and 1 John 3:20: "God is greater than our hearts, and he knows everything."

When Israel or the church praises God, it stretches to find words worthy of God's greatness. When the writer of Psalm 106 asks, "Who can proclaim the mighty acts of the LORD or fully declare his praise?" (v. 2), he expects us to answer confidently, "No one!" The psalmist of Psalm 145 strains to articulate God's praiseworthiness: "I will exalt you, my God the King.... Every day I will praise you and extol your name for ever and ever. Great is the LORD and most worthy of praise; his greatness no one can fathom.... Let every creature praise his holy name for ever and ever" (vv. 1–3, 21). Listen to Paul praise God's inscrutable providence in Romans 11:33–36: "Oh, the depth of the riches of the wisdom and knowledge of God! How unsearchable his judgments, and his paths beyond tracing out! 'Who has known the mind of the Lord? Or who has been his counselor?' 'Who has ever given to God, that God should repay them?' For from him and through him and to him are all things. To him be the glory forever! Amen." And who can refrain from joining in the praise arising from around the throne of God in Revelation 4? The four living creatures around God's throne never stop proclaiming, "Holy, holy, holy is the Lord God Almighty, who was, and is, and is to come" (v. 8). Then the twenty-four elders lay their crowns before the throne and say, "You are worthy, our Lord and God, to receive glory and honor and power, for you created all things, and by your will they were created and have their being" (v. 11).

I admit that some narrative texts seem to imply limitations in God's control or power or knowledge. These texts play a central role in open theists' arguments for a risk view of divine providence. John Sanders surveys these texts in two extensive chapters, totaling over a hundred pages, in his book *The God Who Risks*.[10] Sanders and others emphasize how these narratives portray God as acting in time, responding to human actions, changing plans, learning new information, expressing uncertainty about the future, and experiencing emotions such as surprise, anger, regret, sorrow, and grief.[11] According to Sanders, if there are no compelling reasons to do otherwise, we should take them "as disclosing to us the very nature of God."[12]

Though I believe the open view of biblical interpretation is vulnerable on several fronts, I cannot pursue all those criticisms here.[13] I will make but one point: Whereas scores of texts in Scripture heighten God's transcendence, I know of no texts that *generalize* divine risk and limits. No text confesses, "God cannot do all things," or "God does not know all things," or "God cannot work out all things in conformity with his will." Can anyone imagine a canonical psalm or a Christian hymn saying, "Lord, we praise you, for you are greater than any other being. You can do all things that are under your control, and when your plans fail, it is never your fault! We extol you for doing what you can with what you have at your disposal. We give you thanks for doing your best to protect us. We know that you wish us well and will do what you can to help us achieve eternal life. Praise to your name!"

---

10. John Sanders, *The God Who Risks: A Theology of Providence* (Downers Grove, Ill.: Inter-Varsity Press, 1998), 39–139. For a similar study, see Richard Rice, "Biblical Support for a New Perspective," in Pinnock et al., *Openness of God*, 11–58.

11. See Gen. 6:5–7; 22:12; Ex. 4:2–5, 8, 9; 32:9–14; 1 Sam. 15:29; 2 Kings 20:5; Jer. 3:7; Hos. 11:8, 9; Mark 6:6; Luke 8:43–48; and James 4:2.

12. Sanders, *God Who Risks*, 38.

13. See Ron Highfield, *Great Is the Lord: Theology for the Praise of God* (Grand Rapids: Eerdmans, 2008), 151–53, 359–61; see also Alfred Freddoso, "The 'Openness' of God: A Reply to William Hasker," *Christian Scholars Review* 28 (1998): 124.

I do not hear this kind of "praise" in Scripture. The tendency of Scripture is clear: to magnify God's power, control, and knowledge and all his other attributes to the absolute maximum.

What clinches my belief in God's comprehensive sovereignty, however, is its coherence with a Scripture-based, God-honoring doctrine of God. I do not believe one can deny that God accomplishes his will in all things while affirming that God created all things from nothing, that he sustains all things by his "powerful word" (Heb. 1:3), that he knows all things, and that he "is able to do immeasurably more than all we ask or imagine" (Eph. 3:20). How can we proclaim that God is our only Lord and Savior, that his grace in Jesus Christ is completely gratuitous, that Christ will "reign until he has put all his enemies under his feet" (1 Cor. 15:25), or that "God [will] be all in all" (1 Cor. 15:28) if at the same time we assert that God's plans can be thwarted and his will made ineffective? Denying God's comprehensive control requires placing creation's destiny partly in the hands of chance, or necessity, or the Devil, or humanity. And it requires revising the doctrine of God to be consistent with the assertion that God cannot create whatever he wants or accomplish whatever he chooses. You will have to limit God's power, knowledge, presence, freedom, and wisdom; you will have to make God subject to time and space and change. And these moves will sooner or later lead to the conclusion that God is limited in his eternal being, his very essence. I do not believe we should take one step down this road.[14]

How, Then, Does God Work in Providence?

The question "How?" asks about a means that enables an agent to interact with an object in a certain way. When we watch a magic act in which the magician appears to be sawing his assistant in half, we might ask in amazement, "How did he do that?" "How?" is one of those questions we need to answer if we are to understand an agent's action. Many discussions of divine providence get off track at this point by adopting a careless analogy between human and divine ways of acting. Do we really think we can understand *how* God created the world, *how* the Son of God became incarnate, *how* God raised Jesus from the dead,

---

14. My book *Great Is the Lord* is a sustained defense of the traditional doctrine of God against the criticisms of open theism and process theology.

or *how* God controls the world comprehensively?[15] Gregory of Nyssa speaks for the church fathers when he warns: "We have no doubt ... that God underwent birth in human nature. But *how* this happened we decline to investigate as a matter beyond the scope of reason.... The fact of creation we accept; but we renounce a curious investigation of the way the universe was framed as a matter altogether ineffable and inexplicable."[16] Lacking Gregory's caution, some writers propose philosophical or logical or psychological theories of how God controls the world without sacrificing human freedom. Other writers, finding these theories implausible, argue that since the "how" project fails, a robust view of divine sovereignty is not compatible with genuine human freedom. Thus we reach an impasse.

These theories overlook Scripture's answer to the question of means. According to Scripture, the one God acts through the Word and the Spirit to create, guide, govern, reconcile, and redeem the world—without diluting his Godhead or displacing creation. In Scripture, the Word becomes incarnate and is raised from the dead through the Spirit. Faith comes by hearing the Word of God, and the Spirit sanctifies us and gives life to our "mortal bodies" (Rom. 8:11). Hence, God's power to give being to something not himself, to unite himself to a full human nature without sacrificing his deity, to indwell his creation without displacing it, and to work concurrently with intelligent beings without compromising their freedom—all are rooted in God's immanent and eternal triune life. Attempting to explain God's relationship to the world in philosophical, logical, or psychological terms transforms a revealed mystery into a speculative obscurity. It revives a fundamental mistake of second-century Gnosticism—seeking semidivine mediators to span the gap between the transcendent God and the material universe—a heresy

---

15. Karl Barth rejects all answers to the question of how God operates in creation other than the operation of the Word and Spirit: "And now we can and must give the simple positive answer that the operation of God is His utterance to all creatures of the Word of God which has all the force and wisdom and goodness of His Holy Spirit. Or, to put it in another way, the operation of God is His moving of all creatures by the force and wisdom and goodness which are His Holy Spirit, the Spirit of His Word" (*CD* 3/3, 142).

16. Gregory of Nyssa, "Address on Religious Instruction," in *Christology of the Later Fathers*, ed. Edward R. Hardy (Philadelphia: Westminster Press, 1954), 288, emphasis in original. Irenaeus, in his debate with the Gnostics, urged that God "Himself in Himself, after a fashion which we can neither describe nor conceive, predestinating all things, formed them as He pleased" (*Against All Heresies* 2.2.4 [ANF 1:361]).

that Irenaeus so ably refuted with his doctrine of the economic Trinity. Irenaeus asserts, "For this is a peculiarity of the pre-eminence of God, not to stand in need of other instruments for the creation of those things which are summoned into existence. His own Word is both suitable and sufficient for the formation of all things"[17]

Divine Action in Creation, Incarnation, and Salvation

Now, let us allow the analogy of faith to inform our thinking about the way God acts in the world by comparing the acts of creation, incarnation, and salvation with that of providence. In *creation*, God gave the world its total being through the Word and the Spirit, so that the triune God is the only "cause" of creation. Creatures did not exist to participate in their creation, so God acted unilaterally for their benefit before and apart from their own choice and action. God made this choice for them. Yet, as a result of God's unilateral act of creation, creatures possess their own distinct and real being, with all its properties and powers—including the power of freedom. Let us underline this point: Human freedom comes into being through a sovereign divine act. In the case of creation, at least, divine sovereignty and human freedom do not conflict; indeed, human freedom depends absolutely on divine power.

The *incarnation* was not merited or caused by the goodness of the Virgin Mary or of the man Jesus. It was pure grace. Nevertheless, the incarnation did not diminish the human nature in any respect. And just as the human and divine natures are united in the person of the Son by the power of the Holy Spirit—without confusion or change or division or separation—the human and divine wills are likewise united.[18] The Spirit enabled Jesus' human will to affirm the divine will perfectly. He triumphed over sin, not because his human freedom was overpowered by divine grace, but because divine grace empowered him for genuine freedom. Human freedom was not restricted by the divine decision and

---

17. Irenaeus *Against All Heresies* 2.2.4 (ANF 1:361). For a study of this theme in Irenaeus, see Colin E. Gunton, *The Triune Creator: A Historical and Systematic Study* (Grand Rapids: Eerdmans, 1998), 52–56.

18. These four qualifications on the relationship of the human and divine natures were laid down in the Symbol of Chalcedon (451), and the affirmation of two wills working in complete harmony, with the human in perfect submission to the divine, was laid down in the Sixth Ecumenical Council, held in Constantinople in 680. See Philip Schaff, ed., *The Creeds of Christendom*, vol. 2, rev. David S. Schaff (1931; repr., Grand Rapids: Baker, 1990), 63–64, 72.

direction involved in the incarnation any more than it was by divine creation. Quite the opposite: God's abundant grace given in the incarnation enabled human freedom to achieve the goal for which it was created.

In its teaching about *salvation*, Christian orthodoxy rejects Pelagianism, which says human beings do not need grace, and Semipelagianism, which says human beings can merit grace by their free openness to grace.[19] Instead, drawing on Paul's letters, orthodoxy asserts that prevenient grace enables the free reception of more grace.[20] The Spirit enables us to believe the gospel, gives us new birth, sanctifies us, and pours God's love into our hearts (Rom. 5:5). Our freedom to live for God is always a Spirit-empowered response to his grace freely bestowed on us. God's grace creates and empowers human freedom for God, for faith, love, and good works. Again, we find it to be a principle that in his sovereign freedom God acts first to cause, empower, and liberate human freedom. The notion that God's sovereign action toward us in creation, incarnation, and salvation somehow threatens our freedom is completely foreign to Scripture.

Divine Action in Providence

Many evangelical theologians would agree that God works through the Word and the Spirit in complete gratuity in creation, incarnation, and salvation. They would not argue that human beings cooperated with God in their creation or that the man Jesus freely agreed beforehand to be united with the eternal Son of God or that sinners begin or empower their own salvation.[21] But when it comes to providence—God's direction of the ordinary course of human history—some theologians begin to look for

---

19. Though the term "Semipelagianism" was coined in the sixteenth century by opponents of Molina, this idea was condemned at the Council of Orange (529). See F. L. Cross and E. A. Livingstone, eds., *The Oxford Dictionary of the Christian Church*, 3rd ed. (Oxford: Oxford University Press, 1997), s.v. "Semipelagianism."

20. One of the best examples of medieval thought on grace and freedom can be found in Bernard of Clairvaux, "On Grace and Free Choice," in *The Works of Bernard of Clairvaux*, vol. 7, *Treatises III*, trans. Daniel O'Donovan (Kalamazoo: Cistercian, 1977), 53–111.

21. Perhaps I am being too optimistic. Karl Barth correctly points out that Luis de Molina and his Jesuit colleagues developed the theory of middle knowledge to support their Semipelagian theology of grace; that is, "to aid a new semi-pelagianism to gain its necessary place and right in the new situation in opposition to the Augustinian-Thomistic teaching of the Dominicans, which they accused of being dangerously near to Luther and Calvin" (*CD* 2/1, 569). Evangelicals under the influence of Molina will have a difficult time escaping his Semipelagianism, even if they wish to do so.

other mediators and modes of divine action. They argue that God cannot simply "cause" human freedom to do his will freely. For them, the idea of a caused free act is as contradictory as the concept of a square circle. Out of respect for freedom, God attempts to persuade people to do his will by fallible means: ideas, inspirations, conscience, circumstances, or words. Since the idea of infallible persuasion, short of seeing God face-to-face, seems problematic, it appears likely, according to this way of thinking, that God will fail to accomplish his providential will in all cases.[22]

I argue that providence does not constitute an exception to the way God works and that God's freedom and action precede and empower human freedom and action at every point. In creation, God gives human beings their real and distinct existence, and because God is faithful, his creative Word continues its sustaining force. In providence, which presupposes creation and moves toward salvation, God works before, through, with, inside, around, and after human working to accomplish his will. Apart from God's creation, nothing could exist. Without his sustaining action, nothing could abide, and without his continual cooperation, nothing could happen. Through the Word and the Spirit, God gives real and lasting efficacy to human action by empowering and directing all things, including human freedom, to their God-appointed end. In this way, God frees human freedom from the futility of its blind groping and enables it to achieve its end. If God can create the original power of freedom, create a free human being who could not sin, and reorient fallen freedom toward righteousness without doing it violence, he can direct human freedom according to his will in every other case without doing it violence.[23] For the fourth time: divine freedom creates and supports human freedom. In no way does it diminish it, contradict it, or compete with it!

What about Freedom and Responsibility?

I am sure some are asking themselves, "What kind of freedom can be created from nothing, infallibly directed to God's ends, and reoriented toward righteousness, without being denatured? Can it really be genuine

---

22. John Duns Scotus, distinguishing himself from the views of Thomas Aquinas, advocates a type of infallible persuasion that God exerts in his grace. Thomists reject this theory as impossible apart from the vision of God. For this discussion, see Garrigou-LaGrange, *Predestination*, 113–14.

23. I am not proposing a theory of "how" God does this.

freedom?" What light does the analogy of faith shed on the nature of human freedom and responsibility and its compatibility with God's sovereignty? Many theories of freedom — even theological ones — begin by asking what kind of freedom can ground genuine moral responsibility.[24] Some theologians begin with the premise that Scripture holds human beings responsible for their sins.[25] This gives them a theological warrant for their theory of freedom. For example, Bruce Reichenbach admits that Scripture does not explicitly teach his view of freedom. He asserts, however, that "it is filled with instances of posed choices which presuppose freedom ... commands to act properly and the sanctions imposed on improper conduct only make sense if humans have freedom."[26] Scripture declares that God holds sinners responsible for their sins and that God is just in his judgments, claims from which David Ciocchi infers the following proposition: *"God guarantees that human beings meet the conditions that are necessary and sufficient to ground deep moral responsibility."*[27]

What type of freedom is presupposed by this assertion of "deep" moral responsibility? Many conclude that it requires a strict form of libertarian freedom, a freedom that retains its potential indifference between opposing options even in the moment of decision. In other words, even with identical internal and external conditions and without any change in God's sustaining action, concurrence, or grace, one could have chosen differently. This theory of freedom views responsibility as presupposing radical self-determination. The self is responsible because it alone determines itself and expresses itself in its act. Gregory Boyd asserts that the agent is the "ultimate explanation" of its action.[28] And

---

24. Rather than beginning with moral responsibility, Gregory Boyd takes his point of departure from the thesis that God created the world so that others can participate in his triune love. But love is possible only where there is freedom, and freedom requires risk, and risk entails moral responsibility (see Boyd, *Satan and the Problem of Evil*, 50–53, 165).

25. Philosophers need to find other epistemic grounds for believing in moral responsibility. For a variety of contemporary philosophical opinions on the issue, see John Martin and Mark Ravizza, eds., *Perspectives on Moral Responsibility* (Ithaca, N.Y.: Cornell University Press, 1993).

26. Bruce Reichenbach, "God Limits His Power," in *Predestination and Freewill: Four Views of Divine Sovereignty and Human Freedom*, ed. David Basinger and Randal Basinger (Downers Grove, Ill.: InterVarsity Press, 1986), 104.

27. Ciocchi, "Suspending the Debate," 586, emphasis in original. To be fair I need to point out that Ciocchi is agnostic about the exact nature of human responsibility and the freedom that grounds it.

28. Boyd, *Satan and the Problem of Evil*, 19.

John Sanders contends that human beings are "minicreators" who create their deeds "*ex nihilo*, since it originates within us and is not merely the effect of divine causation."[29] Had the self been determined by its external or internal conditions or by God, it would not be responsible for its act. The act would have expressed the character of these alien forces rather than the will of the self. Hence, many (if not most) theologians who hold to the libertarian theory of freedom deny its compatibility with complete divine control.

In the light of biblical anthropology, the libertarian view of freedom and the allied concept of radical self-responsibility appear profoundly misguided and overflowing with hubris and self-flattery. They attribute to human beings complete self-possession, sovereign control over their being, and exclusive self-causation of their actions—powers that belong to God alone![30] The libertarian concept of self-determination gives to the one true God no more than historical relevance: God created us and gave us this awesome power. And the idea that we cannot come to possess sincere love for God or render genuine submission to his will unless *as sinners* we possess power to accept or reject any conceivable advance of divine grace makes us the cause, or at least the co-cause, of our salvation. It would take a much lengthier treatment to sustain these critical assertions; however, I will leave that critique for another occasion and focus on two problems that lie closer to the theme of this chapter.[31]

First, theologians who take this approach seem to be satisfied with a bare assertion that Scripture holds sinners responsible for their sin and move quickly to their discussions of freedom. They neglect to ask about the *level* of responsibility Scripture attributes to free human acts. Clearly, Scripture views sinners as blameworthy and liable to punishment, but central to the gospel are repentance, forgiveness of sins, and sanctification. The Scriptures teach that sin is forgivable and sinners are sanctifiable—through God's grace. This understanding of sin and forgiveness presupposes a certain self-investment on the part of

---

29. John Sanders, "God as Personal," in *The Grace of God, the Will of Man: A Case for Arminianism*, ed. Clark Pinnock (Grand Rapids: Zondervan, 1989), 176.

30. Reflection on God's freedom, or aseity, is very relevant to this discussion. See chapter 8 of my book *Great Is the Lord*, 222–54.

31. For a readable critique of the necessity or coherence of rooting human responsibility in autonomous freedom, see Susan Wolf, *Freedom within Reason* (New York: Oxford University Press, 1990), 3–22.

the sinner in his sin. Otherwise, we would not need forgiveness. But this self-investment cannot be an act of absolute self-determination. By definition, such radical acts cannot be forgiven or undone since they express the self definitively.[32] Nowhere in Scripture are sinners described in such Promethean or Miltonian terms, as defiant gods or rebellious angels.

Though it discerns an element of defiance in sin, Scripture also describes the condition from which Christ saves as deception (Rom. 7:11; Titus 3:3), ignorance (Eph. 4:18), slavery (Rom. 6:6; 7:14; John 8:34), blindness (2 Cor. 4:4; 1 John 2:11), misery (Rom. 3:16), corruption (2 Peter 2:10), and death (Eph. 2:1). In each of these conditions, some alien power or defective lack of power blocks the self from true self-determination and self-realization. The power of radical self-determination is not ascribed to human beings in Scripture; it is not even presupposed by Scripture. Jesus' words from the cross, "Father, forgive them, for they do not know what they are doing" (Luke 23:34), are some of the most hopeful words in Scripture. And they clearly refute the notion that possessing a measure of responsibility requires absolute self-determination. You cannot possess such a power if you "do not know" what you are doing.[33] Paul also makes this connection as he reflects on his conversion: "Even though I was once a blasphemer and a persecutor and a violent man, I was shown mercy because I acted in ignorance and unbelief" (1 Tim. 1:13). Paul did these horrible things willingly, but his willingness was coupled with ignorance and unbelief. This ignorant willingness, however, hardly merits the name of freedom,[34] nor does it reveal a "deep" self-responsibility, which entails complete self-knowledge and self-possession. To determine yourself

---

32. See my article "The Freedom to Say 'No'? Karl Rahner's Doctrine of Sin," *Theological Studies* 56 (1995): 485–503. I deal there extensively with Rahner's view of freedom, responsibility, and the possibility of the forgiveness of sins. Rahner defines sin as a free self-determining "no" to God. But how can such a refusal be forgiven and reversed, if it really is free and self-defining? See also my book *Barth and Rahner: Toward an Ecumenical Understanding of Sin and Evil* (New York: Peter Lang, 1989), 99–110.

33. I do not think Jesus meant that those sinners who crucified him had no idea of what they were doing. However, they certainly did not know *fully* what they were doing. Jesus' intersession for their forgiveness assumes that had they known what they were doing, they would not have done it. Responsibility comes in degrees, but we never know fully what we are doing.

34. For a clear distinction between mere willingness (what Bernard calls "freedom from necessity" or "free choice") and genuine freedom (what Bernard calls "freedom from sin" and "freedom from sorrow"), see Bernard of Clairvaux, "On Grace and Free Choice," 53–111.

absolutely for a certain deed requires that you know all the alternatives to that deed and all its consequences. We do not possess such knowledge, and the possibility of repentance (hence, of forgiveness) is rooted in this lack.

There is a second problem with deriving a theory of freedom from the mere idea of moral responsibility. This strategy seeks to derive its understanding of freedom from something not directly addressed by the Scriptures while ignoring the *explicit* teaching of Scripture on the subject of freedom. A Scripture-based theology must allow the explicit teaching of Scripture to set the parameters for any effort to discern its implicit teaching. In those great chapters Romans 6–8, we do not find Paul extolling a natural human freedom to sin or not to sin or to choose between option A and option B. Instead, Paul rejoices in the freedom won for us by Christ and applied to us by the Spirit. He glories in a freedom *from* our settled disposition toward God as enemies, rebels, and ingrates; he delights in our liberation *from* deception, ignorance, slavery, blindness, misery, corruption, and death. The apostle praises God for setting us free through Christ and the Spirit from our sinful way of life in which we blindly chose our way to destruction. For Paul, sin is not something you can stop doing through your own effort and choice, apart from divine help. It is a master from which we need release. And death even more clearly shows itself as something from which we cannot liberate ourselves. It represents all the consequences of sin — corruption of every kind: moral, spiritual, and physical.

In Romans 6 Paul describes sin as a slavemaster who holds us in bondage and drives us to "surrender to ... the concupiscent hunger of self-centered earthly and carnal life."[35] On four occasions in this chapter, the apostle asserts that we have been "freed" from sin (vv. 7, 18, 20, and 22). In chapter 8 he proclaims that we have been freed from "sin and death" through the work of Christ and the Spirit (v. 2).[36] The apostle's words make no sense on the assumption that we possess self-determining freedom as a natural power or can achieve it on our own. In that case, we would be naturally free from sin! According to Robert T. Osborn, "Freedom in the New Testament is not a self-determination

---

35. Heinrich Schlier, "Eleutheros," *Theological Dictionary of the New Testament*, 2:497. Hereafter cited as *TDNT*.

36. "In the Spirit of the freedom of Jesus Christ, there arises our freedom" (*TDNT* 2:499).

but a determination of the self."[37] Our need for a freedom beyond our natural powers becomes clear in Paul's discussion of the law. The law comes to us externally and demands that we obey. According to Paul, we do not, as Rabbinic Judaism taught, possess the natural power to obey or refuse the law's demand. Nor can we, as Stoics maintained, attain freedom by bringing the lower part of the soul under the domination of the higher part. Paul teaches that "even in the retreat into inwardness man is not free."[38] Only Christ and the Spirit can free us from the impossible requirement that we achieve our freedom from sin and death by our own power. What Paul speaks of is "freedom from an existence which in sin leads through the Law to death."[39] We can no more free ourselves from sin than we can raise ourselves from the dead.[40]

For Paul, however, freedom is not merely a negative concept referring only to God's act of removing the alien powers that block our true self-realization. It is also a positive state of full actuality and perfection. In Romans 8 Paul speaks of the glorious freedom of the children of God. Creation itself groans while it waits to be freed from its "bondage to decay and brought into the freedom and glory of the children of God" (v. 21). Paul describes this anticipated liberation as "adoption," "redemption," and salvation (vv. 23–24). The fullness of freedom, then, is not a natural possession or a power acquired through our own efforts. It is a future reality, identical to salvation, redemption, and eternal life, that will be fully realized at the resurrection of the dead. According to Hans Dieter Betz, Paul's "doctrine of salvation is very clearly and consciously formulated as a doctrine of freedom."[41] Genuine freedom is the perfect realization of human nature and destiny, the full flowering of the true self, the "revealing of the sons of God" (Rom. 8:19 ASV). Karl Hermann Schelkle has well said, "The fullness of freedom is a gift reserved for the end. It is liberation from the slavery of the perishable

---

37. Robert T. Osborn, *Freedom in Modern Theology* (Philadelphia: Westminster, 1963), 12.

38. *TDNT* 2:496.

39. Ibid.

40. Jürgen Blunck, "Freedom," *New International Dictionary of New Testament Theology*, ed. Colin Brown (Grand Rapids: Zondervan, 1986), 1:715–20. According to Blunck, Paul teaches that the power to liberate oneself from sin is not "within the realm of his own capacities."

41. Hans Dieter Betz, *Paul's Concept of Freedom in the Context of Hellenistic Discussions about Possibilities of Human Freedom*, Protocol Series of the Colloquies of the Center for Hermeneutical Studies in Hellenism and Modern Culture 26 (Berkeley, Calif.: The Center, 1977), 7.

to the freedom of the glory of the children of God (Rom 8:21)."[42] We participate in this freedom now only as we take on the attitude of the Spirit (Rom. 8:6 TNIV).[43]

Viewing the issue of freedom according to the analogy of faith places our discussion in a new light. In the explicit teaching of the New Testament, the fullness of freedom is not the beginning, but the goal, of human life. It is not the power to choose between this and that or between good and evil; it is the power for, and the actual state of, loving God perfectly and willing his will invariably. The free will we have in the natural state is not adequate for achieving freedom's goal, which is righteousness, holiness, the love of God, and eternal life. Without divine grace, we cannot hope to achieve it. The title of this chapter is "God Controls by Liberating." It could also have been titled "God Liberates by Controlling." For it is clear that Scripture's explicit teaching on freedom asserts that it is only through a sovereign act of God's grace that we can be freed from the guilt and disposition of sin. Scripture does not see God's sovereign grace as a problem for human freedom. Rather, Scripture proclaims it as the only power able to bestow genuine freedom on us!

Now it should be very clear that the *New Testament* view of freedom fits perfectly with a strong view of divine sovereignty. God's providential and saving actions — even when they overrule and defeat our misguided and sinful intentions — are designed to liberate us from sin and death. Even if we cannot explain how God works in providence to accomplish his will perfectly, we can now see that the objection that such a view of providence contradicts human freedom and responsibility — however enticing to philosophical intuition — possesses no biblical warrant.

---

42. Karl Hermann Schelkle, "New Testament Theology: Pauline Theology," in *Encyclopedia of Theology: The Concise Sacramentum Mundi*, ed. Karl Rahner (New York: Seabury Press, 1975), 1078. According to Schelkle, Paul's teaching on freedom is to be understood as within the horizon of Hellenism, "where freedom was regarded as a precious possession and a prize to be sought after in philosophy, ethics and religion.... It was a point at which the world and the gospel met and parted. In the former, in the Stoa, for instance, freedom is won by the wise man's own effort. In the latter it is the gift of the liberating grace of God" (ibid.). See also Max Müller, "Freedom," in *Encyclopedia of Theology: The Concise Sacramentum Mundi*, 542, where he says, "The free man is the man at one with God. Only if he abandons himself to God does he receive himself back as his own personal possession."

43. *TDNT* 2:499. For more on the freedom theme in Paul, see Richard N. Longenecker, *Paul, Apostle of Liberty* (New York: Harper & Row, 1964), 156–80; Lincoln E. Galloway, *Freedom in the Gospel: Paul's Exemplum in 1 Cor 9 in Conversation with the Discourses of Epictetus and Philo* (Leuven: Peeters, 2004).

What about Evil?

If nothing can happen apart from the will of God and God accomplishes his will in all things, does this not mean that everything that happens is the will of God? And if you think everything that happens is the will of God, are you making God responsible for evil or, even stronger, the doer of evil? William Hasker charges that views like mine imply that "God has deliberately chosen to cause all the horrible evils that afflict our world."[44] Clearly, those defending God's complete sovereignty must refute this charge or be defeated by this objection.

This objection gains much of its force by trading on an ambiguity in the word "evil." Hence, we must clarify this first. What do we mean by "evil"? There are two issues here that we ought not to confuse: (1) What is the basic definition of evil? and (2) How do we identify evil concretely? Keeping these two issues in mind, consider the following argument:

> Evil is that which ought not to be.
> God, being perfectly good, never brings into being that which ought not to be.
> But evil happens (here are given examples of horrible violence and innocent suffering).
> Therefore, not everything happens according to the will of God, and the complete divine sovereignty view of providence is defeated.

What can the defender of divine sovereignty say to this argument? Consider first its definition of evil (proposition 1). Let us grant for the moment that evil is that which ought not to be. This definition still leaves unanswered the question of the ground of the distinction between what ought to be and what ought not to be. It grants us no real insight into the ontological difference between good and evil, and it gives no help in identifying concrete evil. It does not clarify the relationship of the God of the Bible to "what ought not to be." Clearly, this definition is not basic enough. Proposition 2 must be granted by every Christian theologian. The third step in the argument identifies concrete evils (proposition 3). Notice here how the argument depends on human beings' possessing the ability to identify real evil by observation

---

44. William Hasker, "A Philosophical Perspective," in Pinnock et al., *Openness of God*, 152.

or experience. The assertion "This case of innocent suffering is evil" is a human judgment about a concrete event. What justifies this verdict?

It seems to me that this conclusion identifies something as evil by how much it offends our natural sensibilities. It designates the violence, suffering, pain, and loss we find dreadful and horrifying as "evil." We simply know that it ought not to be because of how we feel about it. Gregory Boyd asserts this epistemic principle: "Radical evil can be known only when incarnated and experienced concretely." He then relates the gut-wrenching story of Zosia, a little girl who was tortured and killed during the Holocaust. Rejecting "abstract" definitions of evil, Boyd explains, "When I speak of 'evil' throughout this work ... I am referring to every concrete horrifying experience that in various ways *looks and feels* like this one."[45] Boyd claims that evil can be identified by the way it "looks and feels." This way of knowing evil was at the heart of the argument made by Manichaeans and other metaphysical dualists in the patristic era.[46] Gregory of Nyssa pinpoints their mistake when he says, "Such people distinguish good and evil on the basis of sensation, and do not realize that that alone is evil which is alien to what is genuinely good. To judge good and evil on the basis of pain and suffering is appropriate [only] in the case of irrational natures, since by not sharing in intelligence and understanding they are unable to grasp what is genuinely good."[47]

In my view, a doctrine of providence that judges theological truth by the way it "looks and feels" is deeply flawed for at least two reasons.[48] First, it violates an essential principle of the Christian doctrine

---

45. Boyd, *God at War*, 34–35, emphasis added. In *Satan and the Problem of Evil*, Boyd adopts the same strategy for defining evil. There he tells the story of Greta, a seven-year-old girl who was kidnapped, raped, and killed (214–15). For my analysis and critique of Boyd's theodicy, see Ron Highfield, "A Response to Gregory Boyd's Open Theist Solution," *Restoration Quarterly* 45 (2003): 165–80.

46. The role Gregory Boyd gives to Satan (in *God at War* and *Satan and the Problem of Evil*) is strikingly similar to metaphysical "darkness" in Manichaean thought. Even if Satan is a created and fallen being, he performs the role that metaphysical evil plays in dualistic systems. He limits God's sovereignty, crowds his space, corrupts his creation, defeats his will, and spoils his plans. In effect, Satan is the creator of the concrete world in which we live.

47. Gregory of Nyssa, "Address on Religious Instruction," 285.

48. To avoid misunderstanding, I am not saying that evil is not at work in such horrifying events as Zosia's murder. It is. I am criticizing a certain way of claiming knowledge of this fact and a certain carelessness of language that pronounces such events as "evil" without qualification. This way of speaking may satisfy our need to express our horror, but it should not be imported into the doctrine of providence without qualification.

of providence: the doctrine of providence is a doctrine of faith based on Scripture. The above argument boils down to a criticism of a doctrine of faith, using human experience as a norm. Throughout Scripture, we are warned not to draw conclusions about God's goodness, justice, providence, or power from our negative experiences. This criticism of the traditional view of providence recommends that we do just that! It is a faithless substitution of fragmentary human experience for the comfort of the Scriptures. Faith in God's care is not always easy to maintain in the face of suffering and persecution. Scripture never said it would be.

Second, the objection from experience operates with a defective, or at least imprecise, understanding of evil. No moral law exists outside and above God by which we may judge him. God is the moral law in his own being. Though it is correct to say evil is "that which ought not to be," Christian theology must speak more precisely, saying with Karl Barth that evil is a manifestation of that which "God has not willed and does not will and will not will."[49] Whatever God does not will is evil and ought not to be, precisely because he does not will it. And if this is our definition of evil, we can see that any judgment deeming an event to be evil is also a theological claim. We claim to know that God did not will that event. But what gives us the right to identify our feelings with the voice of God?

Now we need to explore how this more precise definition of evil works out in the doctrine of providence. If evil is that which God does not will and God's will is always effective, then evil can have no genuine and lasting being. The Christian tradition of both Western and Eastern theology contends that everything that possesses being is good insofar as it is. As Augustine says, "So every being, even if it is corrupt, insofar as it is a being is good, and insofar as it is corrupt, is evil."[50] Hence, both branches rejected the Gnostic and Manichaean view that evil is a substance (that is, something with a real, independent existence), maintaining rather that it is a defect or perversion in something that

---

49. Barth, *CD* 4/1, 409. Barth uses the term "nothingness" (or *das Nichtiges*) where I use the term "evil." For Barth, "nothingness" is a broad term that includes sin, evil, and death (*CD* 3/3, 310).

50. Augustine, in *The Augustine Catechism: The Enchiridion on Faith, Hope, and Love*, ed. John E. Rotelle, trans. Bruce Harbert (New York: New City Press, 1999), 4.13, p. 43.

is.[51] This view is often misunderstood. The terms "defect," "absence," "privation," and "perversion" do not refer to the intrinsic limits of our created being. It is not evil that we are vulnerable to nonbeing, possess physical bodies, and can experience pain. Nor is it evil that humanity is fallible in its imagination, intellect, will, and action. In other words, it is not evil that creatures are not God and therefore depend on God for being and for all good things. Karl Barth correctly referred to this aspect of creation as its "shadow" side and contended that it is part of the perfection of the creature.[52] Genuine evil is the falseness of the images in the human imagination and the misdirection of the human will. It is the lack of the love of God and neighbor in the human heart.

A second misunderstanding of this view concludes that if evil has no real and lasting being, it is nothing at all and therefore is innocuous. To the contrary, the moral disorder that is evil does as much damage to the soul as the malfunction of disease does to the body, though neither adds a substance to God's creation. According to Scripture, evil plunges the creature into bondage, misery, suffering, and death. And God takes evil with the utmost seriousness, responding to it with punishment and with purgative and redemptive suffering. The very heart of the Christian faith is our belief that the incarnate Son of God won the victory over evil through his vicarious suffering, death, and resurrection. So even though evil is nothing in itself, it is a deadly enemy of creation and therefore an enemy of the Creator.

If evil is nothing in itself, how can there really be *evil* acts, events, or states of affairs? Does my position not imply that they cannot exist? To most people, this seems manifestly absurd. But if I admit that such things really exist and God's will is invariably done in and through them, how can I escape the charge that I am making God the doer of evil? Let us pursue this thought even further. No one denies that acts such as murder, rape, and torture really happen, really exist. And we know murder

---

51. For the Western understanding, see Augustine *Confessions* 7; for the Eastern understanding, see Basil the Great, *God Is Not the Author of Evil* 8: "Do not consider God the cause for the existence of evil, nor imagine evil as having its own existence. For evil is not subsistent the way an animal might be; nor can we see its essence substantiated. For evil is the absence of good ... evil does not have its own subsistence, but it follows upon the wounds of the soul" (quoted in Dumitru Staniloae, *The Experience of God: Orthodox Dogmatic Theology*, vol. 2, *The World: Creation and Deification* [Brookline, Mass.: Holy Cross Orthodox Press, 2000], 148).

52. Barth, *CD* 3/3, 295–302.

is evil because the command "You shall not kill" expresses the will of God.[53] Now, combining these ideas produces a strange situation: God commands that murder not be done, yet since nothing can happen apart from God's creative power, every murder happens because God enables it to occur. Does this not make God responsible for the murder? My answer is no. God does not murder or do any evil. How can this be so?

In ordinary judgments, we speak of some acts as evil, plain and simple, just as we speak of some people as bad or evil. Of course, when we speak of a person as evil, we are not saying that he or she is an evil substance. We mean that this person is so morally defective, possessed, or blinded by evil that he or she seems wholly given over to evil. Because we believe in creation and in the power of divine grace, however, we would not declare such individuals completely beyond reclamation. Likewise, some acts seem purely evil and beyond redemption. But this is no truer of an act than it is of a person.

An act is not a simple thing. It is complex and involves at least five aspects: intention, deliberation, decision, exertion using means, and results.[54] In intention, one imagines a desirable state of affairs. In decision, one breaks off deliberation and commits oneself to work toward this desired state. One then exerts energy and uses means to achieve the end. Finally, the results are achieved as an actual state of affairs. It is important to emphasize that things almost never turn out exactly the way we imagine. We cannot create a new state of affairs from nothing. Our efforts to influence the future are severely limited by our lack of power and knowledge and by the stubbornness of the world within which we work. Even if we are relatively successful in the short term, the final outcome of an action is largely out of our control and unknown, since it will not be fully achieved until the end of history. Hence, the final meaning of an act must be left open as long as history lasts.

---

53. Medieval and post-Reformation Reformed theologians distinguished between several senses of the will of God. Clearly, there is a difference between expressions of the divine will such as "Let there be light," "This night your life will be required of you," or "Lazarus! Come forth!" and "You shall not murder." The first three clearly express the divine intention to bring about a new state of affairs. The latter may have several purposes: to render humanity guilty, for instance, or to enlighten us. For the Reformed view, see Muller, *Post-Reformation Reformed Dogmatics*, 3:432–75.

54. For Aquinas's view of action, see Alan Donagan, "Thomas Aquinas on Human Action," in *The Cambridge History of Later Medieval Philosophy*, ed. Norman Kretzmann, Anthony Kenny, and Jan Pinborg (Cambridge: Cambridge University Press, 1982), 642–54.

From even this commonsense analysis, we can see clearly that an evil intention cannot wholly determine the final outcome or meaning of an act. The complete divine sovereignty view argues that God acts before, in, through, and beyond our acts — even our evil acts — to accomplish his will.[55] I could not act at all if I did not exist, and I exist because God created me. I could do nothing if God were not sustaining me and the world around me during my act. God's empowering of my action throughout its duration is often called "concurrence," or cooperation. If God were not also acting in our acts, we could do nothing. Hence, whatever my act *truly and lastingly* accomplishes is the will of God because it is also the act of God.[56] And even if my act is motivated by a false image and driven by a perverted will, God is not tainted by my evil and his will is not defeated. God's faithfulness and patience in sustaining a person during his evil act does not make God a slave to the person's evil intentions. Nor does God merely sustain and empower human acts while leaving the direction to the human actor in the name of freedom. God leaves the defects of a person's will behind and achieves his will in and through the human agent's actions.[57]

Hence, the doctrine of providence locates the evil aspect of human action, not in the created being of humanity and not in its final results, but rather in the sinfulness of a heart that is bereft of the knowledge of God and the love of God and neighbor. Sin is not God's creature. It has no positive existence, and the false images it projects can never become real. Therefore, God does not do evil when he works in and through and after stupid, ignorant, and evil human acts. God overcomes the stupidity, ignorance, and evil to accomplish his good will perfectly.

---

55. See Alfred Freddoso, "Suarez on God's Causal Involvement in Sinful Acts," in *The Problem of Evil in Early Modern Philosophy*, ed. Elmar Kremer and Michael Latzer (Toronto: University of Toronto Press, 2001), 10–34, for a very sophisticated analysis of divine concurrence with sinful acts from a middle knowledge perspective.

56. The emphasis on "truly and lastingly" is very important. The true meaning of an act cannot be known until all its effects have played out, and this perspective is completely beyond our horizon.

57. The Jesuits argued that God's concurrence empowers human free action but is not efficacious in determining acts. The Dominicans argued that God's concurrence is efficacious in the case of good acts but not in the case of evil acts. I would say it differently. In evil acts, God's concurrence overcomes the evil in the act, not allowing it to be truly and lastingly realized but instead bringing good out of evil. See Freddoso, introduction to *On Divine Foreknowledge* (Molina), 18–19.

I believe this line of thought enables us to say with some inner consistency and biblical faithfulness that God's will is finally accomplished in all things *and* that God never wills or does evil. But a significant issue remains, one that is potentially lethal to my view; and I must face it head-on. What about the question that Ivan stated so powerfully in Dostoevsky's *The Brothers Karamazov*? Is any higher "harmony" worth the suffering of even one child?[58] What about children's cancer wards? What about the children crushed in earthquakes? What about the children beaten to death by abusive adults? What about tsunamis, typhoons, tornados, and famines? What about the human brutality exhibited in wars, ethnic cleansing, and the slave trade? There seems to be no end and no limit to human suffering and cruelty. Let me be quite clear. On my own, of my own wisdom and strength, I have absolutely nothing to offer a weeping world but my tears, my questions and doubts, my embraces, and my suffering.

I have only one hope: that in the suffering, death, and resurrection of Christ, the end of history has been revealed.[59] He took on himself and into his person all the evil and suffering of the world from the beginning to the end. He drank the bitter cup and absorbed the violent blows. And he won the victory for us. The view I am developing here is opposed to Leibniz and others who see the world as a timeless work of visual art, where shadow and light, good and evil, suffering and joy, and sin and righteousness contribute to the perfection of the whole. Nor do I, like Hegel, see good and evil related in a dialectical movement toward perfection. My view of providence is christocentric and unfolds in dramatic, agonistic, and eschatological ways. It does not timelessly survey the world and conclude that it is the best of all possible worlds. Nor does it say that from the end the world will appear to have been perfect all along. It sees in the suffering, death, and resurrection of Christ the drama of history played out.

In Christ's resurrection, we find revealed the final victory over evil and the ultimate destiny of the children of God. In this human being, sin has been atoned for and the consequences of sin have been removed. In him, God brings it about that his will is done on earth as it is in heaven. Human freedom has been set free and redirected toward

---

58. See the section titled "Rebellion" (5.4), in Fyodor Dostoevsky, *The Brothers Karamazov*, trans. Constance Garnett (New York: Barnes & Noble, 1995), 218–27.

59. This revelation is the basis, the only possible basis, of my argument about the nature of evil events and their final and lasting results.

righteousness, and the history of creation and providence has been ful-filled. He is our life, our Savior, and our hope. And he is my paradigm for how God works out his will in all things without doing violence to human freedom or becoming the author of sin and evil.

But before the resurrection came the crucifixion. Scripture teaches that God willed the suffering and death of Christ. Though it was dreadful and horrible for Jesus, surely no Christian would say that the Father's will was evil! God accomplished his will "by the hands of law-less men" (Acts 2:23 ESV). The evil will of Christ's betrayer and mur-derers did not prevent God from accomplishing his good will through their actions. And the evil wills of those who persecute us or the seem-ingly blind forces of nature that crush us cannot prevent our Father in heaven from bringing us to the kingdom he has promised. But we cannot expect to see the end of things with our eyes any more than the Good Friday disciples could anticipate Resurrection Sunday. And to reconstruct the doctrine of providence from a Good Friday perspective would be to abandon the resurrection faith and hope.

Conclusion

I began this chapter with the observation that the Western world is obsessed with freedom and wary of any encroachment on its cherished liberty. Unfortunately, the freedom it seeks is not the glorious liberty Jesus offers, freedom from sin and death. It craves, rather, lordship over itself and power over its circumstances. We live in a culture that sees physical suffering and death as the worst possible evils, to be resisted and protested and avoided at all costs. It cannot comprehend the mind of the writer who sings that one day in the presence of the Lord is worth more than a thousand days anywhere else (Ps. 84:10) or understand the heart of Paul, who declares that "our present sufferings are not worth comparing with the glory that will be revealed in us" (Rom. 8:18). Until we see our true bondage and misery and can cry with the apostle, "Who will rescue me from this body that is subject to death?" (Rom. 7:24), we will not be able to grasp our absolute need of God's grace and providen-tial care. Not until, by God's grace, we long for freedom from sin more than we desire another day of life can we rejoice in the divine providence that controls by liberating and liberates by controlling.

PAUL KJOSS HELSETH

A Kindred Spirit

An air of worship pervades Dr. Highfield's discussion of providence that is both deeply satisfying and profoundly encouraging to those who are jealous to maintain the methodological priority of Scripture in the study of theology. While some might be tempted to write Dr. Highfield off as just another Calvinist whose understanding of God's sovereignty has compromised his otherwise good judgment, in fact he is not trying to be "a good Calvinist" at all. For his theologizing is informed neither by a confessional commitment to the Reformed tradition nor by a "Calvinistic" reading of the text, but by his self-conscious devotion to the analogy of faith. Whatever affinities exist between Dr. Highfield's views and those of Reformed believers generally, they testify not to what some might suggest is Dr. Highfield's unacknowledged Calvinism but to the remarkable like-mindedness that often characterizes believers who recognize that God-honoring theology has much less to do with philosophical speculation than it does with faithful attention to what God has revealed in his Word. As a Reformed believer, my hope for Dr. Highfield is not that he would abandon his methodological commitment to the priority of Scripture and the analogy of faith but that through his careful attention to what the text of Scripture actually says he would come to embrace the Reformed worldview in all of its fullness and affirm with B. B. Warfield that Calvinism is not just another species of theism, religion, and evangelicalism but just theism, religion, and evangelicalism come to full flower. "In Calvinism," Warfield notes in a comment that is sure to rankle those not presently members of the Reformed camp,

> ... objectively speaking, theism comes to its rights; subjectively speaking, the religious relation attains its purity; soteriologically

speaking, evangelical religion finds at length its full expression and its secure stability. Theism comes to its rights only in a teleological conception of the universe, which perceives in the entire course of events the orderly outworking of the plan of God, who is the author, preserver, and governor of all things, whose will is consequently the ultimate cause of all. The religious relation attains its purity only when an attitude of absolute dependence on God is not merely temporarily assumed in the act, say, of prayer, but is sustained through all the activities of life, intellectual, emotional, executive. And evangelical religion reaches stability only when the sinful soul rests in humble, self-emptying trust purely on the God of grace as the immediate and sole source of all the efficiency which enters into its salvation. And these things are the formative principles of Calvinism.[60]

Points of Agreement

Dr. Highfield's discussion of providence is informed by a number of judgments that I am eager to embrace as a Reformed believer. Among those judgments are the following: (1) He believes that "no-risk" views of providence are difficult for many of our contemporaries to take seriously because we live in a culture that has been "bewitched" by the notion of creaturely autonomy. Indeed, he correctly notes that many in the evangelical camp have endorsed an understanding of human freedom that, when considered "in the light of biblical anthropology," is idolatrously "misguided" and "overflowing with hubris and self-flattery." (2) He acknowledges that advocates of no-risk views of providence must concede that "they do not know a way to bring belief in God's perfect lordship into complete harmony with human freedom." Those who take Scripture seriously, he argues, must grant that some things are ultimately inscrutable, and for this reason, they must resist the temptation to transform "revealed myster[ies] into … speculative obscurit[ies]." (3) He maintains that theologians attempting to formulate a distinctively Christian understanding of providence must exhaust the analogy of faith before making "cautious use of speculative methods to probe the

---

60. B. B. Warfield, "Calvinism," in *Calvin and Calvinism*, vol. 5 of *The Works of Benjamin B. Warfield* (1931; repr., Grand Rapids: Baker, 1991), 355.

inherent rationality of the faith." We ought not to confound theology and philosophy by granting methodological priority to philosophical speculation, he reasons, for when we do so, we subvert the authority of Scripture and mistake eisegesis for exegesis. (4) He insists that it is simply unbiblical to pretend that God's "complete sovereignty" and human freedom are inherently incompatible, for he recognizes that because of the fallen condition, "God's freedom and action [must] precede and empower human freedom and action at every point." Failing to take the fallen condition seriously not only obscures the clear biblical teaching that "divine freedom creates and supports human freedom," he reasons, but more important, it opens the door to a Manichaean tendency that subverts the gospel by making us "the cause, or at least the co-cause, of our salvation." Finally, (5) Dr. Highfield affirms that the liberation of those who are in Christ will be fully realized only in the new heavens and the new earth. "The fullness of freedom," he wisely concludes, "... is not a natural possession or a power acquired by our own efforts. It is a future reality, identical to salvation, redemption, and eternal life, that will be fully realized at the resurrection of the dead."

A Methodological Quibble

Although I am obviously very sympathetic with many aspects of Dr. Highfield's discussion of providence, I have a minor though no less real concern about the methodological strategy that informs his analysis. While I understand and appreciate Dr. Highfield's reluctance to transform "revealed myster[ies]" into "speculative obscurit[ies]" by confounding theology and philosophy, I wonder if his reluctance to address the "how" of God's providential relationship to the world that he has made fosters a measure of confusion that, in the end, is largely unnecessary. If I am inferring correctly, Dr. Highfield is a theological determinist who endorses the distinction between primary and secondary causation, and thus he would explain the "how" of God's relationship to the world that he has made in terms of an understanding of concurrence that embraces some form of compatibilism. While he rejects "risk" views of providence because he recognizes that there is "no biblical warrant" for the understanding of creaturely autonomy that those views take for granted, nevertheless he is reluctant explicitly to embrace determinism, the distinction between primary and secondary causation, and compatibilism. For doing so would apparently entail an unwarranted intrusion of philosophy into the realm of theology, a presumptuous attempt to probe the "how" of what is inherently inscrutable.

For the record, I greatly admire Dr. Highfield for his integrity and for his determination not to confound theology and philosophy. I wonder, though, why he is persuaded that endorsing any of the aforementioned stances would constitute an unwarranted philosophical presumption. While it certainly would be presumptuous to pretend that we know, for example, precisely *how* the mystery of compatibilism works, is it really all that presumptuous to say, along with scholars like D. A. Carson and Paul Helm, that compatibilism gives the best account of the biblical teaching on the relationship between the sovereignty of God and human freedom, even if the doctrine itself is not taught explicitly in Scripture, as Helm maintains?[61] After all, if something looks like a duck and walks like a duck and quacks like a duck, is one really engaging in a kind of presumptuous speculation to say that it more than likely is a duck, particularly when that is the general conclusion to which exhausting the analogy of faith leads?

This quibble is particularly relevant to what, at least for me, is some confusion regarding Dr. Highfield's discussion of the problem of evil near the end of his chapter. About midway through his analysis, Dr. Highfield alludes in a footnote to the medieval and Reformed insistence that there are "several senses" in which we can conceive of "the will of God." Yet he does not relate the distinctions between these senses to the problem of evil, most likely because he believes that doing so would confound theology and philosophy and suggest that God is the author of evil in some sense. Instead, he insists that evil is "that which ought not to be," or as Dr. Highfield puts it using the language of Karl Barth, "evil is a manifestation of that which 'God has not willed and does not will and will not will.'" But, I wonder, if "nothing can happen apart from God's creative power," as Dr. Highfield argues, and if evil is "that which ought not to be," as he maintains, then why *is* it? Even if we grant that evil is best understood as a "defect or perversion" in a created reality

---

61. For example, see D. A. Carson, "Reflections on Assurance," in Schreiner and Ware, *The Grace of God, the Bondage of the Will*, 2:405–8; Paul Helm, "Response by Paul Helm [to John Sanders]," in *Perspectives on the Doctrine of God: Four Views*, ed. Bruce A. Ware (Nashville: B&H, 2008), 242.

that is inherently good, it seems that the answer to this question begs for a fuller discussion of "the will of God," particularly when Dr. Highfield later insists that "God's will is finally accomplished in all things" *and* "God never wills or does evil." It is certainly true that discussions of the distinction between, for example, the "hidden" and "revealed" wills of God can get quite technical and can devolve into mere wrangling about words. Is it not conceivable, however, that such discussions could lend needed clarity to Dr. Highfield's understanding of the problem of evil—including his endorsement of Barth—without becoming excessively speculative? If so, then why the reluctance to engage in such a discussion, particularly when—at least as far as Reformed evangelicals are concerned—the distinction between, for example, the "hidden" and "revealed" wills of God flows more or less naturally out of the attempt to take everything that Scripture says about "the will of God" seriously?[62]

Conclusion

No matter how Dr. Highfield might respond to this methodological challenge, I want to make it clear how much I appreciate his work, and I want to emphasize how eager I am to stand with him in his concluding reminder to those who would do God-honoring Christian theology in an age that is "obsessed with freedom." "Until we see our true bondage and misery and can cry with the apostle, 'Who will rescue me from this body that is subject to death?' (Rom. 7:24)," he wisely reminds us, "we will not be able to grasp our absolute need of God's grace and providential care. Not until, by God's grace, we long for freedom from sin more than we desire another day of life can we rejoice in the divine providence that controls by liberating and liberates by controlling."

---

62. For a good discussion of the distinction between the hidden, or "decretive," and the revealed, or "preceptive," wills of God, see, e.g, Turretin, *Institutes of Elenctic Theology*, 1:220–22.

WILLIAM LANE CRAIG

So far as I can tell, Ron Highfield does not advocate a view different from that of Paul Kjoss Helseth, so that we have, in fact, only
three rather than four views represented in our book. He, like Helseth, affirms universal, divine, causal determinism along with a compatibilistic view of human freedom.[63] Most of what I say in response
to Helseth's contribution applies to Highfield's paper and need not be
repeated here. I shall restrict myself to comments on a few of Highfield's defenses of his position.

Highfield's fundamental contention is that "God accomplishes
his will in all things." As for why he embraces such a view, he says,
"What clinches my belief in God's comprehensive sovereignty ... is its
coherence with a Scripture-based, God-honoring doctrine of God." He
warns:

> Denying God's comprehensive control requires ... revising the doc-
> trine of God to be consistent with the assertion that God cannot
> create whatever he wants or accomplish whatever he chooses. You
> will have to limit God's power, knowledge, presence, freedom, and
> wisdom; you will have to make God subject to time and space and
> change. And these moves will sooner or later lead to the conclusion
> that God is limited in his eternal being, his very essence.

Is that true? I agree with Highfield that open theism's doctrine of providence is very difficult to square with Scripture on the whole, but the
same cannot be said of Molinism, given that Scripture does not pro-

---

63. Although Highfield says next to nothing about how God controls everything that happens, his commitment to universal determinism, as well as to human freedom, is evident in his
remark that some theologians, with whom he disagrees, "argue that God cannot simply 'cause'
human freedom to do his will freely. For them, the idea of a caused free act is as contradictory
as the concept of a square circle."

nounce on whether God brings things to pass only by strongly actualizing states of affairs or also by weakly actualizing states that involve human free choices.[64] It is correct that Molinism holds that God cannot create whatever he wants or accomplish whatever he chooses, since some possible worlds are infeasible for God. So he is not free to create just any world he pleases. But I deny that that places any nonlogical limit on his power, any more than does his inability to create a married bachelor.[65] Nor is he limited in his knowledge, presence, or wisdom or thereby subject to time, space, or change. Thus, Molinism does not in any way limit God's essential attributes. On the contrary, it is Highfield's and Helseth's view that limits God's essence by impugning his essential goodness and wisdom. For according to universal divine determinism, God makes people sin and then punishes them for it, and the world becomes a farcical charade. Such a view is neither faithful to the full testimony of Scripture nor honoring of God.

Molinism requires that we draw a distinction between God's absolute intentions and his conditional intentions. His absolute intention is that all persons be saved and come to a knowledge of the truth. But due to human freedom and obstinacy, that absolute intention is frustrated. God's conditional intention is to save certain persons and bring about certain events without abrogating human freedom, and God's conditional intentions are always fulfilled. Thus, while God's absolute will is not accomplished, his permissive will is. Such an understanding is faithful to Scripture's witness to the universal salvific will of God and the tragic fact that many persons will be damned. Calvinism cannot really take seriously Scripture's testimony to God's universal salvific will.

Highfield recognizes that "many evangelical theologians would agree that God works ... in complete gratuity in creation, incarnation, and salvation.... But when it comes to providence ... some theologians ... argue that God cannot simply 'cause' human freedom to do his will freely." Right; they reject compatibilism. Here is an argument for that conclusion.

---

64. See my response to Helseth.

65. See Thomas P. Flint and Alfred J. Freddoso, "Maximal Power," in *The Existence and Nature of God*, ed. Alfred J. Freddoso (Notre Dame: University of Notre Dame Press, 1983), 81–113.

1. An agent S is morally responsible for an action A only if doing A is ultimately up to S.
2. A is ultimately up to S only if determinism is false.
3. Therefore, S is morally responsible for A only if determinism is false.

So how does Highfield respond to such an argument? First, he denounces libertarian freedom: "In the light of biblical anthropology, the libertarian view of freedom and the allied concept of radical self-responsibility appear profoundly misguided and overflowing with hubris and self-flattery. They attribute to human beings complete self-possession, sovereign control over their being, and exclusive self-causation of their actions—powers that belong to God alone!"

This sort of response misfires, not merely because it represents a tendentious reading of Scripture, but more fundamentally because the argument for the incompatibility of determinism and free will does not presume that there is free will. The above argument could be put forward by the determinist who denies that human freedom exists (indeed, one wonders why his view is not represented in this book!). Incompatibilists, then, may be either libertarians or determinists.[66]

More to the point, Highfield seems to deny premise 1 on the grounds that libertarian freedom is inconsistent with responsibility. He denies that "possessing a measure of responsibility requires absolute self-determination." I found his argument for this denial simply astonishing. Highfield argues that God's forgiving our sins is dependent on our not being fully responsible for those sins. The possibility of repentance and forgiveness is rooted in our ignorance of "all the alternatives to that deed and all its consequences." Had we sinned with full knowledge of the alternatives and the consequences, then "such radical acts cannot be forgiven or undone since they express the self definitively."

This denial of the power of God's grace and the efficacy of Christ's atonement is very disturbing and will be, I hope, repudiated by every other contributor to this volume. Of course, had Highfield given some reason to think that acts that "express the self definitively" are unforgivable, that would be something with which to grapple. But he merely asserts it.

---

66. As I was recently reminded by my assistant and former grad student Shaun McNaughton.

Not only so, but how does his point work to refute the argument? If our deeds are forgivable because they are to some extent due to factors outside our control, that only reinforces the claim that one is morally responsible for an act only to the extent that the act is up to that person. To the degree that it is not, one is exonerated and may be forgiven. If one were utterly determined to do the act, one would be completely non-culpable. Hence, Highfield's objection actually supports the argument for the incompatibility of freedom and determinism.

Highfield's second objection to the argument for the incompatibility of freedom and determinism is that it derives its understanding of freedom from something other than Scripture. According to the New Testament, freedom in all its fullness "is not the power to choose between this and that or between good and evil; it is the power for, and the actual state of, loving God perfectly and willing his will invariably." This scriptural doctrine of full freedom, however, is not relevant to this argument. The argument does not try to give a positive account of full freedom but simply attempts to show that moral responsibility is incompatible with determinism. Highfield's comments neither have relevance nor do anything to defeat the argument's conclusion. If full freedom is compatible with determinism, then it excludes moral responsibility.

Finally, Highfield attempts to come to grips with the claim that universal divine determinism makes God responsible for evil. I agree with Highfield that one cannot assume that so-called natural evils are really evil and "ought not to be." Suffering is not necessarily evil. But let us therefore stick with moral evil as our point of contention, sins that we commit. Since Highfield thinks that God's will is invariably done and nothing escapes his will, it follows that God wills moral evil and even causes it to occur. Given that that is impossible, there must be no moral evil. Here is an argument to that effect.

1. Nothing that God unconditionally wills is evil.
2. God wills unconditionally everything that happens.
3. Therefore, nothing that happens is evil.

The Molinist escapes this argument by denying premise 2. Sinful acts are willed only conditionally by God. But Highfield affirms both premises and is therefore logically committed to denying that anything that happens is evil, an unscriptural and evidently false conclusion.

Incredibly, but consistently, Highfield appears to embrace 3.[67] He says, "If evil is that which God does not will and God's will is always effective, then evil can have no genuine and lasting being." One cannot mollify this conclusion by saying that God will do away with evil or that evil is a privation with no positive being. I am not claiming anything about the ontological status of evil as such but just affirming that people do act sinfully, contrary to 3. Highfield has to deny that people act sinfully.

Highfield seems to appreciate the difficulty in which this puts him: "If evil is nothing in itself, how can there really be *evil* acts, events, or states of affairs? Does my position not imply that they cannot exist? To most people, this seems manifestly absurd. But if I admit that such things really exist and God's will is invariably done in and through them, how can I escape the charge that I am making God the doer of evil?"

How, indeed? Highfield tries to break down a sinful action into various aspects, such as intention, deliberation, decision, exertion, and results. He points out that acts committed with evil intention can result in God's will being done, a point no one would care to dispute. But Highfield recognizes that evil intentions do occur. He says, "The doctrine of providence locates the evil aspect of human action, not in the created being of humanity and not in its final results, but rather in the sinfulness of a heart that is bereft of the knowledge of God and the love of God and neighbor. Sin is not God's creature. It has no positive existence, and the false images it projects can never become real."

Clearly, this answer will not suffice. For in universal divine determinism, the intention, the deliberation, the decision, and the exertion are all caused by God to occur. God is therefore the source of evil. Highfield tries to escape this result by saying, "In evil acts, God's concurrence overcomes the evil in the act, not allowing it to be truly and lastingly realized but instead bringing good out of evil." Alas, this is all to no avail: of course, God can bring a good result out of evil, but the evil intent and decision are not therefore somehow rendered morally neutral so that sin becomes an illusion. Highfield's view that God determines everything that happens leads to the conclusion either that moral evil and sin are illusory or that God is the source of evil.

---

67. Ironically thereby frustrating Highfield's aspiration, "I do not want to sacrifice even one biblical truth to make a theological system more internally consistent."

Finally, I have to say that I am troubled by what seems to me an incipient irrationalism in Highfield's approach to theology. He offers almost no account of how God sovereignly controls the universe, much less how such control is compatible with human freedom. He excuses himself because "God's nature and his relationship to the world are ultimately incomprehensible by human reason." While allowing that "it is possible to achieve some rational insight" into divine providence, he is afraid of allowing "biblically based theology to be overwhelmed by speculative metaphysics or logic or psychology or 'passion for systematic consistency.'" He insists that

> before Christian theologians take up the role of metaphysicians or logicians or psychologists, they should exhaust the method evangelicals ought to hold nearest to their hearts: the analogy of the faith. With this method, obscure elements of the faith are laid beside clearer parts. And each scriptural teaching is understood in the light of every other. Only after this method has been exhaustively applied should we feel free to make cautious use of speculative methods to probe the inherent rationality of the faith.

If the admonition here is simply to do careful biblical theology prior to engaging in systematic theology, then such advice is unremarkable. We evangelicals all agree with such a procedure. But it is hard not to detect here a certain distrust of logical analysis and philosophical reflection, which is both unfortunate and naïve: unfortunate because it would deprive us of the insights such reflection might bring and naïve because such methods are already from the start quietly at work when one does biblical exegesis and theology. While we may not be able to explain how God providentially governs the world, we can at least provide models of such governance that show the logical coherence of the Christian worldview — a project that Highfield admits exceeds the capacity of Reformed theology.

GREGORY A. BOYD

I applaud Highfield's attempt to sustain a christocentric methodology as well as his obvious, earnest desire to articulate a view of providence that honors God and reflects his Word. Yet I believe there are some serious problems with the thesis he articulated and defended in his essay. I will group my criticisms around three topics: Highfield's inadequate and confusing views on freedom, an incoherence I find in Highfield's central thesis, and Highfield's inadequate handling of the problem of evil.

Issues Related to Freedom

I have three closely related issues regarding Highfield's various comments on the nature of freedom.[68] The first concerns the role of free will in salvation. I am in full agreement with Highfield when he argues that the God-appointed end of our freedom of choice is eventually to give way to a much more beautiful form of freedom: the freedom to love God and to be conformed to the image of Christ. Highfield correctly notes that *this* is the freedom Paul and other New Testament authors celebrate. Moreover, I wholeheartedly agree with Highfield that we never could have entered this "fullness of freedom" by our own power of choice. Without the liberating empowerment of the Holy Spirit, we are dead in our sin (Eph. 2:1, 5).

Where Highfield and I part ways, however, is that I do not see how this highest form of freedom could be characterized as a freedom for

---

68. Highfield's use of the term "freedom" is at times confusing, largely because he uses the term in at least three distinct senses without ever clearly indicating which sense he means. Sometimes the term refers to a person's freedom to love God and be free from sin—what Highfield calls the "fullness of freedom" or "genuine freedom." Other times he uses the term in a compatibilistic sense, referring to a person's freedom to choose what they want. And still other times Highfield uses the term to refer to libertarian freedom, which he of course rejects. I feel this pervasive ambiguity makes his essay more challenging to follow than is necessary.

genuine love of God if the process that led up to it was itself exhaustively controlled by God. Love that is not chosen is not, in my view, genuine love. Related to this, I see no scriptural or rational reasons why we should see the liberating empowerment of the Holy Spirit as *all-controlling*. It is one thing to grant that we who are dead in sin cannot love God *without* the Holy Spirit, and quite a different thing to say that *with* the Holy Spirit we who are being liberated *must* love God. So far as I can see, Scripture consistently teaches the first but never teaches the second. To the contrary, we are repeatedly encouraged to *yield* to the Spirit rather than *resist* or *suppress* the Holy Spirit.[69]

Second, as is to be expected given his deterministic convictions, Highfield is no fan of "the libertarian view of freedom." He believes this concept is driven by the modern need to be autonomous and self-determining. "We want control," he argues, "and we insist that controlling ourselves and our circumstances accompanies any meaningful liberty." This view, he argues, is "profoundly misguided and overflowing with hubris and self-flattery."[70]

Now, for all I know, Highfield may be correct in alleging that some people embrace libertarian freedom because they are "overflowing with hubris and self-flattery." But so far as I can discern, my own motives as well as the motives of all the Christians I know who espouse libertarian freedom are centered on biblical, theological, and philosophical considerations. It might have been more helpful if Highfield had focused his critique on these considerations rather than resorting to an *ad hominem* argument.

I also find it hard to accept Highfield's argument that the concept of libertarian freedom is a modern, prideful, humanistic idea. The early church uniformly and emphatically defended free will against all forms of determinism and held that evil originates in the misuse of these wills, not in a mysterious plan of God. Only with Augustine in

---

69. E.g., Isa. 63:10; Gal. 5:16; Eph. 4:30; 1 Thess. 5:19.

70. It does not help that Highfield imagines that libertarian freedom "attributes to human beings *complete* self-possession, sovereign control over their being, and *exclusive* self-causation of their actions—powers that belong to God alone!" (emphasis added). I am quite certain that all philosophically trained defenders of libertarian freedom would agree with me that this is a caricature of libertarian freedom. A person's freedom cannot even be theoretically isolated from the myriad of physical, social, psychological, and spiritual factors that influence a person moment to moment.

the fifth century do we find Christians embracing a Stoic, compatibilistic understanding of freedom and espousing a Stoic-type theodicy that contended that evil was part of God's grand plan.

Third, Highfield frequently expresses his compatibilistic understanding of freedom by saying things like, "God works before, through, with, inside, around, and after human working to accomplish his will." Hence, he holds, humans are free and yet God accomplishes exactly what he wills in and through us. When one considers some of the demented and diabolic ways humans have freely acted, the thought that God was meticulously accomplishing his will through them is rather disturbing, especially when we remember that Highfield contends that God controls *by liberating*. What is liberating about the God-controlled activity of Hitler, Stalin, or Pol Pot? This leads to the second major point I want to make in response to Highfield's essay.

A Foundational Incoherence

As the title of his essay suggests, Highfield's thesis is that divine providence "controls by liberating." At the same time, Highfield believes God exercises "comprehensive sovereignty," which for him means, "God controls the world comprehensively." Nothing happens outside of God's will. My fundamental difficulty with Highfield's essay is that I frankly do not see how these two theses are compatible.

If God controls by liberating while also controlling everything, should not everything be liberated? Even more fundamentally, if God controls by liberating while controlling everything, how is it that anything or anyone ever *needs* liberating in the first place? Where did bondage come from? And does God control whatever it is that we and creation are in bondage to? If yes, it seems that at least one thing violates the thesis that God controls *by liberating*. If no, it seems that at least one thing violates the thesis that God controls *everything*. Either way, I cannot see how Highfield's position is internally consistent.

In various ways, this foundational incoherence crops up throughout Highfield's essay. For example, Highfield rightly argues that without "divine help," we cannot free ourselves from our sin. Sin "is a master from which we need release." I could not agree more. Yet, based on the assumption that God controls everything, there would be no such master from which we need releasing *unless God willed it*. I thus must wonder, once again, how Highfield can claim God controls *by* liberating when God also controls the bondage *from which* we need to be liberated.

Similarly, Highfield argues, "God's providential and saving actions—even when they overrule and defeat our misguided and sinful intentions—are designed to liberate us from sin and death." Yet it is not clear why God should need providentially to "overrule" and "defeat" anything if everything is already providentially controlled by God. Nor is it clear to me how Highfield can claim that all God's providential actions are liberating when they include preserving in existence the sin and death from which God seeks to liberate us. In this light, it seems to me Highfield should have titled his essay "God Controls by Oppressing *in Order to* Liberate," though, so far as I can see, even this modified thesis would be acceptable only if Highfield embraced universalism.

The Nature of Evil

The foundational incoherence I find in Highfield's position is most clearly evidenced in his discussion of evil. For example, at one point Highfield says, "Whatever God does not will is evil and ought not to be, precisely because he does not will it." This is a decent (though abstract) definition of evil.[71] Yet I cannot conceive of how anything can exist that God does *not* will if everything that exists does so only *because* God wills it, as Highfield argues.

For a moment I wondered if Highfield was going to suggest that evil does not exist, which, so far as I can see, is the only logical conclusion available to him. He came close when he argued that "evil can have no genuine and lasting being" and "evil has no real ... being." Now, I cannot pretend to know what Highfield means by denying that evil has "genuine" or "real" being, for I frankly cannot form a clear conception in my mind of what would constitute "disingenuous" and "unreal" being. So far as I can see, being is simply *being*. Whatever Highfield might

---

71. In *God at War*, I argue that abstract definitions of evil never capture the essence of evil. I thus give a concrete nonfictional illustration of evil involving a little Jewish girl who had her eyes plucked out by Nazi soldiers. Highfield argued that my argument "boils down to a criticism of a doctrine of faith [viz., his understanding of providence], using human experience as a norm." It is, he says, "a faithless substitution of fragmentary human experience for the comfort of the Scriptures." I am puzzled as to why Highfield views my concrete *illustration* as a *norm* against which his deterministic doctrine of providence falls short, especially when Highfield explicitly acknowledges his *agreement* that my illustration constitutes an evil.

mean, however, I struggle to see how evil can exist at all if the all-good God controls everything, let alone controls everything "by liberating."

My confusion was hardly lessened when Highfield went on to insist that it would be a mistake to conclude that since "evil has no real and lasting being, it is nothing at all and therefore is innocuous." To the contrary, Highfield argues, "The moral disorder that is evil does as much damage to the soul as the malfunction of disease does to the body, though neither adds a substance to God's creation." Now, I again cannot begin to guess at what Highfield might mean when he denies that evil is "nothing at all" while affirming that evil "has no real and lasting being." How does "no real ... being" differ from "nothing at all"? Nor can I guess what Highfield might intend to communicate by denying that the evil of moral disorder and of physical disease "adds a substance to God's creation." What does adding a "substance" to "God's creation" mean — especially if the "substance" has "no real ... being"? What really puzzles me, however, is how the damage done to the soul or body can be evil when God controls both, and nothing controlled by God can be evil. To the contrary, everything God controls (that is, everything) is supposed to be liberating.

My confusion was not alleviated when I later came upon Highfield's argument that "even though evil is nothing in itself, it is a deadly enemy of creation and therefore an enemy of the Creator." I again confess to having no idea what Highfield means when he says evil is "nothing in itself" and yet is "a deadly enemy." I honestly cannot get clear on what it means to say that something (?) is "nothing in itself," still less what it means to say that something (?) that is "nothing in itself" can relate to everything else as an "enemy." But what really baffles me is how "something" (?) that is "nothing in itself" could ever be "an enemy of the Creator" when the Creator is said to control everything (by liberating!), for it seems to me that everything must include even things that are "nothing in itself." To his credit, Highfield acknowledges that "to most people this seems manifestly absurd," and I readily count myself among this majority.

Highfield concludes his essay by claiming, "Not until, by God's grace, we long for freedom from sin more than we desire another day of life can we rejoice in the divine providence that controls by liberating and liberates by controlling." I would like to claim I long to be free from sin more than I desire another day of life, though I honestly doubt that this is altogether true. But I am also quite certain this has little to do with my inability to rejoice "in the divine providence that controls by liberating and liberates by controlling." My inability, rather, is rooted in the simple fact that I honestly cannot get a clear idea of what Highfield means when he asserts this.

GOD LIMITS HIS CONTROL

GREGORY A. BOYD

Few theological topics have more practical significance than the topic of divine providence. How we understand the nature of providence affects how we understand God and the role we play in his plan. It also directly affects how we interpret suffering and evil in the world and thus how we minister to hurting people. And it obviously affects the level of hope, courage, and peace we have as we live in this world that sometimes feels as if it is spinning out of control. In short, this is an extremely important topic, and I feel honored to be given the opportunity to share my thoughts on it.

In what follows I will first lay out my understanding of the proper starting point for our reflections on providence and the criteria by which I think any proposed Christian model of providence should be assessed. I will then flesh out and defend the model of providence that I believe best meets these criteria. I will label this "the open model of providence" since its most distinctive feature is its assertion that the future is, to some extent, open, consisting of possibilities rather than a single, eternally settled story line. And I will conclude by arguing that the open model best meets the criteria for an adequate model of providence, though space limitations force me to reserve much of my critique of competing providential models to the response sections of this book.

Starting with Jesus

The Christocentric Starting Point

It is my conviction that all theological reflection must begin with Jesus and be carried out with a focus on Jesus. He is the one and only eternal

Word of God (John 1:1), the only perfect image of God (Col. 1:15), and the only "exact representation" of God's essence (*hypostasis*; Heb. 1:3). All the fullness of God was embodied in the Son (Col. 2:9; cf. 1:19). Hence, when we see Jesus, we see God the Father (John 14:7–9). As Paul says, "The light of the knowledge of the glory of God [is displayed] in the face of Christ" (2 Cor. 4:6 ESV; cf. 1 John 1:1–3). Jesus even goes so far as to claim that "*no one* knows the Father *except the Son* and those to whom the Son chooses to reveal him" (Matt. 11:27, emphasis added; cf. 1 John 2:23).

There is no reason to think a christocentric starting point is any less crucial for our reflections on divine providence than for any other topic. Indeed, Jesus is the one *through whom* everything came to be, *by whom* everything continues to be held together, and *for whom* everything exists.[1] How could we not expect to find in him the key to understanding the nature of God's governance of the world? Of course, as with every other topic, we must allow the whole counsel of Scripture to inform our reflection. Yet, as Luther so clearly understood, Jesus is the centerpiece of Scripture.[2] Hence, Scripture must be interpreted through the lens of Christ (see John 5:39–47; Luke 24:25–27, 44).

In light of this, I propose four christocentric criteria by which models of divine providence should be assessed.

God Wages Spiritual Warfare

As I have argued elsewhere, from his deliverance and healing ministry to his countercultural lifestyle, radical kingdom teachings, and voluntary crucifixion, everything Jesus was about centered on manifesting the reign of God against forces of evil that oppose God (namely, the Devil, principalities and powers, demons).[3] While there is never a question whether these foes will be ultimately vanquished by the work of Christ,

---

1. Col. 1:15–17; cf. John 1:1–3; 1 Cor. 8:6; Eph. 3:9–10; Heb. 1:2–3; 10.

2. As Luther famously quipped to Erasmus, "Take Christ out of the Scriptures, and what will you find remaining in them?" Martin Luther, *The Bondage of the Will* [1525], in *Luther's Works*, ed. J. Pelikan and H. Lehmann, 55 vols. (Philadelphia: Fortress; St. Louis: Concordia, 1955–1986), 33:26.

3. See Gregory A. Boyd, "The Christus Victor View," in *The Nature of the Atonement*, ed. J. Beilby and P. Eddy (Downers Grove, Ill.: InterVarsity Press, 2005), 23–49; idem, *God at War*, 171–268. On Jesus' life as a sustained revolt against the powers, see idem, "The Kingdom as a Socio-Political Spiritual Revolution," *Criswell Theological Review* 6, no. 1 (Fall 2008): 23–42.

it is also perfectly clear in the Gospels, as throughout the entire Bible, that these cosmic foes genuinely resist the reign of God and exercise a formidable destructive influence in the world today.[4] In this light, I believe that the ability of a proposed model of providence to render intelligible the reality and scope of evil in the world and the need for God to battle against it should constitute a central criterion by which it is judged to be acceptable or not.

God Relies on Power and Wisdom

It goes without saying that God sometimes relies on sheer power to overthrow his cosmic enemies and to accomplish his purposes. This superior power is displayed in Jesus' "power encounters" with demons, in his healing ministry and nature miracles (e.g., multiplying food and calming a storm), and especially in his resurrection. Hence, viable models of providence must ascribe to God the level of power needed to accomplish these things.

Yet, as important as God's power is, Christ's display of superior power in overthrowing enemies is actually the *least* distinctive aspect of his revelation of God. Indeed, reflecting our fallen inclination to worship power over others, pagans throughout history have tended to equate greatness with power. The more power a god has, pagans have typically assumed, the greater the god must be. What distinguishes the revelation of God in Christ from pagan views is that God *does not* rely primarily on power to conquer his spiritual foes.

In allowing the cosmic powers as well as wicked humans to crucify him, Jesus revealed that God also relies on his *superior wisdom*. In his wisdom, which he purposely kept "secret" and "hidden" throughout the ages (e.g., 1 Cor. 2:7; Eph. 3:9), God allowed the powers to help orchestrate Jesus' crucifixion (John 13:27; 1 Cor. 2:6–8), knowing that it was by this means that these forces of evil would bring about their own demise (Col. 2:14–15; cf. Heb. 2:14; 1 John 3:8).[5] Not only this, but by this same wisdom, the wicked intentions of humans played into

---

4. For example, John claims that "the whole world is under the control of the evil one" (1 John 5:19; cf. John 12:32; 14:30; 16:11; 2 Cor. 4:4; Eph. 2:2). See Boyd, *God at War*.

5. That God kept his wise plans hidden explains why, throughout Jesus' ministry, demons recognized *who Jesus is* but had no clue *why he had come to earth* (Mark 1:24; 3:11; 5:7; Luke 8:21). For a fuller discussion, see Boyd, "Christus Victor View," 36–38.

God's plan in bringing about Christ's crucifixion (Acts 2:23; 4:28). In this light, I believe that any proposed model of providence that hopes to be considered viable for followers of Jesus must be able to render intelligible why God often relies on his superior wisdom to defeat foes and accomplish his purposes.

God Relies on Other-Oriented Love

As distinctive as God's reliance on wisdom is, the *most* distinctive aspect of the revelation of God in Christ is Jesus' demonstration that God relies on love to defeat foes and accomplish his purposes. More than anything else, it was the perfect love of God revealed in the incarnation, ministry, and self-sacrificial death of Jesus that in principle defeated evil. As he commands us to do, God overcame evil not with violence but by suffering violence on Calvary for the sake of love (1 Peter 2:20–23; cf. Rom. 12:17–21). This is the very definition of the kind of love that God eternally is (1 John 4:8, 10; cf. 3:16) and the kind of love that followers of Jesus are commanded to express to all people, including our enemies (Luke 6:27–35; cf. Eph. 5:1–2). In this light, I believe that plausible models of providence must have at their center a God whose eternal nature is other-oriented, self-sacrificial love, as revealed in Jesus, and must render intelligible God's reliance on other-oriented love to defeat evil and accomplish his purposes.

Yet there is another facet of God's love that is centrally important for a Christian understanding of divine providence. Jesus reveals that God is a loving community of three divine persons. Moreover, that Jesus was fully human reveals that God wants to embrace humans in this loving divine community and carry out his purposes in the world in community with humans. Indeed, Jesus revealed that God's desire is for the human community to participate in and reflect the perfect loving community of the triune God (see, e.g., John 17:20–26).

A central aspect of this participation, as revealed in Christ, is that the God of communal love empowers humans genuinely to affect him. The cross reveals this from God's side, as the one who is fully God suffered out of love at the hands of those for whom he died. And Jesus' prayer in Gethsemane reveals this from the human side, as the one who is fully human asked if it was possible for the Father to alter the divine plan and accomplish the mission in some way that avoided the hellish spiritual and physical agony of the cross (Matt. 26:39). In this particular instance, of course, it was not possible. Yet this prayer — by the only one who truly knows the Father (Matt. 11:27) — reveals that God is in principle open to modifying his plans in response to human input, as we find him doing throughout the biblical narrative (e.g., Ex. 32:12–14).[6] In this light, I believe that any model of providence that hopes to be considered plausible by followers of Jesus must be able to render intelligible the loving, communal way God operates in the world as well as God's loving willingness to be affected and influenced by humans.

God Wins by Bringing Good Out of Evil

Finally, the resurrection of Jesus demonstrates that, as formidable as God's cosmic foes are, *he wins in the end*. In fact, through Jesus' life, death, and resurrection, God has in principle *already* won and *already* accomplished all of his purposes for creation.[7] Displaying his power, wisdom, and love, God brought the ultimate good of a restored creation and a redeemed people out of the evil of what was done to Christ on Calvary. It is now just a matter of time before God will bring unity to all things in heaven and earth under the lordship of Christ (Eph. 1:10; cf. Col. 1:20). In this light, I believe that any model of divine providence that hopes to be considered viable by followers of Jesus must be able to render intelligible God's ability to bring good out of evil and ultimately defeat evil and accomplish his overall purposes for creation.

The Open Model of Providence

I will now flesh out the open model of providence that I believe best meets the four christocentric criteria just outlined.[8]

---

6. Other classic examples of God changing his mind in response to human activity are Ex. 33:1–3, 14; Deut. 9:13–29; 1 Sam. 2:27–31; 1 Kings 21:21–29; 2 Chron. 12:5–8; Jer. 18:7–10; 26:2–3; Ezek. 4:9–15; Amos 7:1–6; Jonah 3:10. John Sanders offers an insightful discussion of this motif in *The God Who Risks*, 48–84. For a popular-level discourse on this theme by one of the world's most famous evangelists ("God's Smuggler"), see Brother Andrew, *And God Changed His Mind* (Grand Rapids: Chosen, 1999).

7. The qualifier "in principle" is necessary because, obviously, we do not yet experience everything that Christ accomplished (see Heb. 2:7–9). We live in between the "already" and the "not yet" of God's eternal kingdom on earth.

8. While there is a good deal of agreement regarding the nature of divine providence among open theists, there are also significant differences. Hence, it should not be assumed that I speak for all open theists as I develop my open model of providence. For a sampling of other openness perspectives on themes related to divine providence, see Sanders, *God Who*

Love and Freedom

As noted above, Jesus has revealed that God is other-oriented love. This means that everything he does is motivated by love. Hence, according to the open view, God created the world as an expression of his love and for the purpose of inviting others to share in his love.[9] This is reflected in Scripture's proclamation that all things were made *by* and *for* Jesus Christ, the one who incarnates God's love and who alone perfectly expresses God's eternal, loving nature (Heb. 1:2–3). More specifically, as it concerns humans, the purpose for creation is for us to receive and reflect God's love by being incorporated into Christ.[10] Before the creation of the world, God predestined that he would acquire a people—a "bride"—who would receive the Father's perfect love for the Son and participate in the Son's perfect love for the Father. In other words, God's anthropological purpose in creating the world was to express his eternal nature (that is, "glorify himself") by sharing his eternal, other-oriented, triune love with us.[11]

If love is the goal of creation, however, then the creation must include free agents, according to the open view. As the early church uniformly understood, for contingent beings such as humans, love (as well as every other moral virtue) must be freely chosen.[12] Had God created us such that we *had* to love, our love could not be genuine.

Risks; William Hasker, *The Triumph of God over Evil* (Downers Grove, Ill.: InterVarsity Press, 2008); Richard Rice, *God's Foreknowledge and Man's Free Will* (Minneapolis: Bethany House, 1985); Peter Geach, *Providence and Evil* (Cambridge: Cambridge University Press, 1977); Clark Pinnock, *Most Moved Mover* (Grand Rapids: Paternoster/Baker Academic, 2001); and Michael Saia, *Does God Know the Future?* (Fairfax, Va.: Xulon, 2002). Particularly noteworthy is the recent intriguing use Alan Rhoda has made of game theory to discuss issues related to providence in "Beyond the Chess Master Analogy: Game Theory and Divine Providence," in Oord, *Creation Made Free*. Other essays by advocates of open theism in *Creation Made Free* are pertinent to this topic as well.

9. Thomas Oord justifiably argues that open theology is first and foremost a "theo-logic [*sic*] of love" ("An Open Theology Doctrine of Creation and Solution to the Problem of Evil," in Oord, *Creation Made Free*, 28–52).

10. The classical expression of the "in Christ" motif, which in fact permeates all of Paul's writings, is Eph. 1:3–14.

11. This motif is beautifully expressed in Christ's prayer in John 17:20–26. It is worth noting that this prayer arguably refutes the typical Reformed view that God's "glory" refers to his sovereignty (understood as meticulous control), for Jesus says he gave his disciples the "glory" the Father had given him (v. 22). My thanks to Paul Eddy for pointing this out to me.

12. See, e.g., Tatian *Address to the Greeks* ANF 2: 7. For the early church's understanding and emphasis on free will, see Dale R. Stoffer, "The Problem of Evil: An Historical Theological Approach," *Ashland Theological Review* 24 (1992): 60–62; Roger Forster and Paul

To illustrate, suppose a scientist invented a microchip that could control every neuron in a person's brain and that was so sophisticated it could be implanted without the person knowing it. If this scientist programmed the microchip to do so, she could coerce any person to feel, think, speak, and behave in perfectly loving ways toward her, and her subjects would even believe they were doing this of their own volition. While they would certainly *appear* to love this scientist, and while they themselves would *believe* they loved this scientist, would we not consider her demented if she mistook the coerced appearance of love to be *actual* love? In *making* subjects "choose" to love her, the scientist was actually *preventing* them from genuinely choosing to love her, for they no longer had the capacity to do this of their own volition. In reality, this demented scientist was just *loving herself* through these subjects, as much as if she were manipulating puppets on her hand to mimic loving expressions toward her.

So too, had he wanted to, the all-powerful God certainly could have created a world in which everyone was predestined to feel, think, speak, and behave in perfectly loving ways toward him and each other. But God would know, even if we did not, that we would be mere puppets on his hand. If God instead wants a people who *genuinely* love him and each other, he must create us with the capacity to choose to love *or not*. He must give us genuine say-so to affect what comes to pass as we choose lovingly to align our wills with his *or not*.

We might make the same point from a different direction. Christ's ministry, along with the rest of Scripture, provides many examples of people rejecting God's will and grieving God's heart. Does this itself not prove that God created us with the capacity to reject his will and grieve his heart? That we find God giving people choices and holding them responsible for their choices throughout Scripture confirms this point.[13] Yet since everything God does is done with a loving motive,

---

Marston, *God's Strategy in Human History* (Wheaton, Ill.: Tyndale House, 1973), 243–57; Boyd, *Satan and the Problem of Evil*, 39–49. The necessity of libertarian freedom for love to be genuine does not hold for God, I argue, for unlike contingent beings who *by definition* could be otherwise, God is *by definition* a necessary being whose eternal, God-defining character could not be otherwise.

13. For a succinct review of passages revealing our ability to choose to reject God's will, quench God's Spirit, thwart God's purposes (to a degree), and thus grieve God's heart, see Boyd, *Is God to Blame?* 61–77.

we can only conclude that God gave us the capacity freely to reject his loving will *because it was necessary for love*. A similar argument could be made regarding the many angels who rebelled against God (e.g., 2 Peter 2:4; Jude 6). Hence, it seems to me that Scripture as well as logic and intuition teach us that *love requires freedom*.

The Uncontrollable and Irrevocable Nature of Free Will

God's decision to create a cosmos that was capable of love and that was, therefore, populated with free agents was also a decision to create and govern a world he could not unilaterally control. So far as I can see, these are two aspects of one and the same decision. What it means for God to give agents some degree of morally responsible say-so over what comes to pass is that God's say-so will not unilaterally determine all that comes to pass. Of course, throughout history some pastors, theologians, and philosophers have tried to argue otherwise. God determines the free choices of agents, we are in various ways told, *in such a way* that these agents remain responsible for the evil they choose while God remains all-good in ordaining them to do these evil acts.[14] I cannot begin to enter the labyrinth of issues involved in this position, except to say that I find myself unable to ascribe coherent meaning to it. Language has meaning only insofar as it connects, at least analogically, with our experience. But I find nothing in my experience — or *any conceivable experience* — that sheds the least bit of light on what this mysterious "in such a way" (or related expressions) might mean.

To illustrate, suppose the earlier mentioned demented scientist secretly implanted her neuron-controlling microchip in a person's brain, which led this person to murder someone. Can we conceive of any form of justice that would find the scientist to be innocent of the crime while holding the controlled subject responsible? I cannot, and it would not make the least bit of difference if all the lawyers in the world insisted she programmed the chip to control neurons "in such a way" that the controlled subject was morally responsible for the crime while the demented

---

14. For example, the Westminster Confession affirms that "God from all eternity did, by the most wise and holy counsel of his own will, freely and unchangeably ordain whatsoever comes to pass; *yet so as* thereby neither is God the author of sin; nor is violence offered to the will of the creatures, nor is the liberty or contingency of second causes taken away, but rather established" (3.1, emphasis added). Similarly, Augustine speaks of the unspeakably strange "ways" agents who act in opposition to God's will thereby fulfill his will. Enchndim, ANF 3: 100.

scientist remained innocent. Nor can I see what difference it makes if we replace the demented scientist with God and replace the microchip with a concept of "sovereign decree" or "predestination" or "divine ordination" or anything of the sort. Whoever or whatever rendered the murder certain to occur is morally responsible, whether by means of a microchip or a mysterious deterministic decree.

I and other open theists thus hold that God limits the exercise of his power when he creates free agents. To the extent that God gives an agent free will, he *cannot* meticulously control what that agent does. Yet the "cannot" in this statement is not a matter of insufficient power, for God remains all-powerful. It rather is simply a matter of definition. Just as God cannot create a round triangle or a married bachelor, so too he cannot meticulously control free agents.

This point is important inasmuch as some critics have caricatured the open view as suggesting that God arbitrarily restricts the use of his power on a case-by-case basis. If so, the argument continues, open theists must accept that if God refrains from preventing a particular evil, it is simply *because he did not want to*, just as deterministic understandings of providence hold. Hence, some conclude, the open model of providence offers no advantage over classical models, while depicting God as a rather arbitrary deity.[15]

Just as important, it is not just that God cannot meticulously *control* the free will of agents; I would go further and argue that God cannot *revoke* it.[16] In fact, as it concerns theodicy, I am not convinced that there is a significant difference between affirming that God can unilaterally control a free agent, on the one hand, and affirming that God can unilaterally revoke the free will of an agent whenever he sees fit, on the other.[17] Libertarian free will is the capacity to choose to go *this* way or

---

15. This is the central argument in Helseth, "What Is at Stake?" 275–307.

16. For the purposes of this essay, I am painting with rather broad strokes. A much more nuanced discussion would specify innumerable variables that condition the extent to which God can maximize the good and minimize evil in any given situation. See Boyd, *Satan and the Problem of Evil*, chaps. 6–7.

17. This touches on the ongoing philosophical discussion generated by H. Frankfurt in "Alternative Possibilities and Moral Responsibility," *Journal of Philosophy* 66 (December 1969): 829–39. Suffice it for the present to note that even if one grants the validity of Frankfurt's counterexamples to the principle of alternate possibilities, the fact that there *is* evil in the world is proof enough that God does not utilize a "Frankfurt device" to revoke free will when it suits him.

that way. If God revoked an agent's capacity to go *that* way because he disapproved of it, then he clearly did not genuinely give the agent the capacity to go this way *or that way*. Conversely, if he truly gave an agent the freedom to go this way *or that way*, he must, by definition allow them to go *that* way, even if he abhors it.

This, of course, does not mean that God can do *nothing* to prevent an agent from freely engaging in evil. Short of coercively revoking an agent's will, God can do a myriad of things to influence this agent in a different direction or to influence other agents to help prevent, or at least minimize, the evil this agent intends. But the one thing God cannot do, by definition, is meticulously control or unilaterally revoke a free will once given.[18] God, of course, has sufficient power to do anything he pleases. But the constraint free agency places on God is not about power; rather, it is about the metaphysical implications of the kind of world God decided to create.

The Limited Scope of Free Will

While it is important that we understand the logical constraints that the decision to create a free world places on God, it is also important that we understand that there are significant constraints on the free will God gives us. The open view insists that we are morally responsible to the extent that we are free, but it does not specify the extent to which agents in general or any individual agent in particular is free. Indeed, given the innumerable variables outside of our control that influence us moment to moment, I do not see how anyone other than God could possibly specify the extent to which any agent is free, in a libertarian sense, in any given moment.[19]

Hence, as important as free will is to the open model of providence, it does not naïvely deny that the scope of free will is significantly restricted. It thus has no problem affirming that God's knowledge of what will come

---

18. The irrevocability of free will is important for all the same reasons as the uncontrollability of free will. If God had the power to revoke free will whenever he wished, we would once again have to conclude that when God does not revoke an agent's will once he sees that he is going to use it for evil purposes, it can only be because *he does not want to*. This in turn forces the conclusion that God allows each specific instance of evil he does not prevent for a specific, good divine reason, which is precisely the position the open view denies.

19. Among the variables that influence us are our genetic inheritance, our upbringing, current physical and spiritual influences (e.g., God as well as good and evil spirits), the ongoing effects of previous decisions others and we have made, and, most important, the amount of say-so God has given us at the start. For a more comprehensive and nuanced discussion, see Boyd, *Satan and the Problem of Evil*, chaps. 5–7.

to pass in the future is incomprehensibly superior to ours, simply because he perfectly knows all past and present variables that effect what comes to pass, including his own will. Yet, amid all the things we do not have say-so over, the open view holds that free agents have (or at least had) *some degree of* say-so, however slight it may be in the total scheme of things. It is this limited domain of say-so for which we are morally responsible.

Character Solidification

Not only is free will obviously limited in scope; it is also limited *in duration*. As I have argued elsewhere, there are a number of indications that the irreversible directionality of time means something vis-à-vis libertarian free will.[20] The New Testament depicts life in this present epoch as an ever-closing window of opportunity, in which we are either growing in Christlikeness or becoming increasingly hardened to God's Spirit (e.g., Heb. 3:13–15). We eventually reach a point of no return, when we are either solidified in our relationship with God or solidified in our rejection of God.[21] This present epoch is a probationary period during which God is acquiring and preparing his bride, the purpose of which is eventually to lead to a glorious wedding and eternal marriage (e.g., John 3:29; Eph. 5:25–26, 31–32; Rev. 19:7).

On top of this, our own experience confirms the popular ancient maxim, repeated in various forms throughout history, that *our choices become our habits; our habits become our character; and our character becomes our destiny.*[22] As we all know, the longer we continue down a chosen path, the harder it is for us to veer from this path, and we eventually reach a point of no return. We begin by making our choices, but in the end, our choices make us. We are gradually but inevitably becoming the decisions we make.

---

20. Boyd, *Satan and the Problem of Evil*, 185–206.

21. Several passages that suggest people can become solidified in their stance against God are Matt. 12:31–32 (and parallels); Rom. 1:24–28; 1 John 5:16. On the other hand, that heaven is consistently depicted as a secure place where God's redeemed will delight in him forever suggests that people eventually become solidified in their loving orientation toward God. On the fate of those who die with characters yet unsolidified, see Boyd, *Satan and the Problem of Evil*, 380–85.

22. The earliest form of this teaching, so far as I have been able to discover, appears in Heraclitus, who in the fifth century BC remarked that "character is man's fate." Walter Kaufmann, ed., *Philosophic Classics*, 2nd ed. (Englewood Cliffs, N.J.: Prentice-Hall, 1966), 17. On some historical examples of this teaching, see Boyd, *Satan and the Problem of Evil*, 187–89.

In this light, it seems evident that while love must be freely chosen, it does not have to be *eternally* chosen in a libertarian sense. Rather, the purpose of libertarian freedom is provisional, intended eventually to lead us to a much greater, eternally solidified form of compatibilistic freedom. God gives us the libertarian capacity to choose for *or against* love in hopes that we will eventually become not merely people who choose love but people whose very beings are love. At this point, we are conformed to the image of Jesus Christ, the one who incarnated God's love. Tragically, Scripture suggests that those who persist in the opposite direction suffer the opposite fate. They eventually lose their capacity to turn from their hard-heartedness and enter into God's eternal love.

This point is important not only because it renders intelligible the biblical portrait of heaven and hell as irrevocably solidified but also because it explains how God can sometimes know what agents will freely choose under certain conditions. For example, given God's perfect knowledge of the kind of character Peter had formed up to the time when he betrayed Jesus, there is little difficulty in understanding how God could have known that Peter would betray Christ when it was in his self-interest to do so (Luke 22:34). Peter was morally responsible for his cowardly decision, not because he could have chosen otherwise *in that moment*, but because he freely developed the kind of character that rendered it certain that he would deny Christ when it was in his self-interest so to do.[23]

Freedom and Possibilities

We come now to the most distinctive, and most controversial, aspect of the open model of providence. According to this model, if an agent possesses the free will to choose between alternate possibilities, then what is real, prior to the agent's choice, are the alternate possibilities.

---

23. Also at play in the betrayal narrative is that Peter had been clinging to a mistaken militant concept of the Messiah (see, e.g., Matt. 16:21–23). This is why Peter *appeared* so bold while Jesus was working miracles and the crowds were following him, yet revealed himself to be a coward once Jesus was arrested and the crowds turned against him. God's purpose in having Jesus give the prophecy of Peter's denial was to reveal to Peter the sinfulness of his own character and help him discover the true, self-sacrificial nature of leadership in the kingdom. The kingdom Jesus ushered into the world advances not by conquering people but by loving, serving, and dying for them (as Jesus was already showing Peter in the garden; see John 18:10–11; cf. Luke 22:50–51). I do not believe it is a coincidence that after the resurrection Peter was made to affirm *three times* his love for Christ and that Jesus then uttered another prophecy over him. Far from denying Christ, Peter was now ready to follow Jesus to the point of dying just as he died (see John 21:15–19).

Hence, insofar as agents have been given genuine say-so freely to resolve possibilities into actualities and thereby influence what comes to pass, the open view holds that the future is comprised of alternate ontological possibilities.[24] In contrast to the classical view that assumed the future could be exhaustively described by propositions asserting what *will* or *will not* come to pass, the open view holds that, insofar as agents face ontological possibilities, the future must be described by propositions asserting what *might* and *might not* come to pass.[25] (For convenience, I will henceforth refer to the first class of propositions simply as "will" propositions and the second class as "might" propositions).

Most controversially, open theists hold that if God is omniscient and thus knows reality exactly as it is, and if the future is in fact partly comprised of ontological possibilities, then God must know the future as partly comprised of such possibilities. Since an omniscient God must know the truth-value of *all* propositions, in other words, he must know the truth-value of "might" propositions as well as "will" propositions.

This obviously conflicts with classical theism, which has generally assumed that God, by metaphysical necessity, eternally knows the future exclusively as a domain of settled facts, exhaustively describable by "will" propositions. In this view, it is assumed that an omniscient God, *by definition*, must know the future as exhaustively settled. The pervasiveness of this assumption is reflected in the fact that many (if not most) conservative Christian critics continue to accuse open theists of denying the perfection of God's knowledge simply because we affirm that possibilities are included in the content of what God perfectly knows.[26]

---

24. By referring to "ontological possibilities," I am claiming that possibilities are not merely *logical* or *epistemological*. Some possibilities reflect a *state of being*.

25. This must be qualified. In cases in which an agent's choice between alternatives is rendered certain ahead of time by virtue of the solidified character they have freely acquired, their resolving of alternate possibilities precedes their conscious choice. In such cases, what is ultimately real relative to the alternate possibilities facing an agent is not what they *might* and *might not* choose but what they *will* or *will not* choose.

26. This is reflected in some of the titles of books critiquing the open view, such as Steven Roy, *How Much Does God Know?* (Downers Grove, Ill.: InterVarsity Press, 2006); Millard Erickson, *What Does God Know and When Does He Know It?* (Grand Rapids: Zondervan, 2006). In fairness, however, I have to concede that some open theists in the past have invited this misunderstanding in that they unwittingly accepted the classical view of the future as exhaustively settled in the process of denying that God knows it as settled, thus giving the impression that there are things God does not know. See, e.g., Clark Pinnock, "God Limits His Knowledge," in *Predestination and Free Will*, ed. D. Basinger and R. Basinger (Downers Grove, Ill.: InterVarsity Press, 1986), 141–62.

The truth is that the most distinctive aspect of open theism is simply its willingness to question why the reality God created and perfectly knows must, by metaphysical necessity, be exhaustively and eternally settled. Why must there be a determinate fact of the matter about which causally possible future is "the" actual future? By what metaphysical necessity does the perfect nature of God's knowledge dictate the content of the reality that God creates and perfectly knows? In other words, what is it about divine omniscience that renders it *metaphysically impossible* for God ever to create a world in which the future was causally open to alternate possibilities and therefore known by God as such?

Not only are there no compelling arguments supporting this assumption; there are a number of good arguments against it, four of which I will mention. First, as has been frequently argued, it is hard to reconcile the belief that all of history is an eternally settled story line with the belief that temporal agents possess the power to resolve contrary possibilities into actual courses of action. One way of formalizing the difficulty, suggested to me by Alan Rhoda, is as follows":

1. Necessarily, if there is an eternally settled story line, then agent A chooses this *and not that*.
2. Necessarily, there is an eternally settled story line.
3. Therefore, necessarily, agent A chooses this and not that.

Yet if it is necessary that agent A choose this *and not that*, it is hard to see how agent A is genuinely free in the flow of history to choose this *or that*.[27]

Second, regardless of what we may believe, we all live as though the future is partly open and partly settled. For example, every time we deliberate between alternatives in the process of making a decision, we presuppose that it is up to us to resolve alternate possibilities into one definite course of action. There simply is no other way to deliberate. Yet if it is metaphysically impossible for God to create a world with a

---

27. It is sometimes argued that those who argue for the incompatibility of exhaustively definite foreknowledge and libertarian free will are guilty of transferring the necessity of God's knowledge of a future event to the event itself. See, e.g., William Lane Craig, "The Middle Knowledge View," in *Divine Foreknowledge: Four Views*, ed. James Beilby and Paul Eddy (Downers Grove, Ill.: InterVarsity Press, 2001), 126–27. While this criticism applies to some ways of construing the problem, I do not see that I have committed this modal fallacy in the argument just offered.

partly open future, then we who argue that our everyday experience of the world as deliberating decision makers corresponds to the way reality is are not only mistaken in making this claim; we are actually asserting a metaphysical impossibility. Similarly, those of us who argue that God's experience of the future is analogous to our own inasmuch as he too chooses between genuine possibilities must also be asserting a metaphysical impossibility. And even biblical authors who depict God as speaking and thinking about the future in terms of what might and might not come to pass (e.g., Ex. 13:17) must be asserting a metaphysical impossibility, even if we interpret them to be speaking anthropomorphically when they do so. It is difficult, to say the least, to see how this is so, which in turn suggests that the claim that an omniscient God must necessarily know the future exclusively as a domain of eternally settled facts is mistaken.

Third, it seems to me that if God knows the truth-value of all "will" propositions, he must, by logical necessity, know the truth-value of all "might" propositions. For the logical contradictory of "x will occur" is not "x *will not* occur" but rather "not [x will occur]," which is equivalent to "x *might not* occur." So too, the contradictory of "x will not occur" is not "x will occur" but rather "not [x will not occur]," which is equivalent to "x *might* occur."[28] Hence, God's knowledge of the truth-value of all "will" propositions entails a corresponding knowledge of the truth-value of all "might" propositions.

One might concede that God knows the truth-value of all "might" propositions while nevertheless holding that the future is exhaustively describable by "will" propositions if one insists that "might" propositions merely assert the logical precondition for "will" statements. That is, if anything *will* come to pass, then it must be *possible* for it to come to pass. Hence, if God knows that "x will occur," he thereby knows that "x might occur," and if God knows that "x will not occur," he thereby knows that "x might not occur."

This is the only interpretation of "might" propositions one can entertain *if it is assumed* that the future is exclusively a domain of eternally

---

28. In the schema I am proposing, "x will not occur" is the *contrary* (not contradictory) of "x will occur," and vice versa. For a fuller development of this position, see Rhoda, Boyd, and Belt, "Open Theism, Omniscience, and the Nature of the Future," 432–59; Boyd, "Two Ancient (and Modern) Motivations," 1–19.

settled facts. But, as I have already argued, this assumption has no logical or metaphysical basis. It is unclear, moreover, what we are to make of a proposition that asserts "*x might* and *might not* occur." If such a proposition is true, it falsifies *both* the propositions "*x* will occur" and "*x* will not occur," for these are the contradictories of "*x* might occur" and "*x* might not occur." In this case, therefore, the "might" proposition cannot possibly serve as the logical antecedent to the "will" proposition. It thus seems to me that a proposition asserting what "might and might not" come to pass must be allowed to have an ontological referent, namely, the domain of real possibilities.[29]

Finally, while open theists have employed a number of compelling philosophical, scientific, and pragmatic arguments in defense of their position, the primary reason evangelical open theists affirm that the future is partly open is because we believe this conclusion best fits the scriptural evidence. While Scripture certainly depicts *aspects* of the future as settled either in God's mind (foreknowledge) or by God's will (predestination), no Scripture forces the conclusion that the future is *exhaustively* settled, let alone necessarily settled from all eternity. To the contrary, a wealth of Scriptures seem to preclude this perspective.[30]

For example, as we noted earlier, it is significant that Jesus asked the Father if the plan that involved his crucifixion could possibly be changed (Matt. 26:39, 42) — this despite the fact that if any event in Scripture was predestined and foreknown, it was that Jesus would die for the sake of sinners.[31] The very fact that Jesus inquired about this possibility presumes that it is in principle possible for God to change his

---

29. William Craig has argued that the logic of open theism, as I espouse it, forces me to deny that propositions concerning future contingents have any truth-value and forces me to deny bivalence (Craig, "The Middle Knowledge View," 55–57). I want to be clear why I believe Craig is mistaken on both counts. Bivalence requires a nonopen view of the future only when it is combined with the assumption that "will" and "will not" propositions exhaust the possibilities and are therefore contradictory. I instead argue that "will" and "will not" propositions are contraries, not contradictories, because there is a third "might and might not" possibility that excludes both "will" and "will not." I thus affirm that all propositions concerning future contingents have a truth-value and affirm bivalence.

30. The biblical case for the open view has been presented many times, so I will in this essay provide only a brief overview. For several expositions, see Sanders, *God Who Risks*; Pinnock, *Most Moved Mover*; Rice, "Biblical Support for a New Perspective"; Boyd, *God of the Possible*; idem, *Satan and the Problem of Evil*; idem, "The Open Theism View," in James K. Beilby and Paul R. Eddy, eds., *Divine Foreknowledge: Four Views* (Downers Grove: IVP Academic, 2001), 13–47.

31. See, e.g., Isa. 53; Zech. 12:10; Matt. 20:18, 28; Acts 2:23; 4:28; Rev. 13:8.

mind in response to prayer.[32] Yet it is hard to see how God could ever modify his plans in the flow of history if every one of his plans had been unalterably settled from all eternity.

Similarly, if the future is eternally settled in God's mind and/or by God's will, it is challenging to see how God could genuinely *regret* some of his decisions in light of how events played themselves out (Gen. 6:6–7; 1 Sam. 15:11, 35). How can you regret something that turns out exactly as you eternally knew it would? So too, if the future is eternally settled, it is difficult to see how God could express *surprise* over how humans behave, and even confess several times that he *expected* people to act differently (e.g., Jer. 3:7, 19; Isa. 5:1–5).

Along the same lines, it is quite hard to understand why Scripture on numerous occasions would depict God as testing people *to see how they would choose* if their choices were settled an eternity before their testing (e.g., Deut. 8:2; 13:1–3). So too, it is not clear how Scripture could encourage us to *speed up* the time of the Lord's return by how we live if the exact time of his return was eternally set in stone (2 Peter 3:11–12). And, most impressive in my opinion, it is quite a challenge to explain why we repeatedly discover God speaking and even thinking of the future in terms of what *might and might not* take place (e.g., Ex. 4:5, 8–9; 13:17; Ezek. 2:5, 7; 12:3) if the future is eternally settled. Hence, while Scripture certainly depicts aspects of the future as predestined and foreknown, open theists argue that a comprehensive assessment of Scripture suggests that some aspects of the future remain open.

The "Choose Your Own Adventure" Model of Providence

We might understand the open model of providence along the lines of a children's Choose Your Own Adventure book. In these books, the narrative unfolds to a certain point, then the reader gets to choose from several alternatives how the main character should respond to the situation, thus deciding how the narrative should continue to unfold. The narrative then continues along the chosen story line until the reader comes to another point of decision, and so on throughout the book. The combination of choices the reader makes at these decision points leads the main character to one of several possible endings.

---

32. As we find him doing numerous times throughout the biblical narrative. See note 7.

In the open model of providence, the future is partly settled and partly open in just the same way as in these books. God, the author of the adventure of creation, as it were, predetermines the overall structure of the adventure as well as all the possible story lines and all the possible endings within this adventure. Moreover, God predestines certain events to take place *if* certain story lines are chosen and other events to take place *regardless* of what story lines are chosen.[33] Yet within this predetermined structure, free agents are empowered with a certain amount of say-so as to which of the many possible story lines is actualized.

Of course, every analogy has its limitations. One obvious limitation of the Choose Your Own Adventure analogy is that it is too simplistic. The adventure of creation that we are contributing to is infinitely more complex than this analogy suggests. Every day we make hundreds if not thousands of free decisions, each of which opens up new possibilities for us and others while closing other possibilities. Moreover, our individual "adventures" are inextricably wrapped up with one another inasmuch as each decision we make affects others, for better or for worse. The same holds true regarding the decisions of angelic beings (e.g., Psalm 82; Daniel 10). Clearly, the complexity of the open-ended adventure of creation is virtually infinite, which simply reveals the unfathomable intelligence and resourcefulness of its Author.

A second and even more significant limitation of the Choose Your Own Adventure analogy is that the author of these children's books plays no roll in influencing the paths readers decide to take. By contrast, God not only created the overall adventure of creation; he is also the main character in this adventure, influencing how the adventure gets played out. Indeed, Scripture gives us reason to believe that God is present, active, and passionately involved in each and every decision every created agent ever makes (e.g., Acts 17:26–28). We might say that in contrast to the authors of the Choose Your Own Adventure series, the Author of the adventure of creation writes himself into every possible

---

33. For example, I agree with Baxter Kruger and a number of early church theologians that it was predestined, even prior to the fall, that God would become incarnate and adopt humans into the triune community. For an excellent exposition of this theme, see C. Baxter Kruger, *The Great Dance* (Blackwood, Australia: Perichoresis, 2000); idem, *God Is for Us* (Jackson, Miss.: Perichoresis, 1995). Most of what is predestined and/or prophesied in the Bible, however, is conditional and thus open to modification if and when conditions change (see, e.g., Jer. 18:7–10). See Sanders's excellent discussion in *God Who Risks*, 61–65, 72–92, 131–39.

story line of the overall adventure, and thus every possible story line of every possible character in this creational adventure. Yet as passionately influential as God is, according to the open model of providence, he lovingly refrains from coercing agents as they exercise the domain of say-so that he has given them.

The Open Model and the Four Christocentric Providential Criteria

Having outlined the open model of providence, I will now briefly assess it in light of the four christocentric providential criteria developed earlier.

God Wages Spiritual Warfare

Evil originates either in God's will or in wills other than God's. The impossible dilemma of all versions of theological determinism is that they believe God's will is the ultimate explanation for everything that comes to pass, including evil, while also maintaining that God is all-holy and completely free of evil, as Scripture indeed teaches (Hab. 1:13; 1 John 1:5). As I noted earlier, I find this perspective to be completely incoherent, the relentlessly repeated "in such a way" clause notwithstanding.

By contrast, models of providence that ascribe libertarian free will to created agents avoid this dilemma. Evil originates in created wills that choose to go *against* God's will, which is precisely what makes these choices evil. Yet I would argue that the open model has one advantage over most providential models that ascribe libertarian free will to agents while maintaining that God is eternally certain of what free agents will do. In the open model, God grants free will to human and angelic beings, knowing it is *possible* that they will use their free will for evil purposes and harm others but lacking the *certainty* that they will do so. When these agents make themselves evil, God must put up with them, for, as argued above, God cannot revoke the capacity to choose for or against love once he has given it.

By contrast, in models in which the future is eternally settled in God's mind, God is *certain* that particular agents will bring about the exact evils they end up bringing about, *before* he gives them the free will to carry out these evils. One must thus wonder why God would empower Satan, Hitler, Stalin, and other horrifically evil agents to do what they did, knowing full well they would carry out these exact evils if he did so.[34] Since God is all-good, proponents of these models are forced to conclude that it is somehow better that these specific evils be allowed than that they be prevented. This is a formidable problem, and it is a distinct advantage of the open view that it completely avoids this problem.

Of course, open theists must yet account for why God gave Satan, Hitler, and Stalin the *potential* for evil. Like most other free will theists, open theists explain this by appealing to the general principle that love requires freedom. Having explained this, however, open theists alone are free from the burdensome assumption that there is a specific divine reason for each specific evil.

An even more problematic question that burdens those who view the future as eternally settled and thus known by God as such is why God would give certain agents the free will to damn themselves, especially when he tells us he desires all to be saved and is grieved by every person who is lost.[35] More puzzling still is why God sincerely tries to get individuals and groups to turn from their wicked ways and surrender to him if he is eternally certain his efforts will fail (e.g., Acts 7:51; Rom. 10:21; Heb. 3:7–19). Indeed, one must wonder why, throughout the Bible, God attempts a number of endeavors that fail to come to pass if he was certain all along that his efforts would fail because people would not cooperate (e.g., Ezek. 22:30). Does not the fact that God *tried* to get people to acquiesce to his will suggest that God believed at the time that it was at least possible that agents might comply? Yet doesn't the fact that the people ended up rejecting God's will, despite his efforts

---

34. The simple foreknowledge perspective arguably avoids this charge, for in this view, God has no power to affect the future he eternally knows will occur. Unfortunately, this puts God in a position similar to that of the legendary Cassandra, who was cursed with the ability to see the future while being unable to do anything about it. See Boyd, *Satan and the Problem of Evil*, 88–90; idem, "An Open Theism Response" [to simple foreknowledge], in Beilby and Eddy, *Divine Foreknowledge*, 107. A milder but insightful critique is offered by John Sanders in "Why Simple Foreknowledge Offers God No More Providential Control Than the Openness of God," *Faith and Philosophy* 14, no.1 (1997): 26–40.

35. E.g., Ezek. 18:23; 33:11; 1 Tim. 2:4; 4:10; 2 Peter 3:9; 1 John 2:2. It is worth mentioning that if the damned are ultimately annihilated forever rather than consciously punished forever, the problem of why God endowed agents with free will knowing they would certainly use it eternally to damn themselves is significantly lessened, though not altogether abolished. This observation has little relevance, however, since to date the majority of classical theists believe that the damned undergo eternal, conscious suffering.

to the contrary, indicate that God was not *certain* the people would not comply?[36]

For these and other reasons, I submit that the open model of providence satisfies the first of the christocentric providential criteria better than alternative models.

God Relies on Power and Wisdom

Inasmuch as the open model of providence holds that God is the all-powerful Creator of all that exists, it is evident that this model has no problem ascribing to God the level of power we see him exercising in Christ and throughout Scripture. As the Author of the adventure of creation, God can, from the very start, write himself into every possible story line to exercise whatever level of unilateral say-so he sees fit. The only qualification, according to the open model (as well as all models that ascribe libertarian free will to agents), is that God cannot, by definition, exercise meticulous control over agents insofar as he has given them say-so.

Yet the open model also effectively explains why God relies more on his wisdom than on his power when defeating his foes and accomplishing his purposes in Christ and throughout the biblical narrative. God needs only to *outsmart* his opponents if he is not controlling everything they do but rather interacting with agents who possess their own intelligence and their own say-so. A God who accomplished all his purposes simply by exercising his inherent power exhaustively to control others

---

36. The open view has been widely criticized for ascribing to God the possibility of holding false beliefs. See, e.g., Craig, "Middle Knowledge View," 55–56; John Piper, "Grounds for Dismay: The Error and Injury of Open Theism," in Piper et al., *Beyond the Bounds*, 372–73. The charge lacks merit inasmuch as it is predicated on the very view of the future that open theism denies. Obviously, if one assumes the future is exhaustively settled, then God errs if he expects an outcome that fails to come to pass. But if one grants instead, if only for the sake of argument, that the future is partly comprised of possibilities and probabilities, then open theists ascribe no false belief to God when we assert (as Scripture frequently does; see, e.g., Jer. 3:8, 19) that God may expect, and even try to achieve, a certain outcome that ends up failing to come to pass. An omniscient God would accurately expect a more probable event to take place and may rationally attempt to accomplish things that are not certain to succeed because they depend on human cooperation. On this, see Boyd, *God of the Possible*, 59–63. The open view is thus able to explain the surprise, disappointment, and frustration frequently ascribed to God in the Bible, without denying God's infallibility, and so far as I can see, it is the only view that is able to do so. For similar reasons, the open view most easily accounts for the number of divine prophecies that fail to come to pass exactly as prophesied in Scripture (e.g., Ezek. 26). See Sanders, *God Who Risks*, 79–83.

would have no more use for intelligence than a dog does in exercising its inherent power to control the wagging of its tail. Because the open view ascribes a degree of independent intelligence and irrevocable say-so to angelic and human free agents, it explains why God cannot achieve his objectives simply by displaying his omnipotence and why he must, therefore, also rely on his superior wisdom.

God Relies on Other-Oriented Love

Along similar lines, it is difficult, to say the least, to understand how a God who meticulously controlled everything—including every evil that ever befell anyone and even the eternal damnation of certain people—could be described as perfectly loving, especially if we define love by pointing to Jesus' self-sacrificial death on the cross (1 John 3:16). The common Reformed reply that God ordained all that comes to pass, including evil, "for his glory" simply reveals that this model works with a power-centered criterion of greatness ("glory") rather than the criterion of other-oriented love that Jesus demonstrated when he gave his life on Calvary for those who were his enemies.

By contrast, the open model argues that God does not meticulously control everything precisely because God is a God of perfect love. God's other-oriented greatness was displayed when, out of love, God limited the exercise of his power by granting agents their own domain of morally responsible say-so. And God's other-oriented greatness was displayed even more clearly when, out of love, he allowed humans to use the say-so he had given us to crucify him. God glorifies himself not by displaying his inherent ability to damn whomever he wishes. He glorifies himself, rather, by displaying his loving character, as he suffered and died for enemies who would otherwise be damned. It is for this reason that we who follow Jesus most glorify God when we imitate Jesus' self-sacrificial love toward others (not when we try to control them).

For similar reasons, I believe the open view best explains why God relies on humans to accomplish many of his plans and how it is that humans can impact God, at times even to the point of influencing him to modify his plans. To the extent that humans (and, we could add, angels) use their say-so to oppose God's will, God's will is, to that extent, thwarted. The open view thus affirms that to the extent that God has invested agents with say-so to affect what comes to pass, he *needs* them freely to align themselves with his will if his will is to be fully accomplished "on earth as it is in heaven."[37] While those who continue to embrace the power-centered criterion of greatness invariably view such a dependent and vulnerable God as weak, if we allow the crucified Messiah to shape our conception of God, this dependency becomes one more mark of God's greatness.[38]

Because it affirms that God is confident enough to condition some of his plans on the free participation of his people, the open view renders intelligible the remarkable urgency Scripture attaches to prayer and to people's fulfilling their role as God's coworkers.[39] Because the future to some extent remains *up to us* to resolve as we yield to, or resist, God's Holy Spirit, things genuinely hang in the balance when we decide what to do. There is, in this model, no sense in which our lives are a *pro forma* activity by which we merely play out a script that was written an eternity ago. This invests our life with a profound, moment-to-moment significance and sense of responsibility.

Finally, because the open model of providence views the future as partly open, it arguably makes better sense than competing models do as to how God can be affected and influenced by what humans do, even to the point of changing his plans in response to our input and activity. It is not that we provide God with information he otherwise would not have. Rather, it is that the omniscient and omnipotent God wants a genuine, loving relationship with us, and it is in the nature of loving relationships that they are *mutually* influential. Hence, the Author of

---

37. Matt. 6:10. Note that Judges 5:23 explicitly states that God was angry with the people of Meroz because they did not assist he Lord *when he needed them.* On God's self-chosen dependence on humans, see Sanders, *God Who Risks,* esp. 48–65, 280–85.

38. Here I agree with C. S. Lewis, who argued, "To become ... capable of being resisted by its own handiwork, is the most astonishing and unimaginable of all feats we attribute to omnipotence" (C. S. Lewis, *The Problem of Pain* [New York: Macmillan, 1962], 117). By contrast, see Bruce Ware, *God's Lesser Glory: The Diminished God of Open Theism* (Wheaton, Ill.: Crossway, 2000), which is permeated by the presupposition that God is only as great as he is controlling. Throughout this book, the portrait of a God whose knowledge, feelings, and decisions are conditioned by what humans do or who is to any extent dependent on humans to accomplish any of his plans is assumed to be less glorious than an all-controlling deity. With all due respect, I frankly have to confess that I find this criterion of divine greatness to have more in common with ancient Stoicism and Islam than with the crucified Savior.

39. On prayer as illustrating the *mutually* influential relationship between God and humans, see Terence E. Fretheim, "Prayer in the Old Testament: Creating Space in the World for God," in *A Primer on Prayer,* ed. Paul R. Sponheim (Philadelphia: Fortress, 1988); E. Frank Tupper, *A Scandalous Providence* (Macon, Ga.: Mercer University Press, 1995), 274–80; Boyd, *Satan and the Problem of Evil,* 226–41.

the adventure of creation writes into some of the possible story lines that if things unfold in a certain way, and if certain agents with whom he has a relationship pray and/or engage in other activities, he will respond by changing the direction in which he was planning to go. God's ability and willingness to change his plans are much harder to make sense of if the course of history, including God's own future behavior, is exhaustively settled from all eternity.

God Wins by Bringing Good Out of Evil

The final christocentric providential criterion is perhaps the most controversial inasmuch as it has frequently been argued that the God of open theism cannot guarantee that he can bring good out of evil and accomplish his overall purposes for creation. For example, Bruce Ware argues that the open view of God portrays him as a "passive, hand-wringing God" who can do little more than make guesses about the future and hope for the best.[40] Since God can "only guess what much of the future will bring," Ware wonders if "a believer [can] know that God will triumph in the future just as he promised he will."[41]

I believe that this criticism is completely without merit — at least if we grant that God is *infinitely intelligent*. If God's intelligence has no limit, then he can perfectly anticipate, from all eternity, each and every possible decision free agents might ever make. Indeed, an infinitely intelligent God is as prepared for every one of any number of possible future events as he would be for a single future event that was certain to take place. We humans are less effective at anticipating and preparing for possibilities than we are for certainties because the more possibilities we face, the thinner we have to spread our finite amount of intelligence. Hence, if we humans faced an open future of the magnitude that God faces, we would undoubtedly be wringing our hands and could "only guess what much of the future will bring." But a God with *unlimited* intelligence does nothing of the sort, for the simple reason that he has no need to spread his intelligence thin to cover possibilities.

With no limit to his intelligence, God can anticipate and prepare for each and every possibility as effectively as if it was a certainty. He

---

40. Ware, *God's Lesser Glory*, 216.
41. Ibid., 20–21.

knows every one of the innumerable *possible* story lines creation could take as though it was the *only* story line creation could take. While not everything happens *for* a divine purpose, in the open view, everything happens *with* a divine purpose, for God has from eternity been preparing a response to each and every possible event in case it takes place. It is evident, then, that the God of open theism knows the future just as effectively as the God of classical theism, who faces an eternally settled future. The future that the God of open theism knows is *infinitely more complex*, however, which is why some who apparently have trouble imagining a God smart enough to handle such complexity claim he would be anxiously wringing his hands and making guesses if he were placed in such open-ended circumstances.

If we can remain confident in God's intelligence, however, we should have no more difficulty trusting that God can bring good out of evil and triumph in the end when he faces a partly open future than if he faced an exhaustively settled future. If any further reassurance is needed, however, consider that the God of open theism not only perfectly knows and anticipates all the possible story lines creation could take; he himself established the conditions and boundaries of those possible story lines. We may thus rest assured that if there were possible story lines that could not result in God's bringing good out of evil, let alone story lines that threatened God's objectives for creation as a whole, the Author of the adventure of creation would simply exclude them from the adventure.[42]

Conclusion

In this essay I have shared some of the fundamental reasons why I believe the open model of providence is the most compelling for all who make Christ the centerpiece of their understanding of God. It renders

---

42. On this point, open theism (as I espouse it) and Molinism have much in common, for both hold that God excludes possible worlds in the process of actualizing the real world. The primary difference is that open theism believes that the possible worlds God knows prior to creation include truths about what *might* and *might not* come to pass as well as truths about what *would* and *would not* come to pass under certain conditions, while Molinism (arbitrarily, in my view) affirms only the latter. Because of this, Molinism holds that the world that God actualized is constituted by a single, exhaustively settled story line, whereas open theism holds that the world God created includes many possible story lines that free agents must resolve into a single story line. For more on the relation of open theism to Molinism, see Boyd, "Neo-Molinism and the Infinite Intelligence of God," 187–204.

intelligible the reality of evil that Christ and God confront throughout Scripture. It ascribes to God the level of power revealed in Christ and throughout Scripture. Whether parting the Red Sea, raising Jesus from the dead, or predestining certain events to take place, whatever power Scripture ascribes to God, the open view ascribes to God. But because it ascribes a degree of independent intelligence and say-so to agents, the open view also renders intelligible why God does not rely primarily on power but also relies on his unfathomable wisdom and his perfect love. God outsmarts and defeats his opponents through self-sacrificial, other-oriented love. This is the love he eternally is and thus the love that permeates everything he does, including every aspect of his providential rule over creation.[43]

43. My thanks to my brilliant friend Alan Rhoda, who offered helpful feedback on an earlier version of this essay.

PAUL KJOSS HELSETH

Lines of Critique

Dr. Boyd is a compelling writer and gifted communicator. Everything he produces is characterized by an energy that is nothing if not appealing, so it is easy to understand why he has amassed a considerable following among evangelicals who are interested in matters of a theologico-philosophical nature. The substance of what he produces is not, however, without its difficulties, and the essay that he has contributed to this volume is no exception.

In my estimation, Dr. Boyd's presentation of what he elsewhere calls "neo-Molinism" is vulnerable not just to the kinds of challenges that I raise in my response to Dr. Craig's presentation of the Molinist account of divine providence, but to three additional lines of critique as well. First, it may be criticized as descriptively inadequate. While his description of his own view of providence is, as I hope to establish, excessively optimistic, his description of the Reformed view—his chief foil—is woefully deficient. Indeed, it ignores the nuances and flattens out the distinctions that rescue the Reformed understanding of providence from sounding silly and, in the process, sets up a straw man that makes the open view sound almost inspired by comparison.

For example, Dr. Boyd lampoons the Reformed view by comparing the God of Reformed believers with a "demented scientist" who controls her creatures by coercing them through the use of "neuron-controlling" microchips. Just as this demented scientist *makes* people do what she wants them to do by implanting microchips in their brains, so too the God of Reformed believers *makes* people act in a certain way by manipulating them compatibilistically. This analogy, while rhetorically powerful, nevertheless depicts the inscrutable nature of the supernatural relationship between God and his creatures in a way that no serious

Reformed thinker would own, and not just because it presents a less-than-flattering description of the Reformed view of providence. Among other things, the mechanistic imagery is utterly specious, because it fails to take seriously the Reformed insistence that secondary causes are *real* rather than just imaginary causes, and it does so, obviously, because it presupposes that *genuine* freedom necessitates a measure of *genuine* autonomy. But such a notion is just nonsense to Reformed believers, and thus the analogy misses the mark because it begs a host of ontological and exegetical questions.

Second, Dr. Boyd's presentation may be criticized on the grounds that it elevates human experience above what God has revealed in his Word as the standard for determining what is and is not plausible. While Dr. Boyd insists that "a christocentric starting point is ... crucial for our reflections on divine providence," nevertheless he embraces an approach to analogical reasoning that subverts the authority of Scripture by regarding the creature as the primary referent in the Creator-creature relationship, an approach that manifests itself in his disturbing use of the kind of natural analogy cited above. With respect to the Reformed insistence that God works all things — including evil things — *in such a way* that he is sovereign and human beings are genuinely free and responsible for what they do, Dr. Boyd argues, "I find myself unable to ascribe coherent meaning to it. Language has meaning only insofar as it connects, at least analogically, with our experience. But I find nothing in my experience — or *any conceivable experience* — that sheds the least bit of light on what this mysterious 'in such a way' ... might mean." Given such a standard of coherence, one wonders how Dr. Boyd can justify remaining in the Trinitarian camp. After all, there is nothing in our experience that will serve as an adequate analogy for the Trinity. It is and will always remain an article of faith that is ultimately inscrutable and embraced, not because it can be described in ways that make sense in light of our own experience, but because it is received on the authority of what God has revealed in his Word. Is it really necessary to insist that this is precisely the kind of thing that most Reformed believers would say about the mysterious "in such a way" that Dr. Boyd finds so troubling?

Finally, Dr. Boyd's presentation is vulnerable because it is marred by an incoherence that threatens the integrity of the open model of providence itself, an incoherence that is particularly evident in his treatment of Peter's denial of Jesus both in this essay and even more clearly elsewhere. According to Dr. Boyd, Peter's denial of Jesus is noteworthy because it illustrates how God can interact with free agents who have used their self-determining freedom to become the kinds of people with whom he can work compatibilistically. The problem with Dr. Boyd's appeal to Peter, however, is that Peter was not "solidified" as that kind of person when he denied Jesus. He had not yet irreversibly become the decisions that he had previously made, in other words, and thus Jesus could not have known what Peter would do apart from knowing that God would accomplish his purposes for Peter by working in a deterministic or even coercive fashion.

In the discussion that follows, I attempt to substantiate this claim and explain why Peter's denial of Jesus is problematic for the neo-Molinist account of divine providence by exploring what Dr. Boyd says about neo-Molinism and about Peter in a number of his other writings. What I hope to establish is that neo-Molinism, while ingenious on one level, nevertheless is problematic on another: so problematic, in fact, that we really do have grounds for concluding, as I do in my contribution to this volume, that the God of open theism is an ambivalent and arbitrary warrior who cannot be trusted to rule in a way that minimizes evil and maximizes good for his creatures.[44]

"Neo-Molinism" and the "Infinitely Intelligent" Lord of History

According to Jason Nicholls, the standard philosophical critiques of the open model of providence are problematic because they are based on "a misconception about the openness view."[45] Openness theologians cannot affirm that God is the sovereign Lord of history, those who embrace this misconception insist, because they are unwilling "to make room in their system for the possibility of periodic instances of divine intervention ... perhaps even to the point of controlling, overwhelming or overriding libertarian freedom on occasion."[46] The magnitude of this misconception

44. For a fuller exposition of the polemic that follows, see Paul Kjoss Helseth, "On Divine Ambivalence: Open Theism and the Problem of Particular Evils," *JETS* 44 (September 2001): 493–511; idem, "What Is at Stake?" 275–307; idem, "Neo-Molinism: A Traditional-Openness Rapprochement?" 56–73.

45. Nicholls, "Openness and Inerrancy," 631.

46. Ibid., 647.

becomes immediately clear when one considers the manifold subtleties of the neo-Molinist account of divine providence. According to Dr. Boyd, God can retain providential control over the flow of world history because he can have "a significant role in steering human choices."[47] But how can this be? How can the God of open theism retain providential control over the flow of world history if it is logically impossible for him to foreknow the libertarian-free decisions of responsible moral agents, and if genuine freedom really is "incompatible with any form of determinism"?[48] The answer to these questions, Dr. Boyd argues, is found in God's balanced oversight of the kinds of activity that are associated with established and yet-to-be-established characters, the kinds of activity that are associated with what he calls "would" and "might" counterfactuals. While actions that flow from established characters can be foreknown and even determined, thereby affording God a significant reservoir of providence-guaranteeing, "would"-counterfactual knowledge, those that flow from yet-to-be-established characters can be neither foreknown nor determined, for the agent who is performing them retains self-determining or libertarian freedom. The agent retains the "power to do otherwise,"[49] in other words, and thus might possibly do one thing or might possibly do another.

So how does God's balanced oversight of established and yet-to-be-established characters work in the neo-Molinist account of divine providence? According to Dr. Boyd, when God creates moral agents, he gives each agent a "domain of irrevocable freedom" and then "binds himself to interact with ... [them] in ways that honor that [gift of] self-determination."[50] While the extent and duration of the "domain of freedom" that he gives varies from agent to agent and is thus in principle unknowable to the contingent observer, what remains constant (at least in theory) is God's commitment "not to microcontrol a free agent he has created" until that agent either oversteps "the parameters of the gift of freedom God has given" or "solidifies" his character through the use of his self-determining freedom.[51] Until agents with self-determin-

47. Boyd, *Satan and the Problem of Evil*, 123.

48. Ibid., 423.

49. Ibid., 57.

50. Ibid., 182, 183 n. 6. God's self-imposed commitment not to undermine the self-determining freedom of agents possessing libertarian freedom is summarized in what Dr. Boyd calls the "covenant of noncoercion" (cf. 420).

51. Ibid., 420, 191, 188.

ing freedom either go beyond the established bounds of their domain of freedom or their free choices "become crystallized in the form of an irreversible character," God "cannot *by his own choice* coerce ... [or determine their] decisions."[52] Indeed, God's "integrity" demands that he "honor" the gift of self-determining freedom that he has given, for if he does not, he "undermines the authenticity of both freedom and moral responsibility" and thereby demonstrates that the gift of self-determining freedom was never genuinely given in the first place.[53]

When an agent exhausts the gift of self-determining freedom that God gave him, however, God is then "under no obligation to refrain from intervening on [that] agent's freedom,"[54] for that agent has established his free choices in the form of an "eternalized"[55] character that is "irrevocably open or irrevocably closed to God's love."[56] Indeed, it is no longer possible for that agent to be anything "other than [he is]." For his self-determining freedom, which was the "probationary means" of establishing the "kind of eternal being" he would irreversibly become, has given way to a "self-determined character"[57] that is defined in its essence by a moral orientation that is compatibilistically inclined "either for or against God."[58] Since "self-determining acts lead

---

52. Ibid., 427, 183 n. 6.

53. Ibid., 191, 60, 182.

54. Ibid., 191; cf. 171 n. 42.

55. Boyd and Boyd, *Letters from a Skeptic*, 42.

56. Boyd, *Satan and the Problem of Evil*, 190. It is important to note that the domain or quality of freedom that the God of open theism gives to moral agents *does not extend* to those solidified character traits that are the targets of compatibilistic intervention. While it is certainly true that the God of open theism does infuse "basic characteristics" (ibid., 128) into moral agents when he creates them, he does not "preordain" that particular individuals will have the solidified traits that render their activity certain when manipulated compatibilistically. Rather, moral agents *themselves* establish the character traits that make them susceptible to compatibilistic exploitation (ibid., 122 n. 8).

57. Ibid., 189, 188, 122 n. 8; cf. 171 n. 42.

58. Ibid., 189. Dr. Boyd refers to the period of time in which agents possessing self-determining freedom are determining their *own* characters as a "probationary period" (cf. 171 n. 42, 188–89, 427). Note that during this period God cannot work in a deterministic fashion without revoking the irrevocable gift of freedom that he has given to moral agents. Note as well that during this time moral agents are determining not only their whole characters as either for or against God but also those individual character traits that eventually become the targets of compatibilistic exploitation. For confirmation that individual character traits—and not just entire characters—are solidified through the use of self-determining freedom, see, for example, Dr. Boyd's discussion of Peter's cowardice in ibid., 130–33. For examples of other character traits becoming established through the use of self-determining freedom, see Boyd and Boyd, *Letters from a Skeptic*, 41–42; *Satan and the Problem of Evil*, 122–23, 188–89.

to a self-determined character" and "libertarian freedom [thus] becomes compatibilistic freedom,"[59] it follows that there are two kinds of activity for which agents are morally responsible and which we must factor into our understanding of the neo-Molinist account of divine providence. Contingent beings are morally responsible for what they do, Dr. Boyd argues, not only when they *could* do otherwise in a particular situation given their retention of the gift of self-determining freedom, but also when they *could not* do otherwise given the characters they acquired for themselves through the use of their self-determining freedom.[60] "We must remember," Dr. Boyd notes in a passage that is critically important for understanding his exposition of the open view,

> that moral responsibility applies to the acquired character of self-determining agents even more fundamentally than it applies to the particular decisions agents make which reflect and reinforce their character.... There is no contradiction in the claim that a person is morally responsible for an act even though they could not have done otherwise, so long as the character that now rendered their action certain flowed from a character they themselves acquired. It was not "infused" into them by God.... Hence, if God decides that it fits his providential plan to use a person whose choices have solidified his character as wicked, God is not responsible for this person's wickedness.[61]

In light of the fact that morally responsible actions can be fore-known and even determined if those actions flow from self-determined characters, Dr. Boyd concludes that the future is both partly open and partly closed, because it is an unfolding story involving God's balanced oversight of both determined and yet-to-be-determined components. Whereas the unfolding story is open and unknowable to the extent that moral agents retain self-determining or libertarian freedom, it is settled and knowable to the extent that actions flow from self-determined characters that are allowed to act spontaneously or are manipulated

---

59. Boyd, *Satan and the Problem of Evil*, 122 n. 8. Again, it is the *self*, not God, who gives *determinateness* to character. Once this determinateness has been acquired, God is then free to work compatibilistically with the agent, and to do so with integrity (see ibid., 375).

60. Ibid., 392–93.

61. Ibid., 122.

compatibilistically. As the author of an unfolding story involving agents who possess self-determining freedom, God thus retains providential control over the story not only because he knows how moral agents with established characters will act in particular circumstances if the contingencies of history unfold in a certain fashion. He does so, moreover, because he can have a more direct role in steering history, if he so chooses, by "intervening" on the freedom of moral agents who have solidified their own characters through the use of their self-determining freedom. Indeed, not only can God accomplish his loving purposes for the created order by predestining and foreknowing events without ordaining from eternity who will carry out those events, but he can also orchestrate circumstances that exploit the character traits of self-determined agents so that those predestined events are actualized in time.[62] Scripture suggests, for example,

> that the Messiah's betrayal was predestined and Jesus foreknew that Judas would betray him (John 6:64, 70–71; 13:18–19). These contentions do not contradict the view that morally responsible, self-determining actions cannot be predestined or foreknown as long as Judas was not *in particular* chosen to carry out this deed before Judas had *made himself* into the kind of person who *would* carry out this deed. After Judas unfortunately hardened himself into this kind of person, God wove his character into a providential plan.... [In short,] there is no difficulty in understanding how God could predestine and thus foreknow that Jesus would be betrayed and crucified by wicked people without predestining or foreknowing who specifically would betray and crucify him. God orchestrated events to the extent that certain wicked people (and certain wicked spirits, John 13:27; 1 Cor 2:8) acted out their self-acquired characters and did what they wanted to do in conformity with his plan to have his Son betrayed and crucified. But they are still responsible for what they did, for they are responsible for the kind of agents they had freely become. God was simply employing their sinful intentions to his own end.[63]

---

62. Ibid., 122 n. 8.
63. Ibid., 122–23, emphasis in original.

In the end, then, Dr. Boyd can affirm that the future is both partly open and partly closed and that God "is intelligent and powerful enough to ... accomplish all his objectives"[64] only because Dr. Boyd is willing to sanction a form of compatibilism that, ironically, regards compatibilistically free acts as coerced or determined acts for which the acting agent is morally responsible. God is the sovereign Lord of history, Dr. Boyd argues, not only because he is "an infinitely intelligent chess player" who is able "to anticipate *every* possible move and *every* possible combination of moves, together with *every* possible response he might make to each of them, for *every* possible agent throughout history."[65] He is so, moreover, because he "can and does at times unilaterally intervene and work in a coercive way to bring about a certain state of affairs. I would only add that (1) he doesn't do this all the time, and (2) he doesn't coercively use persons in violation to the character they have acquired by their choices and then hold these persons morally responsible for what he made them do."[66]

Neo-Molinism: A Critical Evaluation

What, then, are we to make of Dr. Boyd's willingness to sanction the unilateral or coercive intervention of God in the lives of particular moral agents? Does his endorsement of coercion pose a threat to the coherence and overarching integrity of the openness program? The answer to these questions, I would argue, is found in a consideration of Dr. Boyd's treatment of Peter's denial of Jesus. According to Dr. Boyd, there is such an intimate relationship between established moral character and moral activity that when self-determined agents are "squeezed" in the correct fashion, their behavior is not only "predictable" but "certain."[67] It is no longer open, in other words, but settled, because it flows out of the solidified nature of the acting agent, and for this reason, the agent retains responsibility for performing the act. It

---

64. Ibid., 130.

65. Boyd, *God of the Possible*, 127.

66. Boyd, "A Response to John Piper." I recognize that this comment, written at the height of the controversy in the Baptist General Conference over the foreknowledge of God, is rather dated. To the best of my knowledge, however, it has not been retracted or modified, and it still articulates an idea that seems to be essential to Dr. Boyd's formulation of the open model of providence.

67. Boyd, *God of the Possible*, 33–37.

is the exploitation of character in this particular sense, then, that Dr. Boyd suggests is manifest in the case of Peter's "divinely orchestrated lesson."[68] "God," Dr. Boyd tells us, "knew and perfectly anticipated (as though it was the only possible outcome) that if the world proceeded exactly as it did up to the point of the Last Supper, Peter's character would be solidified to the extent that he would be the kind of person who would deny Christ in a certain situation.... On the basis of this knowledge and his sovereign control as Creator, God decide[d] at some point to providentially ensure that just this situation would come about,"[69] and then actualized the event by orchestrating "highly pressurized circumstances" that "squeezed" Peter's cowardly character out of him three times.[70]

Even if we grant that what might be called "soft" coercion—God working compatibilistically with agents who have established their own characters through the use of their self-determining freedom—is compatible with the foundational assumptions of the openness program, the case of Peter's denial of Jesus still presents insurmountable difficulties for the neo-Molinist account of divine providence. For it establishes, despite what Dr. Boyd would have us believe, that the God of open theism is willing to violate the self-determining freedom of responsible moral agents in order to bring about states of affairs that he really wants to bring about. Remember, Dr. Boyd insists that when God creates moral agents, he gives each agent the gift of self-determining freedom "and binds himself to interact with ... [them] in ways that honor that [gift of] self-determination."[71] In other words, he covenants not to

68. Ibid., 36.

69. Boyd, *Satan and the Problem of Evil*, 131.

70. Boyd, *God of the Possible*, 35–37. Dr. Boyd's comments on character solidification toward the end of this paragraph are remarkably slippery due to an exasperating ambiguity in his understanding of the word "solid." When he says solidified "to the extent that," does he mean "irreversibly" established and "permanently" or "unalterably" acquired? (Boyd, *Satan and the Problem of Evil*, 189). Or does he mean something less than "irreversibly" established and "permanently" or "unalterably" acquired? If solidified "to the extent that" in fact means something less than *really* "solid," then how are we to avoid the conclusion that we are *all* compatibilistically free, even with respect to those character traits that have yet to be "permanently" fixed or settled? Are not *all* of our character traits solidified to one extent or another? What, then, does it mean to say that a character trait is solidified "to the extent that" it can serve as a legitimate candidate for compatibilistic exploitation, particularly when it changes when it is manipulated compatibilistically? These questions lie at the heart of my critique of the neo-Molinist account of divine providence.

71. Boyd, *Satan and the Problem of Evil*, 183 n. 6.

"coerce ... [their] decisions" until they have "spent"[72] their gift of self-determining freedom and their self-determined decisions have given way to a self-determined character that is compatibilistically inclined either for or against God.[73]

What Dr. Boyd's treatment of Peter in fact establishes, however, is that God intervened coercively with Peter *before* Peter's character became "crystallized in the form of an irreversible character."[74] Indeed, Dr. Boyd contends that God's compatibilistic intervention with Peter was the "loving but necessarily harsh" means by which Peter's character "was permanently changed,"[75] thereby conceding that Peter's character was never irreversibly established or "eternalized" in the first place.[76] What the case of Peter really suggests, then, is both the coherence of a more full-bodied form of compatibilism and the utter untrustworthiness of the God of open theism. Since the God of open theism coerced Peter *before* Peter's character was "unalterably"[77] acquired, we may plausibly conclude that the God of open theism is a covenant-breaker who could accomplish his purpose only by revoking the "irrevocable" gift of self-determining freedom that he had given to Peter. In the first place, then, Dr. Boyd's willingness to sanction coercion is problematic because it establishes that the foundational assumptions of the neo-Molinist account of divine providence cannot be applied consistently to the analysis of the flow of history.

It is problematic in the second place because it makes it much more difficult to maintain consistently that "the ultimate cause of any particular evil is the free agent, human or angelic, who produced it."[78] Consider again Dr. Boyd's treatment of Peter's denial of Jesus. The case of Peter establishes that the God of open theism does in fact know what particular moral agents will do in the future, for he *knew* that Peter would betray Jesus if his character were "squeezed" in the correct fashion. God, Dr. Boyd tells us, "saw past Peter's false bravado

---

72. Ibid., 183 n. 6, 191; cf. 171 n. 42.

73. See ibid., 122 n. 8, 189.

74. Ibid., 427.

75. Ibid., 133, 132.

76. Boyd and Boyd, *Letters from a Skeptic*, 42; cf. Boyd, *Satan and the Problem of Evil*, 122 n. 8, 132.

77. Boyd, *Satan and the Problem of Evil*, 189.

78. Ibid., 429.

and *knew* the effect Jesus' arrest would have on him."[79] In light of the fact that God "squeezed" Peter *before* Peter's character was irreversibly established, either Dr. Boyd must concede that the "God of the possible" can know what openness theologians insist it is logically impossible for him to know, namely, the future free decisions of agents possessing self-determining freedom, or he must acknowledge that God *knew* what Peter would do because God *knew* that he would orchestrate circumstances that would *make* Peter betray Jesus, in which case God *forced* Peter to sin.

While some might suggest that such an acknowledgment would undermine the neo-Molinist account of divine providence, Dr. Boyd apparently does not share this concern, for this is precisely the line of argument that he appears to embrace in his remarkable discussion of Genesis 45:5–50:20. Of this passage, Dr. Boyd argues that he is "largely in agreement" with compatibilists who insist that it "illustrate[s] that God ordains evil actions for greater good."[80] "The passage seems to indicate," he concedes, "that God intentionally orchestrated the evil intentions of the brothers in order to get Joseph into Egypt."[81] But while Dr. Boyd agrees with compatibilists "that this text shows that God *may decide* to orchestrate evil actions according to his sovereign will," he denies that it "supports the conclusion that *all* evil actions occur in accordance with God's eternal, sovereign will."[82] Why? Of the three reasons that Dr. Boyd cites in his discussion of these texts, the second is most relevant to the question of who is ultimately responsible and therefore culpable for the evil actions that God actualizes through compatibilistic intervention. If we take Genesis 45:5–50:20 "as evidence of how God always operates," Dr. Boyd argues, then

> we must accept the consequence that this passage always minimizes the responsibility of human agents. This is the conclusion Joseph himself draws from his observation that God used his brothers to send him to Egypt. "Do not be distressed, or angry with yourselves," he tells them, "for God sent me." If this text is taken as

79. Boyd, *God of the Possible*, 36, emphasis added.
80. Boyd, *Satan and the Problem of Evil*, 396.
81. Ibid.
82. Ibid., 397.

evidence of how God *always* controls human action—if God is involved in each kidnapping and murder the way he was involved in the activity of Joseph's brothers—we must be willing to console every murderer and kidnapper with Joseph's words: "Do not be distressed, or angry with yourself ... for God kidnapped and murdered your victims." We cannot universalize the mode of God's operation in this passage without also universalizing its implication for human responsibility.[83]

When we consider Peter's "divinely orchestrated lesson" in light of this remarkable caricature of compatiblism, we are, it seems, left with two options, neither of which speaks very highly of the neo-Molinist account of divine providence. Either God *knew* that Peter would deny Jesus because he *knew* a future contingent (which for an open theist is a bit like saying that God can make a square circle), or more likely, he *knew* that Peter would deny Jesus because he *knew* that he would remove Peter's self-determining freedom and *make* him deny Jesus (which calls God's sinless perfection into question, given the presumption that genuine freedom is "incompatible with any form of determinism"). What the case of Peter establishes, then, is that openness theologians can rescue God from the charge of being the author of coerced sins only by advancing the *ad hoc* hypothesis that some instances of compatibilistic intervention—including those that involve what might be called "hard" coercion—are intransitive. Apparently, in some cases, coercing or forcing an act does not entail that God is responsible for the act.

Finally, and most importantly, Dr. Boyd's willingness to sanction coercion is problematic because it makes it much more difficult to rescue God from being tarnished by the problem of evil. Why? Before we consider the answer to this question, remember that openness theologians would have us believe that their view of evil is superior to traditional views, not only because it helps us understand that evil in general and specific evils in particular are the unfortunate consequences of free decisions to reject the love of God, but also because it explains why "the all-powerful Creator of the world" does not prevent certain events "he wishes would not take place."[84] Whereas traditional views insist that all

---

83. Ibid., 396–97.
84. Ibid., 16.

evils occur because they are part of an inscrutable divine plan, the open view insists that certain evils occur because God cannot prevent them without revoking the gift of freedom that is necessary to love.[85] Indeed, while it is certainly true that the God of open theism is always doing everything he can "to further good and hinder evil," what he in fact can do in each particular situation is "determined" less by what "God would desire" than by the "innumerable [contingent] variables that constitute the 'givens' of ... [that] situation."[86] In short, God can prevent some evils but not others, neither because he lacks omnipotence nor because he is an inherently arbitrary being, but because the "nonnegotiable givens" of some situations prevent him from intervening in a fashion that does not compromise "the domain of irrevocable freedom that he has given to agents."[87] Since it is impossible for contingent beings to know all of the variables that impact God's interaction with free agents in various situations, we must trust that God is always doing everything he can to minimize evil and maximize good "given the situation he must work with."[88] We must trust, in other words, "that when the Father tolerates wickedness, he does so out of his integrity. When he puts an end to it, he does this out of his integrity as well. Whatever good he can do, he does. Whatever evil he can prevent, he prevents. Whatever he must out of integrity allow, he allows."[89]

What, then, are we to make of the assertion that God can intervene to prevent evil in some cases but not in others because his integrity prevents him from compromising the "say-so" that is "the key to morally responsible personhood"?[90] Can we really rescue the God of open theism from being tarnished by the problem of evil simply by insisting that he intervenes in one case and not in another because "the complex constellation of contingent variables that collectively constitute a particular situation" allows him to intervene without rendering the gift of

---

85. Ibid., 429; cf. 16, 423.

86. Ibid., 203, 391, 392, 389 n. 3; cf. 212–13, 232–33. "The metaphysical principles that condition God's interaction with free agents ... together with all the particular decisions and chance occurrences that influenced history to arrive at just this situation, constitute the 'givens' of a particular situation. The givens constitute that which God is up against in responding to a situation" (ibid., 422).

87. Ibid., 196, 231.

88. Ibid., 422; cf. 196–97, 204, 212–13.

89. Ibid., 200.

90. Ibid., 232–33.

self-determining freedom "disingenuous"?[91] The neo-Molinist account of divine providence leaves us with no compelling reason to conclude that we can. Since God can and does intervene coercively to bring about certain states of affairs, and since this coercive intervention can entail, as it did in the case of Peter, real violations of the gift of self-determining freedom given to responsible moral agents, we cannot say that God is always doing "all he could do" to minimize evil and maximize good when what he is doing falls short of violating the covenant that he has established with free agents.[92] Recall again that God intervened coercively with Peter *before* Peter's character was unalterably acquired, thus establishing that covenant infidelity is a viable option for the God of open theism.[93] But how and on what basis does the God of open theism decide when he is going to violate his covenant vows? How does he determine, in other words, which aspects of the future he is going to leave open and which he is going to close when the covenantal standard for making this determination does not obtain in all circumstances? These are the questions that expose the incoherence of the neo-Molinist account of divine providence and establish that the God of open theism is an ambivalent and arbitrary warrior who cannot be trusted to rule in every situation in a way that minimizes evil and maximizes good for his creatures.

Conclusion

That sound you hear in the background is likely one of two things. If Dr. Boyd has responded persuasively to my request to help me, and

---

91. Ibid., 422, 215. Note that in his contribution to this volume, Dr. Boyd puts his finger on the problem that is at the heart of my critique, the problem that he thinks he avoids, but I think he falls into, in his treatment of Peter's denial of Jesus. If God has both the ability and the willingness to revoke the "irrevocable" gift of self-determining freedom whenever he wants to, then, Dr. Boyd acknowledges, "we would ... have to conclude that when God does not revoke an agent's will once he sees that he is going to use it for evil purposes, it can only be because *he does not want to.* This in turn forces the conclusion that God allows each specific instance of evil he does not prevent for a specific, good divine reason, which is precisely the position the open view denies."

92. Boyd, *Satan and the Problem of Evil*, 214.

93. That God coerced Peter *before* Peter's character was irreversibly established is significant because among the "metaphysical principles" that "condition" God's interaction with responsible moral agents is his covenant promise *not* to intervene in their free activity until *they* have established their own characters as either for or against God (ibid., 422). The case of Peter, it seems, calls the nonnegotiability of this "nonnegotiable given" into question, for he was *not* eternalized as a particular kind of person when God intervened coercively. Indeed, God's "squeezing" of Peter was the *means* by which his character was *permanently changed* and he became a "new" man, "a man willing to lay down his life for the lambs the Master entrusted to him" (ibid., 133).

perhaps others, understand why the God of open theism in fact is *not* an ambivalent and arbitrary warrior — if, in other words, Dr. Boyd has demonstrated persuasively that I in fact *am* guilty of caricaturing his views because the God of open theism really *does* honor his covenant vows — then that sound you are hearing is the substance of my critique being systematically dismantled and me pleading with Dr. Boyd to forgive me for having misrepresented his views. If, however, Dr. Boyd has either not responded to my request or not responded persuasively, then that sound you are hearing is the scaffolding of an ambitious philosophical system crashing to the ground. In my estimation, Dr. Boyd's treatment of Peter's denial of Jesus establishes that his system, no matter how ingenious it may appear on the surface, is nonetheless a house of cards, for at its foundation is an account of how the future can be simultaneously both open and closed that is not just implausible, but incoherent. While Dr. Boyd would have us believe that neo-Molinism supplies the theoretical framework for a rapprochement between the open view of providence on the one hand and more traditional views on the other, what he has actually given us, it seems, is a system that works only when its foundational assumptions are violated. Try as I might — and with sincere apologies if I am wrong — I do not know what other conclusion to draw when I consider Dr. Boyd's attempt to reconcile Peter's denial of Jesus with the neo-Molinist account of divine providence.

WILLIAM LANE CRAIG

Gregory Boyd's opening reflections on criteria for an adequate theory of providence afford me the opportunity to state what I understand to be the constraints or guidelines for theological construction. The problem with Boyd's christocentric criteria is not just that what one sees in Jesus as determinative tends to be rather subjective but, more fundamentally, that Boyd's criteria state merely necessary, but not sufficient, conditions for an adequate doctrine of providence. Imagine being told that to become the Wimbledon champion, a player must meet the following criteria: (1) he must be ambulatory, (2) he must understand the rules of tennis, (3) he must be able to hit the ball over the net, and (4) he must not be blind. All those properties are, indeed, necessary, but they are obviously far from sufficient to make a Wimbledon champion! Similarly, Boyd's criteria are not sufficient for an adequate theory of divine providence.

In general, there are two criteria that I think should guide the task of theological construction: (1) consistency with Scripture and (2) consistency with perfect being theology. The first criterion requires that we consult the whole of Scripture's teaching concerning the subject at hand and not just christologically relevant passages. The second criterion draws on St. Anselm's insight that God is by definition the greatest conceivable being, so that scriptural teaching should be extrapolated to the highest degree of perfection possibly attributable to God. In particular, God's attributes, such as omnipotence, omniscience, and goodness, should be understood in the greatest terms possible.

These two criteria will require the open theist to show that his denial of divine foreknowledge of future contingents is (1) consistent with scriptural teaching about divine foreknowledge and prophecy and (2) consistent with divine omniscience, which entails that God has knowledge of all truths, including any truths about future contingents.

Molinism meets not only Boyd's four criteria but also these additional two criteria.

There is much to appreciate in Boyd's essay, particularly his emphasis on the way God glorifies himself by sharing his eternal, other-oriented, triune love with us. This necessitates libertarian freedom on the part of humans. But I find Boyd's analysis of libertarian freedom as involving the power of alternative possibilities to be defective. His example of a person with a microchip in his brain that was implanted by a manipulative scientist illustrates the point. Suppose the scientist is an Obama supporter who has decided to ensure that the person votes for Obama in the next election. He monitors his subject's brain activity as he goes into the polling booth; he is ready to press the button to activate the microchip, but to his delight, the person votes for Obama all on his own, so that the scientist never in fact activates the chip. It seems clear that the person involved freely voted for Obama, even though it was not possible for him to do otherwise. This scenario suggests that what is essential to libertarian freedom is not the possibility of choosing otherwise but rather the absence of causal constraints outside oneself that determine how one chooses. As Boyd puts it, libertarian freedom requires that we have genuine "say-so" about our choices: that they be "up to us."

This understanding of libertarian freedom has the advantage that it enables us to ascribe libertarian freedom to God himself and to Christ in resisting temptation, which Boyd cannot. Boyd's analysis requires him to say that God's love is not freely given and therefore to make an arbitrary exception to the claim that true love requires libertarian freedom. It also forces him to the perverse conclusion that the perfection of libertarian free will in heaven is compatibilistic free will. By contrast, if libertarian freedom amounts to the ability to make externally undetermined choices, then perfect love does not cast out freedom.

A second problem in Boyd's essay is his uncritically equating control with causal determinism. We see the conflation of these notions in his statement that

> God's decision to create a cosmos ... populated with free agents was also a decision to create and govern a world he could not unilaterally control.... What it means for God to give agents some degree

of morally responsible say-so over what comes to pass is that God's say-so will not unilaterally determine all that comes to pass.

Notice how unilateral *control* is here equated with unilateral *determinism*. Ironically, Boyd hereby reveals that he is still a bedfellow with Reformed theologians like Helseth, who makes this equation the centerpiece of his essay. It is no wonder, then, that Boyd finds himself "unable to ascribe coherent meaning" to the statement of the Westminster Confession that:

> God from all eternity did by the most wise and holy counsel of his own will, freely and unchangeably ordain whatsoever comes to pass; yet so as thereby neither is God the author of sin; nor is violence offered to the will of creatures, nor is the liberty or contingency of second causes taken away, but rather established.

This is *precisely* what the Molinist believes, and it is a tragedy that in rejecting middle knowledge, Reformed divines have cut themselves off from the most perspicuous explanation of the coherence of this wonderful confession.

Boyd asks whether we can "conceive of any form of justice" that would exonerate the controlling person from responsibility for the controlled subject's actions. Yes, indeed—our own American system of justice! When the FBI conducts a sting operation to catch a child pornographer or a drug dealer, agents will arrange to put the suspected criminal in circumstances in which they expect that he will freely sell them the pornography or drugs, and when he does so, the agents arrest him. The criminal, of course, will claim entrapment, but if the FBI has done its job carefully, the judge will rule that the pornographer or drug dealer sold the contraband freely and was not compelled to do so and therefore is guilty of the crime. The illustration reinforces what we saw before: that freedom is a matter of the absence of external causal constraints determining one's action. Given middle knowledge, God has no need to resort to causal determinism in order meticulously to control a world of free agents.

Boyd's most serious misunderstandings, however, emerge when he turns to a discussion of the nature of time and of God's foreknowledge of future contingents. Exposing these errors requires an almost line-by-line exegesis. Consider first the claim:

If an agent possesses free will to choose between alternate possibilities, then what is real, prior to the agent's choice, are the alternate possibilities. Hence, insofar as agents have been given genuine say-so freely to resolve possibilities into actualities and thereby effect what comes to pass, the open view holds that the future is comprised of alternate ontological possibilities.

Here two claims are being run together. The first is the affirmation of what philosophers call a "tensed" theory of time. According to this theory, the future is not on an ontological par with the past and the present. Whereas things in the past and the present have been actualized, the future is pure potentiality. This is because temporal becoming is an objective feature of reality. Future events are not somehow "waiting" up ahead for us; rather things come into being in the present. The second claim is causal indeterminism. Given libertarian freedom, the course of events later than any time t is not determined by the causes operative up until t. A free choice at t will result in different events after t depending on what is chosen.

Now, these two claims are distinct. One could embrace a tensed theory of time and be a causal determinist (after all, temporal becoming was real before free agents arrived on the scene). One could hold to causal indeterminism and adopt a tenseless theory of time, according to which future events do exist (many physicists who accept quantum indeterminism would adopt such a view). To avoid confusion, we must keep the claim of a tensed theory of time and the claim of causal indeterminism distinct, even if we accept both claims (as I do).

The sort of confusion I have in mind is evident in Boyd's next sentence:

In contrast to the classical view that assumed the future could be exhaustively described by propositions asserting what *will* or *will not* come to pass, the open view holds that, insofar as agents face ontological possibilities, the future must be described by propositions asserting what *might* and *might not* come to pass.

This sentence creates a false opposition. Classical theists typically embraced a tensed theory of time and causal indeterminism, so that they agreed that agents face ontological possibilities and that there are true propositions about what they might or might not do in a causal sense.[94] But they also affirmed that future-tense statements about what will or will not happen are bivalent, that is to say, either true or false; for example, "Tomorrow Claudius will freely go to the Senate." There is no contradiction whatever in making true, future-tense statements about the occurrence of causally indeterminate events. Hence, we may agree with Boyd that God knows the future as partly comprised of ontological possibilities and, hence, knows the truth-values of "might" as well as "will" propositions.

We can therefore only regard as a serious misrepresentation Boyd's assertion that the God of classical theism knows the future as exhaustively described by "will" propositions. Classical theists who hold to libertarian freedom recognize that even though it may be true that someone will freely choose *x*, still, until the event actually happens, the possibility remains open that he might not choose *x*.

The reason that open theists are accused of denying divine omniscience is because they deny that God knows future contingent truths, such as truths about what agents will freely do. Boyd would avoid this unorthodox conclusion by denying that there are any future contingent truths. He asks, "Why must there be a determinate fact of the matter about which causally possible future is 'the' actual future?" Two reasons, I think. First, Scripture gives examples of such truths, for instance, Jesus' prediction that Peter would deny him three times before the cock crowed. Boyd's attempt to explain this incident away as an instance of character determinism is desperate. Second, the logical principle of bivalence requires that any statement be either true or false. Attempts to deny this principle lead logically to highly implausible results.[95]

In defense of his view, Boyd first puts forward an argument by Alan Rhoda, which asserts, in effect, that

1. Necessarily, if the principle of bivalence is valid for future contingent statements, then agent A chooses this *and not that*.

The premise is false; what is necessarily implied by the principle of bivalence is that agent A chooses this *or* that. The principle obviously does not imply which choice agent A makes.

---

94. In counterfactual discourse, "might" has a technical sense that is quite different from Boyd's usage. Boyd uses the word to affirm causal indeterminism. Counterfactual discourse pairs "might" with "would," not "will" as Boyd does.

95. See Craig, *The Only Wise God*.

Boyd's second argument, that we all live as though the future were partly open, need not detain us, for causal indeterminism does not imply that future-tense statements are not bivalent.

Boyd's third argument is the most confused of all. Boyd proposes a reform of the English language according to which the contradictory of "x will occur" is "x might not occur," and the contradictory of "x will not occur" is "x might occur." The statements "x will occur" and "x will not occur" are on this view contraries, not contradictories. I hazard to say that no English grammar will support Boyd's understanding of these expressions. He is speaking his own idiolect here. The problem with this is that it mixes modal locutions ("might" statements) with nonmodal locutions ("will" statements). In normal English, the statement that something will occur, but might not occur, is perfectly coherent. That is just to affirm that it will occur contingently. Boyd must be assuming that "will" statements are actually disguised modal statements to the effect that something "must" occur and so can be set in opposition to "might" statements. But that is simply not normal English usage.

The point is that insofar as "will" has its normal English meaning of expressing simply the future tense of a verb, on Boyd's view the principle of bivalence must fail for future contingent statements, on pain of denying divine omniscience, resulting in the logical dislocations entailed by such a denial. All this, moreover, is unnecessary, since one can embrace a tensed theory of time and causal indeterminism without sacrificing the bivalence of future contingent statements.

What, then, of Boyd's view of providence? The Molinist, like Boyd, will affirm that God knows all the possible story lines and all the possible endings. But the Molinist adds that God knows as well which story line you will freely choose. In the Molinist view, as in open theism, God does outsmart his opponents without denying to them their rightful "say-so." One curious feature of Boyd's view is that the God of open theism knows the truth of counterfactuals of divine freedom concerning what he would do in any circumstances, but not counterfactuals of creaturely freedom. Boyd insists that God knows each and every story line as if it were a certainty. But he does not take God's freedom to be thereby obviated. If knowing what he would freely do in any set of circumstances is consistent with God's freedom, it is hard to see why his knowing what we would freely do in any circumstances is inconsistent with our freedom.

Which view better handles the problem of evil? Molinism does, for God permits horrible evils only in view of morally sufficient reasons, whereas the God of open theism, once he sees disaster looming on the horizon (Hitler's coming to power, for example), does not interfere to prevent terrible evils that anyone could have seen coming. Any reason he might have for not intervening can be adopted with equal justification by the Molinist.

How might the Molinist handle the fate of the lost? He might maintain that worlds involving universal salvation were not feasible for God or had other overriding disadvantages (like having only a handful of people in them) that made them less desirable.[96] God's trying to reach persons who he knows will freely reject his grace is a measure of how gracious God is. To extend mercy even to those who he knew would spurn it evinces extraordinary benevolence on God's part.

Molinism holds that it remains possible that these persons might comply, as does open theism. Moreover, given his middle knowledge, God can providentially order the world so that everyone who would freely respond to the gospel if he heard it is born at a time and place in history where he will hear it. By contrast in the open theist view, God allows millions of people to languish in spiritual darkness without making any serious effort to bring the gospel to them, with the (presumable) result that many are doomed to hell due to the accidents of history and geography.

Boyd rightly rejects the determinism of our Reformed brethren. But he needs to realize that Molinism provides a sound alternative that allows him to affirm libertarian freedom and a tensed view of time without lapsing into the unjustified excesses of open theism.

---

96. See Craig, "No Other Name," 172–88.

RON HIGHFIELD

In responding to Greg Boyd's view of divine providence, I feel like the elephant who, with the best of intentions, attempted to come to an understanding with the whale. However much the land dweller tried, he could never get close enough to the ocean creature to engage in a meaningful conversation.[97] Compared to the traditional universe I inhabit, the open theist world is rotated ninety degrees to the left. The earth, moon, and constellations are recognizable, but I am looking at them from a skewed angle. To change the metaphor, every word in the new open theist dictionary possesses a meaning different than the words in the old one I still use. The words "God," "providence," "freedom," "love," "Creator," "Savior," "Lord," "omnipotence," "omniscience," "grace," "eternity," "wisdom," and many more have been retained, but their meanings have been revised. If you think in the traditional theological vocabulary, you must not assume that the following sentences (if derived from the open theist dictionary) possess the meaning that naturally arises in your mind when you hear them: "The eternal God is the omnipotent Creator of heaven and earth" or "God is the omniscient Lord of history" or "The infinitely wise God will most certainly achieve his eternal plan for creation." To understand their meaning, you will need to have your open theist lexicon handy.

In view of the near incommensurability between Boyd's model and my understanding of God's providence, I cannot hope to respond to every argument, unspoken assumption, or definition contained in his chapter. Just creating a bilingual (open theist–traditional) dictionary to translate one language into the other would occupy a whole volume. Instead, I will limit my critique to a few decisive differences that may enable the reader to weigh the merits of life in one universe as opposed

---

97. Karl Barth used this metaphor to describe his relationship to Rudolf Bultmann.

to life in the other. I will begin by assessing the overall vision of God I see in Boyd's chapter and then examine what I consider the most decisive arguments of each section.

The Open Theist Vision of God

In my view, the open theist teaching about God's attributes and activity falls far short of how we ought to think and speak of God. Because of his understanding of freedom and his metaphysical doctrine of relationality, Boyd implicitly rejects and everywhere ignores the traditional doctrine of divine simplicity, that is, the idea that God *is* his nature, that he is identical to his attributes. To reject divine simplicity is at minimum to postulate a real distinction between God's existence and his essence. This postulate implies that the Lord is God because his existence conforms to the concept of deity. The idea of divinity and the concepts of love, possibility and impossibility, power, knowing, and all the rest are not defined by the living reality of God; they define what sort of God can exist. In principle, God relates to the concept of deity the way I relate to the concept of humanity. God does not exist as God because he wills to do so any more than I exist as human because I will it. God's deity is his fate.[98] Without guidance from the doctrine of divine simplicity, the philosophical concept of relation, which demands that two related things inhabit the same causal space and hence both be subject to being changed by the relation, is freely applied to God's relationship with his creation.[99] For Boyd, the concepts of love, power, and relation apply to God in the same sense that they apply to creatures. This allows him and other open theists to read the limitations of creatures into God. God is temporal, changeable, and passible because he is related to temporal, changeable, and passible creatures. For God to relate to the temporal phases of creatures, he must live his life also in temporal phases; to relate to suffering creatures, God must suffer; and so on.

---

98. For my extended discussion of divine simplicity, see Ron Highfield, *Great Is the Lord: Theology for the Praise of God* (Grand Rapids: Eerdmans, 2008), 261–74. See the appropriate chapters of this book for discussions of other divine attributes mentioned in this section.

99. If God created the world from nothing, his relationship to creation is utterly different from any relationship of two creatures to each other. Hence, the philosophical concept of relation cannot be applied to God's relation to creation without denying creation from nothing. Process theism is much more consistent in its application of relation to God than open theism is; it *explicitly* denies creation from nothing.

So God is not eternal in the sense of Boethius's famous definition, which traditional theologians found so apropos to God: *Eternity is the simultaneous and complete possession of infinite life.*[100] God too has a future and relates to his future as we relate to ours. God does not possess his eternal life simultaneously because some of it no longer exists and some has not yet come to be.[101] For God, the future exists not as actuality but only as possibility, and the move from possibility to actuality depends not on God alone but also partially on the choices of free creatures. God knows the future only by knowing everything about the present, that is, by believing propositions about states of affairs that "can or cannot" or "will or will not" or "might or might not" come to pass. However, God knows the truth-value of all propositions about what *will or will not be* only insofar as he determines unilaterally to bring about certain states of affairs, no matter what creatures do.[102] Hence, with the exception of those states of affairs God determines unilaterally, God cannot know which present possibilities will be actualized and which will be left behind.

In the open theist lexicon, "divine omniscience" means that God knows everything that is possible for any knower to know. At first, this definition sounds impressive, and Boyd claims that it is just as all-encompassing as the traditional understanding. But this is not true. It clearly places *natural* limits on God's knowledge and power by postulating a ground of what is possible and impossible for God *other than God himself.* God finds himself situated in an eternal world of concepts and laws[103] — expressible as propositions that can be manipulated logically by finite human beings — some of which are incompatible with each other. This world defines God's divinity and constrains his actions. Eternally and necessarily, God cannot create a world where creaturely freedom and love are possible *and* everything happens according to his will by the power of

---

100. Boethius, *The Consolation of Philosophy* 5, trans. W. V. Cooper (London: J. M. Dent, 1902), 160.

101. To think of God as temporal is to understand God's life as perpetual movement from possibility to actuality rather than pure act, which is the traditional view.

102. Apparently, Boyd considers the domain covered by "will or will not" propositions to be exhausted by statements that assert what *God* will or will not bring about. In this way, Boyd can maintain that all such propositions are either true or false *and* that God knows the truth-value of each of them, without being forced into a middle knowledge framework.

103. Both open theism and Molinism tend toward rationalism, make little use of the way of negation, and thus deemphasize the ineffable mystery of God's being.

his will. And why can God not do exactly what he wants? Because God wants two logically incompatible propositions to be true at the same time. God is forced to choose between two good things, each of which is possible in itself. God chooses freedom and love, leaving unrealized a world where his will is accomplished perfectly by the power of his will.

God's choice for freedom and love necessarily forecloses the option of knowing exhaustively what will or will not come to pass in the future. Why? Because God knows only the present, and the present contains the future only by way of possibilities. And those possibilities can be described by propositions about what "can or cannot," "will or will not," and "might or might not" come to pass. The domain of "will or will not" truths is limited to states of affairs God unilaterally determines and excludes as meaningless statements about what free choice will or will not do. Future states of affairs brought about by human choices fall into the categories of "can or cannot" and "might or might not" propositions, which leave the future undetermined and hence unknowable.

Let us summarize. God exists eternally in a context where laws of thought and concepts such as relation, contradiction, justice, and love possess a type of being, necessity, and force independent of God's will and, even in their most primitive form, can conflict with each other.[104] This context makes it impossible for God simply to create the world he wants. If he decides to create, he is forced to choose from among many good options. Boyd contends that all the limits God experiences in relation to creation are self-limitations brought about by God's free decision to create. They are not natural limitations. This is not true. The impossibility of God's simply doing what he wants, his being forced to choose between logically incompatible (but good in themselves) options, is a *natural* limitation. Only the prior presence of a natural limitation explains why God must limit himself further to create free beings who can love. God finds himself limited by an eternal other that delimits his space.[105]

---

104. Another disastrous consequence of denying divine simplicity.

105. For my criticism of divine self-limitation theories, see Ron Highfield, "Divine Self-Limitation in the Theology of Jürgen Moltmann: A Critical Appraisal," *Christian Scholars Review* 32 (2002): 47–71; idem, "The Function of Divine Self-Limitation in Open Theism: Great Wall or Picket Fence?" *Journal of the Evangelical Theological Society* 45 (2002): 279–99; idem, "Does the World Limit God? Assessing the Case for Open Theism," *Stone-Campbell Journal* 5 (2002): 69–92; idem, "The Problem with the 'Problem of Evil': A Response to Gregory Boyd's Open Theist Solution," *Restoration Quarterly* 45 (2003): 165–80.

Anselm of Canterbury famously affirmed that we ought to think of God as "that than which nothing greater can be conceived."[106] But a God who is the ground of his own possibility and who can never be forced to choose between goods is clearly greater than one whose ground of possibility is something other than himself and who can be placed in the dilemma of a forced choice by a necessity outside the scope of his freedom.

Boyd's Four Christocentric Principles

Boyd presents his view of providence as an explication of four christocentric principles. In my view, however, Boyd's doctrine of providence does not rise to the genuinely christocentric. A theory does not merit the designation "christocentric" just because it quotes texts about Christ's work and treats a few topics discussed in Christology textbooks. Boyd's four principles by no means articulate the cardinal truths of the revelation of God in Christ. A christocentric doctrine of providence would ask how God's being and action in Christ provide a model for God's working in the world. It would show how the saving work of Christ is intimately related to God's work of creation and eschatological redemption in Christ. A christocentric doctrine of providence would look at the incarnation and the work of Christ for revelation of who God is and how he works to achieve salvation for humanity. It would take seriously the Son of God's assumption of human nature without ceasing to be God and the human and divine nature of Jesus' deeds. Such a theology would put central emphasis on the truth that God's freedom and human freedom were completely realized in the same person and that Jesus freely refrained from sinning both as God and as man. A genuinely christocentric doctrine of providence would take into account that God defeated Satan, sin, and death with the free cooperation of only one human, Jesus Christ, who is also the eternal Son of God filled with the Spirit of God. Christocentrically understood, our deliverance from Satan, sin, and death is not dependent on our freedom, but our freedom is dependent on Christ's free act of deliverance!

---

106. Anselm of Canterbury, in *Saint Anselm: Basic Writings*, 2nd ed., trans. S. N. Deane (LaSalle, Ill.: Open Court, 1968), 7.

Spiritual Warfare

According to Boyd, the narratives of Jesus' spiritual warfare against Satan, demons, and every form of evil indicate that evil possesses power not only against human beings but also against God. God can be defeated in at least some of his specific aims. Supposedly, open theism's theory of divine self-limitation and the ability of creaturely free will to remain obdurate forever to God's overtures explain why such vulnerability does not diminish God's omnipotence. God cannot merely annihilate the cosmic evil forces since he must respect the freedom he has given to angels as well as to humankind. In view of the powerful influence of cosmic evil, we cannot expect that God will always be successful in persuading people to make good choices. But in response to this last point, why should we think that the Devil possesses greater powers of persuasion *in relation to God* than any other creature? Why shouldn't God be infinitely better at persuasion than Satan, so that God wins every time? Hence, Boyd's specific take on spiritual warfare adds nothing to his general free will explanation.

God Relies on Power and Wisdom

Boyd (mistakenly) defines God's power as coercive, and as a consequence, since free will cannot be coerced, he contends that God must use wisdom rather than power to accomplish his will.[107] Rather than working through coercion, wisdom accomplishes its goals through manipulation and persuasion. God may choose to "outsmart" his enemies and, without coercion, thwart and redirect their actions to bring good out of evil. Or God sometimes attempts to persuade free agents in a variety of ways to choose wisely. But God is not always able to find a way to negate evil or to persuade every free being to act justly. And here lies the problem with Boyd's theory: God wants everyone to choose the good always and uses all his wisdom to achieve this goal. Why, then, can God not achieve this end? Boyd's oft-repeated answer is that it is logically impossible for God to give someone libertarian freedom for A without at the same time giving him or her freedom for $\sim A$. That is just what libertarian freedom is. I will address libertarian freedom below.

---

107. This mistaken opposition between divine power and divine wisdom is another unhappy consequence of denying divine simplicity.

But let us consider here that the argument derived from the logical contradiction in the notion of a coerced freedom does not address the question of divine persuasion. Persuading an agent to choose *A* instead of ~*A* does not violate the agent's freedom. Indeed, it violates no law of logic to say that God is able to persuade all free agents to choose the good freely on every occasion. And if it is not logically impossible, there must be another reason why God does not do this: either he does not really want to do so or he does not know how to do it. What other options are possible based on open theist premises? Hence, in Boyd's framework either God sometimes intentionally allows evil to win or his wisdom is limited.

God Relies on Love

According to this "christocentric" principle, God relies on love to defeat evil and accomplish his purposes. (This love, I assume, works by persuasion.) To give his creatures some "say-so," the loving God restrains his power and opens himself to be affected and changed by those he loves. He chooses to depend on creatures for help in accomplishing his will, and he suffers when things go wrong. Despite the sentimental appeal of this picture of divine love, it finds little support in the New Testament and is by no means christocentrically derived. Even though Boyd quotes scriptural texts to support his relational theism, it is clear that this interpretation is driven by the assumption that divine love falls under a general concept of love extrapolated from human experience. Boyd signals this when he says, "It is in the nature of loving relationships that they are *mutually* influential." A genuine christocentric doctrine of God's love would begin, not with human love, but with the eternal love among the Trinity, in which there is no suffering, no change, and no possibility of refusal to love in return. God loves the world in his eternal love for his Son and through the Son loves even his enemies (Rom. 5:6–10). He shows his love for us sinners, not by allowing us to say yes or no, but by refusing to take our idiotic no seriously. His love manifests itself in breaking open our self-enclosed existence and freeing us from our senseless no for the yes of love in return. God does not need to change to be our highest good; he is that good eternally. We need to change so that we can receive him as our supreme good. And only he can bring about that change.

God Wins by Bringing Good Out of Evil

According to Boyd's fourth "christological" principle, Christ's work of atonement and his resurrection show that God can bring good out of evil. Indeed, they show that God has "in principle *already* won and *already* accomplished all of his purposes in creation." This is a bold claim, which I accept. But can the open theist view of providence do justice to it? At first, it seems plausible that the self-limited God of open theism can accomplish the purpose for which he created the world. Of course, that plausibility rests on God's plan being defined in such general terms that it can encompass an almost infinite spectrum of specific outcomes. That is to say, God has lots of "might be" worlds (a narrower class than "possible" worlds) that fit the general criteria for creation's goal, and as one world becomes unrealizable, God can work for another. But several problems plague this view. First, even with a very generally defined view of God's plan, such as "The purpose of creation is for us to receive and reflect God's love by being incorporated into Christ," the God of open theism cannot know that this goal will be realized. Even explaining that the word "us" in this sentence refers not to specific individuals but generally to "a people" does not ameliorate the problem. Given the unknowability of future free choices, there must be some "might be" worlds that do not fit the general criteria. It might be that all the angels fall and no human beings choose to receive God's love. Boyd anticipates this objection: "If there were possible story lines that could not result in God's bringing good out of evil, let alone story lines that threatened God's objectives for creation as a whole, the Author of the adventure of creation would simply exclude them from the adventure." This is a stunning statement and should result in a massive revision of open theism. I can see only two ways for the God of open theism to do this. God could make sure some angels and some human beings freely say yes to God by a mysterious type of causality that does not coerce freedom or by infallibly effective persuasion, both of which are defined by Boyd as impossible. Or God could simply never allow the circumstances to arise that would realize the rejected world. But the only way for God to do this while maintaining libertarian freedom is through middle knowledge of what a specific free being would do under certain conditions. But to make this exception is to inflict a mortal wound on open theism. If God can rule out worst-case scenarios, why can he not in the same way rule out every world but the one that corresponds to his perfect will? Or at least pick the "might be" world that best approximates his perfect will? I suspect, however, that Boyd will want to avoid these implications and maintain his basic open theist framework. Hence, in Boyd's doctrine of providence, God cannot know for certain in advance that even his general purpose for creation will be accomplished.

Consider a second challenge to open theism's God achieving his goal for creation. Even if an infinite number of "might be" worlds fit the general criteria of divine success and God manages to have one of them realized, surely some of them are better than others, measured by the best-case scenario. In Boyd's providential framework, there can be no assurance, much less certainty, that God will be able to realize anything close to the best "might be" world. God may "succeed" in achieving a minimum goal, but the open theist view cannot inspire confidence that God is able to bring about his most perfect will and his greatest glory.

A third problem concerns the impersonal nature of the open theist view of providence. Even if I can take comfort that God will accomplish his general will and in a general way bring good out of evil, I can possess no confidence that God can make *my* salvation certain or bring good out of every evil that befalls *me*. In the open theist world, at the point of God's decision to create the world, he could not know the certain realization of any possibility that depends on a free decision at any point in its causal history. Hence, in contemplating whether or not to create, God knew nothing for certain about anyone alive today. My Creator did not know from the beginning that I would be born, would survive until I wrote these lines, or would come to faith in Christ. He cannot know even a day in advance that a decision by some free agent driving down a freeway or robbing a convenience store or shooting an arrow randomly would not end my life. He cannot know an hour in advance that I will remain faithful for a day, much less faithful unto death. Hence, the open theist view of providence can give me no assurance that God knows how to make my salvation sure or that the evil that befalls me tomorrow cannot thwart God's plan for me.

The Heart of the Open Theist Model of Providence

As this section of Boyd's chapter makes clear, the open theist view of providence stands or falls with the ideas of libertarian freedom and the free agent who exercises this power.[108] According to open theism, a free agent acts with libertarian freedom when he determines his own will for *A* or ~*A* apart from a determining or codetermining cause of any kind — divine, physical, or psychological — other than himself. And the agent could have chosen differently under the exact same conditions. Boyd argues that logic, intuition, and Scripture show that libertarian freedom is the necessary condition of genuine love. And since God wanted to create beings who could return his love, he had to give them freedom to love or not to love him. Hence, by creating such beings, God limited his ability to control completely what happens in his creation. Boyd illustrates this predicament with his story of the "demented scientist" who "makes" the object of her affection love her by implanting an emotion-controlling microchip in his brain. However much such "love" looks like the real thing, it is not. Genuine love must arise freely in the heart of the beloved. The same rule holds true in God's relationship with us. He cannot "make" us love him. When Boyd asserts that God "cannot" make us love him, he means that it is logically impossible, as impossible as "a round triangle or a married bachelor." As long as God does not revoke his decision to create beings capable of love, he "cannot" revoke the creature's freedom. This would place him in self-contradiction.

In response to this line of thinking, I first want to point out that libertarian freedom and free agency are highly abstract and logically polished concepts. They are defined so that they will work efficiently in open theist arguments. And they work beautifully at the logical level of the relations among propositions. But propositions should not be mistaken for the things to which they ostensibly refer. Real, existing human beings and the living God are not clear concepts susceptible to logical manipulation. It seems to me implausible that the abstract concept of libertarian freedom could adequately conceptualize the depth of the human self. But it seems highly dubious and, indeed, presumptuous to think we are able to conceptualize adequately God's being and his way of relating to creation in an abstract proposition. The image of a philosopher-logician declaring triumphantly that it is impossible for God to relate to his creation in a certain way, because two abstract propositions contradict each other, possesses what Kierkegaard called a "comic" quality.

---

108. Of course, this is also true of Molinist and Arminian systems.

In a second observation about libertarian freedom, it is good to remember that we do not experience libertarian freedom psychologically. The concept has to be abstracted from experience and refined. And in this form, it is highly contested. Indeed, compatibilistic freedom is much closer to lived experience. We seem to be pretty clear in most cases about what we want to do, and it is usually pretty obvious when conditions are favorable for doing what we want. No great abstraction is needed.

My third and more serious concern with libertarian freedom is the obvious fact that Scripture does not teach the libertarian theory. Scripture does not talk (as does Boyd) about created free agents. Nor does it speak of a natural power to love or not love God. It speaks, rather, of our "powerlessness" and of our settled enmity toward God (Rom. 5:6–10). Sadly, the fall lies between creation and the sinful, ungodly, blind, enslaved, corrupt, lost, and suffering human beings who are the objects of God's love and of his saving will. Boyd speaks as if the fall had no effects on our wills or our reason, as if we had not been born already turned away from God. Scripture is unambiguous: All have sinned! And sin is not a superficial condition touching only the body and its evanescent emotions but leaving the sovereign self untouched; apart from divine grace, the heart is corrupt and the will is turned toward evil.

Boyd's illustration of the "demented scientist" completely reverses the biblical order. To reflect the narrative of salvation, the story should go this way: a good scientist falls in love with a woman who cannot love him back because an evil genius planted a microchip in her brain at birth, programming her for selfishness, envy, and suspicion. The good scientist believes that were it not for the alien influence, he could win his beloved's affection. Driven by his love, he discovers a way, without his beloved's knowledge or permission (which she could not give in any case), to disable the chip so that she can return his love. In a similar way, the God who comes to us in Christ finds us, not in pristine innocence possessing sovereign power over ourselves, but already corrupted, enslaved by evil, and unable to love God or our neighbors. In his infinite love and powerful grace, he frees us from slavery, opens our eyes, unbinds our wills, and melts our hearts. In the New Testament, freedom is defined not as the power to choose between good and evil but as the power of a new life, in which sin no longer controls us and we love God with all our heart, mind, and strength.[109] We were indeed created for freedom and love as Boyd contends, but only in Christ and by the grace of the Holy Spirit are we gifted with the power freely to love him with our whole being. In my view, the Christian doctrine of providence should be inspired by the confidence that everything God does in his interaction with his creation aims at this goal, the most certain achievement of which reveals both the infinite glory of God and the glorious liberty of his beloved creation. Now the reader must decide whether the open theist doctrine of providence can do justice to the God of Scripture, who revealed himself in our sovereign Lord and Savior, Jesus Christ.

---

109. For this view of freedom, see my chapter in this book.

CONCLUSION

DENNIS W. JOWERS

In the introduction to this volume, we established that Scripture contains no unambiguous doctrine of providence. Rather, it presents extensive data about God's influence on the world and leaves it to the reader to synthesize the teachings scattered throughout its pages. In the foregoing, Paul Kjoss Helseth, William Lane Craig, Ron Highfield, and Gregory Boyd articulate four such syntheses and comment on each other's views. Helseth, in particular, defends his understanding of providence as divine omnicausality. He argues, that is to say, that by causing every creaturely event that occurs, God exercises comprehensive control over even the minutest aspects of his creatures' activities. Craig, by contrast, advocates Molinism, according to which God employs "middle knowledge," his knowledge of what human beings would decide to do under any conceivable set of circumstances, to control creaturely affairs without depriving human beings of libertarian freedom.

Highfield, without employing the language of divine omnicausality, stresses all creatures' dependence on God for their being and their operation. He argues, moreover, that this dependence in no way compromises human freedom, because Scripture identifies true freedom with a life of obedience to God. Boyd then counterposes his open theist perspective on providence to the more conventional views expressed by the others. If one views the incarnate Christ as the supreme revelation of God's nature, Boyd argues, one cannot consistently deny that God desires what is best for all human beings and that God fails to achieve this only because he cannot ensure that human beings will obey him without depriving them of libertarian freedom. In the following, we attempt to clarify the perspectives advocated in this volume by identifying and discussing areas of agreement and disagreement between the authors and their contrasting views of providence.

Areas of Agreement
Divine Transcendence

On at least three points of inestimable significance, all of this volume's authors agree. First, each of the authors repudiates panentheistic identifications of the world as God or as an aspect of God. It is not surprising, admittedly, that four authors who are evangelical Christians oppose panentheism. This sets the authors of this volume apart, however, from broad swaths of contemporary theologians who regard the inclusion of the world within the divine being as essential to any credible conception of God and his action on the world.

Their agreement on God's distinctness from the world notwithstanding, Helseth, Craig, Highfield, and Boyd differ sharply about the extent to which God qualitatively transcends his creation. Helseth and Highfield, for instance, conceive of God as a simple, immutable, atemporal, impassible being whom the world can in no way influence. Craig, while displaying greater flexibility, stakes out a position that, in many respects, approximates the classical theism of Highfield and Helseth.

Boyd, however, takes the life of Christ *qua* human to be the paradigmatic revelation of the divine nature and, on this basis, effects a wholesale transformation of the classical idea of God. He depicts God, for instance, as capable of change and suffering, as able and eager to receive influences from the world, and as subject to temporal succession. Boyd's God is even partially ignorant of the future, although, given Boyd's assumptions, not ignorant of any truth that is knowable at any given time.

One would radically misunderstand the significance of these four authors' ideas, however, if one failed to place them in the context of contemporary theology: that is, if one failed to observe that, in an academic theological environment awash with panentheism, they stand united in refusing to identify God even partially with his world. The four authors are allies therefore, not enemies, in larger struggles over the relationship between God and the world.

Divine Intervention

Each of this volume's authors, moreover, grants that the God who transcends the world intervenes in worldly affairs nonetheless. All four authors, for instance, believe not only that God can bring about those extraordinary events Christians call "miracles" but also that he has done so on numerous occasions. All four, likewise, acknowledge that God can and does intervene in human affairs in ways that, although nonmiraculous, amount to more than mere localized results of the causality he exerts always and everywhere. These shared convictions place the four authors of this volume well outside the mainstream of contemporary academic theology.

Helseth and Highfield, furthermore, maintain that God originates, supports, and brings to completion every creaturely act. Craig, as a Molinist, likewise considers divine causality essential to the accomplishment of any human act. He denies, however, that divine causality determines how the will uses the impetus that God's cooperation, or *concursus*, supplies. Helseth, Highfield, and Craig, therefore, agree that God, in a certain sense at least, causes all human actions. They differ, however, over the nature of God's causality: deterministic (Helseth and Highfield) or indeterministic (Craig).

Boyd, by contrast, repudiates the notion that God causes every human act. For he explicitly characterizes free agents as "the *ultimate originators* and *ultimate explanation* of their own acts" (Boyd's emphasis).[1] Boyd, in other words, imputes to free agents other than God the capacity to effect a creation *ex nihilo* of sorts, that is, the capacity to realize states of affairs that do not ultimately originate in God. Those who sympathize with the perspectives of Helseth, Highfield, and Craig typically find such ideas alarming and wonder whether one does not subtly compromise monotheism if one postulates the existence of multiple uncaused causes, as Boyd appears to do when he identifies the ultimate source of free human acts as human beings rather than God.

Bañezian Thomists and Reformed scholastics, moreover, typically argue that Molinists like Craig also implicitly posit the existence of more than one uncaused cause. For although Molinists regard an influx of divine causality as essential to the occurrence of any human act, they hold that the human agent, rather than God, determines whether the act God causes will be virtuous or vicious.[2] From whence,

---

1. Boyd, *Satan and the Problem of Evil*, 78.
2. See Molina, *Concordia*, disp. 32, in q. 14, art. 13, p. 134a.

ask the Bañezians, does the agent's determination derive? If it derives from something intrinsic to the agent, but not from God, as the logic of Molinism suggests, then this intrinsic something creates a reality that does not ultimately originate in God. For reasons we will explore later, however, Craig is unlikely to find this criticism troubling. The fissures between the four thinkers' understandings of the relation between divine action and the actions of free creatures, then, are severe. In the face of widespread opposition to the very idea that God intervenes in human affairs, however, the four authors' unity in affirming this idea is encouraging and significant.

The Veracity of Scripture

Remarkably, all four of this volume's contributors regard the witness of Scripture to God's nature and action as authoritative and comprehensively true. In some respects, this is unsurprising. All four authors are members of the Evangelical Theological Society, whose members reaffirm annually: "The Bible alone, and the Bible in its entirety, is the Word of God written and is therefore inerrant in the autographs." Admittedly, exegetical considerations appear peripheral to the overall argument of Craig's essay, and the confessions and writings of Reformed theologians speak at least as loudly as Scripture in Helseth's case for divine omnicausality. Although Boyd refers to Scripture extensively, moreover, the christological hermeneutic he employs shifts his discussion away from scriptural texts that many regard as crucial to answering the questions he poses about God and divine action.

Nevertheless, the commitment to Scripture's authority and inerrancy that this volume's authors share is rare in the upper echelons of contemporary academic theology and, to this extent, worthy of notice and celebration.

Areas of Disagreement

This volume's authors also disagree about a number of weighty issues. Besides their disagreement on the nature of divine providence, they dissent from each other's opinions on free will, divine omniscience, and the problem of evil. In the following, we intend to explore these areas of disagreement and thereby disclose the nature and the roots of their differences.

Free Will

Of the volume's four authors, Boyd sets forth his view of human freedom most clearly. He embraces a qualified form of the principle of alternate possibilities, according to which acts cannot be sufficiently free to incur praise or blame, reward or punishment, unless their agent can refrain from performing them. From this principle, Boyd excepts only actions performed out of irreversible character traits. These acts he considers free, even though their agent cannot refrain from them, because they spring from dispositions the agent himself has forged by a long pattern of free decisions.

Although the originator of Molinism, Luis de Molina, subscribed to an understanding of freedom similar to that of Boyd,[3] William Lane Craig, writing on Molinism's behalf, sets forth a conception of freedom that sharply diverges from Boyd and resembles in important respects the conception ordinarily advocated by Calvinists. Specifically, Craig proposes (1) that so-called "Frankfurt examples" prove the principle of alternate possibilities false and (2) that an agent can be morally responsible for his decisions, even if he cannot decide otherwise, as long as he is the decisions' ultimate originator.

Both Craig's and Molina's views on freedom might seem to conflict with their belief that God, in a certain sense, causes all human acts. Craig and Molina, however, attempt to resolve the seeming conflict by claiming that God causes the acts of free creatures only by means of a "simultaneous concurrence," that is, a divine cooperation with human acts that enables them to occur without determining precisely what they will be. Not God, but the human will, argue Molina and Craig, ultimately determines what human beings do with the causality that God supplies.

Opponents of Molinism have objected for centuries, however, that if something other than God ultimately determines how human beings act, some causality in the universe must not derive from God.[4] Craig answers this objection in his response to Helseth. "The problem," he writes,

---

3. Molina, *Concordia*, disp. 2, in q. 14, art. 13, p. 8a; and disp. 24, in q. 14, art. 13, p. 104b.

4. See, e.g., Jean-Baptiste Gonet, *Clypeus Theologiae Thomisticae contra novos ejus impugnatores*, 10th ed., 6 vols. (1659–69; repr., Paris: Vivès, 1875–76), vol. 1, disp. 6, art. 6, §3–4, pp. 505b–506b; Charles René Billuart, *Summa s. Thomae hodiernis academiarum moribus accommodata*, 19 vols. (1746–51; repr., Würzburg: Johannes Jacob Stahel, 1758), vol. 2, disp. 8, art. 3, pp. 193–94, 197–98; Gundisalv Feldner, *Die Lehre des heil. Thomas von Aquin über die Willensfreiheit des vernünftigen Wesen* (Graz: Ulrich Moser, 1890) §74, pp. 167–68.

is supposed to be that in this case the secondary agent is causing something, namely, the motion of its own will, but is doing so without divine concurrence, which contradicts the doctrine. But libertarians do not consider an agent's freely choosing to be an instance of an agent's causing its own choice, for that would lead to an infinite regress of causes. Rather, an agent's freely willing something is just an action of the agent, not an effect of the agent. So it is not as though some effect is produced by a secondary cause without God's concurring.

If the fundamental objection, then, depended on the notion that the human will must cause itself to decide, instead of simply deciding, it would refute itself by causing an infinite regress. The objector's point, nevertheless, seems to be that all creaturely occurrences, that is, all creaturely transitions from potency to act, require causes and that a human being's decisions, although not products of the human being's causality, are creaturely occurrences. One who grants that agents do not cause themselves to decide, therefore, may still reasonably assert that the decision of the will, being a creaturely occurrence, must derive from some cause.

Craig would presumably respond to this objection by identifying God's simultaneous concurrence with a human decision as the cause of that decision insofar as it constitutes an occurrence. Craig would insist, however, that the will's disposition alone, which is more of a characteristic than an occurrence, accounts for its preference for one option rather than another. The objector, nonetheless, could counter Craig's rejoinder by arguing:

1. If the deciding person's will possessed this disposition from the commencement of the person's existence, God, who created him, must have caused it.
2. If the deciding person's will came to possess this disposition after his creation, something must have caused this change.
3. God is the only uncaused cause in the universe.
4. Therefore, the cause referred to in (2) must either be identical with or ultimately derive from God.
5. Either premise 1 or premise 2 must be the case.
6. Premises 1, 4, and 5, then, imply that the will's disposition must ultimately derive from God.

7. The will's preference derives from its disposition.

8. Therefore, the will's preference derives ultimately from God.

Craig's effort to reconcile God's causality of everything other than himself with the human will's power to originate its own decisions, accordingly, seems to fail. Helseth's and Highfield's attempts to counteract the criticism that their affirmation of divine deterministic causality undermines human freedom and responsibility, nevertheless, fail much more spectacularly. Instead of devising an account of human freedom that manifests its compatibility with an all-determining divine causality, they simply declare the matter inscrutable. Craig, ironically, does more than either Helseth or Highfield to vindicate the compatibility of freedom and determinism by criticizing the principle of alternate possibilities.[5]

Divine Omniscience

The second principal subject about which Helseth, Craig, Highfield, and Boyd disagree is that of divine omniscience. Boyd, for instance, differs from the other authors in his very definition of the term. Whereas the other authors and the Christian tradition as a whole conceive of divine omniscience as God's knowledge of all truths that will ever exist, Boyd conceives of divine omniscience as God's knowledge of all the facts that are logically possible for him to know at any time. Because Boyd conceives of the future as indeterminate, he holds that this set of facts does not include definite knowledge about decisions made with libertarian freedom in the future. As far as decisions taken with libertarian freedom are concerned, Boyd believes that there is no fact as to what will happen until the decisions actually occur.

Boyd's conception of divine omniscience makes sense, it seems, only if God exists within time and is subject to change: conclusions that Helseth, Highfield, and, to some extent, Craig reject. Here as

---

5. Highfield's and Helseth's failure in this area, incidentally, constitutes a deficiency in their arguments, not in the position they seek to defend. For articulate, defensible conceptions of freedom and responsibility that accord entirely with the notion that God deterministically causes all creaturely occurrences, see, e.g., Aquinas, *Summa Theologiae* I, q. 83, art. 1; q. 105, art. 4; and I–II, q. 6, art. 1; Jonathan Edwards, *The Works of Jonathan Edwards*, vol. 1., *Freedom of the Will*, ed. Paul Ramsey (New Haven, Conn.: Yale University Press, 1957), 163–74; and Hugh McCann, "The Author of Sin?" *Faith and Philosophy* 22 (2005): 144–59.

elsewhere, questions about the divine being impinge on the debate over providence in a way that relativizes the significance of disputes about the responsibility and freedom of human beings.

Craig, writing on behalf of Molinism, agrees with Helseth and Highfield that divine omniscience includes knowledge of all facts that will ever exist. He includes within the scope of divine omniscience, moreover, what Molinists call "middle knowledge," a kind of knowledge that, though logically prior to God's decree to create, indicates precisely what any creatable free being would do in any given circumstance. Helseth, Highfield, and Boyd find the notion of middle knowledge troubling, because the truths in which it putatively consists are, although distinct from God, prior to and thus independent of his creative decree.

The gravest difficulty for the notion of middle knowledge seems to be the problem of how God could conceivably possess it. That is, inasmuch as the truths that God putatively knows through middle knowledge are both distinct from God's being and logically prior to his decision to create, they concern, by definition, merely potential states of affairs. That which is merely potential, naturally, does not exist.

The nonexistence of some state of affairs, admittedly, does not ordinarily prevent God from knowing it. For although God cannot know of something that does not exist simply by inspecting it, he can know of it indirectly insofar as he can cause it. Since God knows himself perfectly, he knows of everything he could possibly cause.[6]

The truths that God putatively knows through middle knowledge, however, concern things that God cannot simply cause. They concern, rather, decisions made by nondivine beings through libertarian freedom: decisions whose occurrence God can cause but whose content, *qua* free in the libertarian sense of the term, he cannot causally determine. God, accordingly, cannot cause precisely those realities that middle knowledge concerns to become fact.

Furthermore, the truths in which middle knowledge consists, being contingent, cannot form aspects of God's necessary being. He cannot know them, therefore, by contemplating himself. As we have just seen, moreover, they are not things that God can create; they are logically prior to God's creative decree. That which is neither created by God

---

6. See Aquinas, *Summa Theologiae* I, q. 14, art. 5, corpus.

nor integral to his being, however, must exist and hence be knowable, if it exists at all, independently of God's being. Therefore, if God can possess middle knowledge, the truths in whose knowledge it consists must exist independently of his being.

If this were the case, however, (1) something other than God would exist, which he has not created *ex nihilo*, and (2) something external to God, which he cannot control, would place limits on what kind of history he can actualize for subjects who are free in the libertarian sense of the term. For those who subscribe to the doctrines of creation *ex nihilo* and divine omnipotence, it seems, both consequences are problematic in the highest degree.

Whether or not one considers human beings in the universe envisioned by Helseth and Highfield to be genuinely free, furthermore, it seems difficult reasonably to dispute that their position coheres with the classical doctrine of divine omniscience. To contemplate the range of possible universes that God might actualize, according to Helseth's and Highfield's account, God need merely gauge his own creative capacities. To know what events will actually occur, God need merely behold his own decree to cause them to occur precisely as he desires.

Helseth's and Highfield's view of God, then, may pose enormous difficulties when one attempts to resolve the problem of evil or to reconcile divine sovereignty with human responsibility and freedom. Beyond all question, however, a God who deterministically causes all things can know everything that will ever occur. Helseth's and Highfield's high doctrine of divine sovereignty thus meshes seamlessly with classical theism's understanding of divine omniscience.

Evil

The third principal subject about which this volume's authors disagree is how Christians ought to address the problem of evil. This disagreement, unlike the others, manifests itself in even the authors' theological method. Boyd, for instance, seems to regard the problem as of architectonic significance for Christian theology. Manifold aspects of his theology reflect his eagerness to respond adequately to the problem of evil, and theodicy, the enterprise of vindicating God from culpability for evil, appears to influence even his exegesis.

Unlike Boyd, Craig does not view the entire doctrine of God through the lens of theodicy. Craig appears, for example, to regard determining Scripture's teaching about God's omniscience and control over the world as logically prior to the task of resolving the problem of evil. Like Boyd, however, Craig seems to elevate adequacy for the purposes of theodicy to the status of a criterion by which one may distinguish between true and false doctrinal claims.

Highfield and Helseth, by contrast, appear to regard theodicy as altogether secondary to the theological enterprise. For them, apparently, theodicy constitutes a purely apologetic concern: something legitimate and important in its own sphere but logically subsequent to the theologian's task of determining what Scripture teaches. Highfield, in particular, displays acute sensitivity to the danger that if one does not treat apologetics as distinct from and subordinate to systematic theology, one may easily falsify the teaching of Scripture to render it palatable to human tastes.

Highfield, nonetheless, at least gropes toward a rudimentary theodicy. While human beings commit sins with evil intentions, he observes, when God causes them to act as they do, he does so from the purest of motives. Inasmuch as God achieves a great good through the entire course of the world's history, Highfield therefore concludes, the particular evils that contribute to this ultimate good cannot constitute evils in an unqualified sense of the term. While this insight hardly amounts to a comprehensive theodicy, it does represent a promising step in the direction of one.

Craig's highly developed theodicy, by contrast, appears almost entirely to depend on two central claims: (1) that God can empower human beings to make decisions whose content he does not causally determine and (2) that God possesses middle knowledge. We need not repeat our earlier comments on these subjects here. The value of Boyd's theodicy, finally, hinges on the accuracy of his views on the divine nature, that is to say, the crucial question for Boyd's theodicy is not whether he succeeds in absolving God of responsibility for evil; it is whether he absolves the right God.

Conclusion

The contributors to this volume, naturally, disagree about numerous other matters that we cannot discuss here. The authors' views on the divine attributes, the theology of grace, and the extent of the atonement, for instance, all bear significantly on the issues we have explicitly addressed. Notwithstanding the inevitable omissions, however, the primary factors that ought to guide decision making about the various models of providence seem to have received at least limited attention.

In conclusion, we should like briefly to recall the foremost strengths of each author's view of providence. The most attractive element of the Calvinistic option, dubbed "God Causes All Things," presented by Paul Kjoss Helseth is surely its exalted conception of God. One may dispute, admittedly, whether paying God metaphysical compliments constitutes a fit manner of glorifying him. Nonetheless, Helseth's penchant for ascribing to God the utmost in power, knowledge, and grace, for example, lends a reverential tone to his writing that suggests an intimate link between exalted conceptions of God and devotion that befits God's infinite exaltation.

The most attractive characteristic of Craig's Molinism is its combination of breadth of vision with philosophical insight. One cannot contemplate Molina's attempt to reconcile libertarian freedom with complete divine control over the universe by reconceptualizing God's foreknowledge without noticing (1) the breathtakingly ambitious character of Molina's project and (2) the almost mathematical elegance with which Molina executes it. Whether one agrees with Molinism or not, therefore, one cannot help admiring the inventiveness and acumen of its originator.

The most impressive feature of Highfield's doctrine of providence is its unvarnished biblicism. In keeping with the predilections of his Restorationist tradition, Highfield eschews philosophical argumentation and constructs his doctrine, which coheres in all essential respects with classical theism, on thoroughgoingly exegetical grounds. A worshipful tone, moreover, pervades Highfield's presentation of his view so that his readers learn not only of his doctrine's biblical basis but also of the kind of spirituality that it instills.

The most praiseworthy aspect of Gregory Boyd's open theism, finally, is its unconventional apologetic thrust. Boyd's reconfiguration of the doctrine of God, that is, seems to constitute a kind of indirect apologetic: an attempt to render Christianity more attractive, not by presenting evidence for it as in traditional apologetics, but by reformulating its content so as to manifest its intrinsic plausibility. This enterprise, as

Boyd would surely admit, is fraught with perils. It is at least arguably necessary, however, inasmuch as no amount of evidence for the Christian faith will seem persuasive to persons who regard Christianity as inherently unworthy of belief. Whether or not one approves of his ideas, therefore, Boyd seems to perform a vital task.

SCRIPTURE INDEX

SUBJECT INDEX

ABOUT THE AUTHORS

Paul Kjoss Helseth (PhD Marquette University) is Professor of Christian Thought at Northwestern College in St. Paul, Minnesota. He is the author of *"Right Reason" and the Princeton Mind: An Unorthodox Proposal* (Phillipsburg, N.J.: P & R Publishing, 2010), and has co-edited and contributed to *Beyond the Bounds* (Wheaton: Crossway, 2003) and *Reclaiming the Center* (Wheaton: Crossway, 2004).

William Lane Craig (PhD, University of Birmingham, England) is research professor of philosophy at Talbot School of Theology, Biola University and lives in Marietta, Georgia.

Ron Highfield (BA, MTh, Harding University; MA, PhD, Rice University), Professor of Religion at Pepperdine University, is the author of *Great is the Lord: Theology for the Praise of God* (Eerdmans, 2008) and articles in *Theological Studies*, the *Christian Scholars' Review*, the *Journal of the Evangelical Theological Society*, *Faculty Dialogue*, the *Stone-Campbell Journal*, and *Restoration Quarterly*.

Gregory A. Boyd (PhD Yale University Divinity School) is a teaching pastor at Woodland Hills Church in St. Paul, Minnesota. His published works include *Present Perfect*, *The Myth of a Christian Religion*, *The Myth of a Christian Nation*, and his international bestseller *Letters from a Skeptic*.

Three Views on the Rapture

Pretribulation, Prewrath,
or Posttribulation

*Craig Blaising, Alan Hultberg, and
Douglas J. Moo; Alan Hultberg,
General Editor; Stanley N. Gundry,
Series Editor*

The rapture, or the belief that, at some point, Jesus' living followers will join him forever while others do not, is an important but contested doctrine among evangelicals. Scholars generally hold one of three perspectives on the timing of and circumstances surrounding the rapture, all of which are presented in Three Views on the Rapture. The recent prominence of a Pre-Wrath understanding of the rapture calls for a fresh examination of this important but contested Christian belief.

Alan D. Hultberg (PhD, Trinity International University and professor of New Testament at Talbot School of Theology) explains the Pre-Wrath view; Craig Blaising (PhD, Dallas Theological Seminary and president of Southwestern Baptist Theological Seminary) defends the Pre-Tribulation view; and Douglas Moo (PhD, University of St. Andrews and professor of New Testament at Wheaton College) sets forth the Post-Tribulation view. Each author provides a substantive explanation of his position, which is critiqued by the other two authors. A thorough introduction gives a historical overview of the doctrine of the rapture and its effects on the church.

The interactive and fair-minded format of the Counterpoints series allows readers to consider the strengths and weaknesses of each view and draw informed, personal conclusions.